PRAISE FOR Love, Loss, and Longing

"Carol's honesty in this remarkable book provides insight into the deep complexities of adoption. *Love, Loss, and Longing* is a book the adoption community has been waiting for, and an essential book for all those interested in children, women, families, and relationships."

— Kathryn Brackenbury, B.A.,
Birth mother, special education teacher

"For all adoptees, birth and adoptive parents, and indeed all those impacted by adoption—reading Carol Bowyer Shipley's very personal account is an important and powerful gift to give yourself. Carol brings to light experiences that are startling, seldom discussed, and yet fundamental for those of us in the adoption triangle—moments that flash both the luminous and darker aspects of human experience. I emotionally echoed with so many of these moments. Moreover, I felt relief from the wisdom and compassion of Carol's writing which helped me to better understand myself as an adoptee as well as to re-situate the adoption experience from some 'un-discussed margins' to a poignant centre stage. Thank you, Carol, for this moving and inspiring book."

—J. M. Thompson, M.Sc.,
Adoptee, international development advisor

"We first met Carol when, as adoptive parents and volunteers in the Open Door Society, we organized a panel of people in the adoption triangle and she was our moderator. We were immediately struck by her authenticity, her humility, and her passion for her calling as an adoption practitioner. Since then, we have participated in the Birth Mother services with her as the compassionate lead.

Love, Loss, and Longing is a deeply personal, searingly honest book that reflects so many of Carol's personal qualities and provides a valuable and insightful journey into the world of adoption. We found ourselves laughing, crying, and connecting with the people in her stories. Not just a personal account, this book will also be relevant to those wanting to broaden their perspectives on the myriad of positive family possibilities that adoption presents."

—Yasminka Kresic, M.B.A., & Joe Stelliga, H.B.Comm.,
Adoptive parents, co-founders of a leadership consulting firm

"Love, Loss, and Longing is a remarkably comprehensive memoir about healing the hurt of adoption. Adopted at four months of age, Carol brilliantly recounts feeling mildly depressed all her life and how her reunion with her birth mother and other members of her birth family lifted her feeling of melancholy.... Carol leaves nothing out. Blending together careful reflections of her own personal healing, her adoption work with others, her Native daughter's adoption journey, and insights from various adoption studies and literature, her book is a welcomed addition to adoption literature.

Carol helps us understand the complexity of adoption as a camera would capture a series of events without censorship. The accounts of her personal experiences, integrated with the essentials of good adoption practices, are honest, highly informative, and moving. Her story and the story of others inside the adoption circle touch your heart. Her book also lends support for better adoption practices and adoption legislation in the future.

Carol's entry into story telling makes the reader aware of a different culture—the culture of adoption. She engagingly initiates us into the thinking of an adoptee. Her book guides us. We learn how adoption reunions generate complex issues and how the loss of a birth mother and birth family can have a lifetime effect on one's identity, self worth, mental health, and heritage.

With profound respect for her courage to share such intimate details of her life and her willingness to expose her vulnerabilities, I highly recommend *Love, Loss, and Longing* to all members of the adoption triad and professionals working in the field of adoption."

— Jennie E. Painter, M.S.W.,
Adoption licensee, open adoption specialist

"Carol's personal story covers adoption from the point of view of the adoptee, the birth mother, and the adoptive parents as well as of the social worker trying to facilitate this process to the benefit of all. She drives home the importance of openness. The huge potential healing in reuniting the child, longing to know her past; and the birth mother, always anxious about what happened to her child, is vividly portrayed. As someone who knew very little about the history and the different models of adoption in Canada, I learned a lot about the essential work that is being done to reform what was once a traumatic process cloaked in shame, secrecy, and silence."

— Elaine Marlin, B.Sc.H.Ec.,
Community activist

Love, Loss, and Longing

STORIES OF ADOPTION

Updated Edition with Birth Father Revelations

CAROL BOWYER SHIPLEY

For Jack —
Thanks for good
childhood memories —

Best,
Carol

Library and Archives Canada Cataloguing in Publication

Shipley, Carol, 1936-
     Love, Loss, and Longing: Stories of Adoption / Carol Shipley

ISBN 978-1-92753-351-2

1. Shipley, Carol, 1936-. 2. Shipley, Carol, 1936- —Family. 3. Adoption 4. Adoption reunion 5. Open adoption 6. Adoptees—family relationships 7. Birth mothers 8. Birth Fathers 9. Adoptive parents 10. Domestic adoption 11. International adoption. 12. Mothers and daughters.

Order this book online at www.mcnallyrobinson.com
Order online at http://carolshipleyadoptionstories.weebly.com
or email orders: <cbshipley33@gmail.com>

McNally Robinson Booksellers
1120 Grant Avenue
Winnipeg MB R3M 2A6

Photos: front cover photo on license from 123RF.com, back cover photo by Ken Shipley
Cover design by McNally Robinson

Second Edition 2016

Printed and bound in Canada

For my husband, Ken,
who has always believed in me.

And for all of you inside the
adoption circle who shared
your lives with me.

CONTENTS

FOREWORD

Carol Shipley in *Love, Loss, and Longing: Stories of Adoption* challenges many of the once held tenets regarding adoption. For so long adoption has been considered "private" and children never told about their origins. Fortunately, closed adoption has been replaced by open adoption as the most prevalent today, except in the case of most international adoptions.

At a time when adoption is being openly discussed, Carol Shipley's book is a long-awaited and welcome contribution to the adoption literature. The book is essential reading for anyone who is part of the adoption circle—adoptees, birth and adoptive parents, partners, siblings and grandparents, and for adoption professionals and social work practitioners.

The seeds for this book were planted in 1988 when Carol entered the graduate program at Carleton University and started her own personal journey of locating her birth mother. I had the privilege of supervising Carol's graduate research thesis and remember well those first meetings as the research question and approach took form. She interviewed women who had been on the uncertain journey to locate their birth mothers. Upon graduation she became involved in assisting others in the adoption circle. This book, some 20 years later, is informed by Carol's experiences as an adoptive daughter, an adoptive mother, and an adoption practitioner; it is deeply personal and driven by passion and expertise.

The result is a rich tapestry of women's experiences interwoven with the current literature in the area as well as legislative changes regarding adoption. As I read the book, I was deeply moved by the personal accounts and experiences of the women—their determination and strength as they travelled the adoption pathway.

It is also a highly personal account of the author's own life as an adoptee and adoptive mother. Overall, it is a celebration of the lives of those in the circle—adoptees, birth parents, and adoptive parents who set out on the journey, found and embraced each other and a network of other family members.

Carol is to be congratulated for this well written and highly important resource for people who have been touched by adoption, including adoption professionals and social work practitioners. *Love, Loss, and Longing: Stories of Adoption* will change perceptions and understanding regarding adoption.

Colleen Lundy, Ph.D.
Professor, School of Social Work
Carleton University

PREFACE

My adoptive parents did not meet my birth mother when they went to the hospital to get me. They were not told that my birth mother had visited me every day in the hospital nursery for the first four months of my life, partly because she lived in the hospital and worked for the matron. My adoptive parents were not told that my birth mother nursed me every day, and smiled and cooed at me as she laid me down beside her on a blanket outside on warm sunny afternoons. They were not told that moments before they met me, my birth mother cuddled me close in her arms, and sobbed. They were told only that I was a very happy baby who was always smiling.

The baby was unusually quiet and still.

I write of her this way because I am still unable to use the first person, I, to describe myself at this point, the point of my entry into my new family. It's as though I disappeared. I'm viewing 'the baby' as if she were not me. Abruptly, I was no longer who I had been just hours before.

The separation from my birth mother created a rift—in the full sense of how the dictionary defines that word, as "to split asunder by force; to break, as the heart."

I slept so much that my parents often checked the crib to see if I was still breathing. They could not coax me into a smile. One of their friends asked, "Is there something the matter with her?" My parents worried. But another friend, who had ten children, said simply, "There is nothing the matter with her. All she needs is a bit of loving."

I had withdrawn into sleep and unresponsiveness in the few ways that a baby can express grief. I was a very sad baby.

INTRODUCTION

This book is filled with adoption stories—my own and others who have touched my life. Adoption stories are among the most dramatic, heart-wrenching, life-giving, sad-happy, paradoxically true stories you will find anywhere. The themes are universal— abandonment, loss, identity building, intimacy, lack of control, rejection, bonding, separation, severed ties, reunion, fulfillment; and the feelings that accompany them are primal—longing, grief, guilt, shame, selfless love, generosity, gratitude, anger, despair, euphoria, loneliness. They express deep truths.

In the late 1970s, a doctor, Arthur Sorosky, and two adoption social workers, Annette Baran and Reuben Pannor, broke the silence surrounding adoption in a book called *The Adoption Triangle* (1978). This triangle consisted of adoptees, birth parents, and adoptive parents. The book was courageous in its searing condemnation of secrecy in adoption and was regarded as a "must read" for everyone in the triangle.

Fast forward twenty years. The benefits and rewards for each party in the triangle getting a chance to meet, share identifying information, and forge relationships with one another were beginning to be recognized both by those who were in the triangle, and by the adoption professionals working with them. As the bonds strengthened, and the relationships deepened, the original triangle began to expand. It became a circle. The original triangle—adoptee, birth parent, and adoptive parent—is still there. But members of the triangle have been joined by the siblings, spouse, grandparents or offspring of any of the above. A conservative estimate is that one in every five persons in North America is a member of this adoption circle!

This book is written primarily for those of you in the adoption circle who live adoption.

Alongside of you are adoption professionals (my own colleagues for the past twenty years) who work tirelessly as licensees and international agents who coordinate adoptions, as adoption practitioners who assess and prepare families for adoption, and as birth parent counsellors who support those who give children into adoption. And then there are Children's Aid workers and supervisors who do most of the above, as well as that most difficult of tasks—apprehending children at risk, many of whom become adopted. I have learned much and benefited from your encouragement, creativity, wisdom, and commitment. This book is for you.

"The best interests of the child" is a touchstone in child welfare with which everyone agrees. In the case of the adopted child, it was not considered in her best interests to know her origins until "right to know" thinking began to surface in the 1960s. Even now this right can be overridden by the rights of the birth family to privacy based on a promise of confidentiality made long ago. Ontario's Access to Adoption Records Act of 2009 includes a veto which allows a birth parent to prevent an adoptee from gaining information about her origins. The result is that she never fully knows who she is and may never heal psychologically nor feel fulfilled. The birth parent and the adoptive parent have adult voices in their adoption process. But the adopted child is young and vulnerable—without a voice in the adoption process when plans are being made for her future.

Adoption social workers used to operate on the premise that blood ties were not essential to psychological well-being, that a person could be grafted onto the family tree of others, and if transplanted early into desirable surroundings, he or she could develop into a healthy individual. The child would enter the adoptive family and be treated as if born to them. Essentially a myth, this was known as the "as if born" concept (Sachdev 1989, 4). The irony in all of this is that it is based on legalized deception. The importance of the psychological connection between a child and her family of origin was at best, minimized and de-emphasized and at worst, forbidden and pathologized. It would not be until the 1970s that the "as if born" adoption myth was challenged as a result of adoptee activists embracing the adoptees' right to know their origins.

Everyone, especially those whose lives are touched by adoption, has a story to tell. Happy-ever-after used to be the prevailing adoption story. But adoption is founded on loss. And over time, those who lived it courageously broke the silence and spoke their truth. The birth parent's loss is perhaps the most complex kind of loss—loving and letting go, all the while longing for what cannot be. The child is best served emotionally in his or her own family, but there will always be children who need placement outside of their family of origin. An adopted child loses the opportunity to be raised by the family into which he was born, longs to know fully who she is, and finds that grappling with the complex challenge of forming a personal identity is more difficult. Adoptive parents long to have children. They mourn not being part of the first days or years of their child's life about which they may know nothing. They often mourn the loss of the child who would have been born to them.

I have three adoption personas—adoptee, adoptive mother and adoption professional. It is primarily my adopted child persona who informs my work in adoption as I strive to ensure that the child's voice is listened to, and her best interests are heeded. My three adoption personas inform this book.

Part I of this book contains my own story from infancy to reunion with my birth family and the integration that followed, and my adopted daughter's story from childhood to reunion with her birth family after which she embraced her Aboriginal heritage. Each of our adoptions was closed—no identifying information was exchanged nor was contact possible between adoptive family and birth family; each was a public agency adoption. In the last two chapters of Part I, I bid loving goodbyes to my two mothers: Dorothy who died in 1999, and Vera who died in 2010. My own story is just that—it contains my bias, and my interpretation of events and memories. Those individuals who live in my story will undoubtedly have memories and interpretations of events different from mine, and equally true.

Part II describes my move, as a seasoned social worker, into the adoption field—as an adoption worker in two child welfare agencies, and then as an adoption practitioner in the Ontario private adoption system. I worked with birth parents, adoptive families, and adoptees. I am proud to have had a hand in creating an important ritual that honors birth mothers—an annual event called Birth Mother's Day. The stories of three life-giving birth mothers who placed babies for adoption in different decades are told. The element of choice available to these women, the quality of support from family and friends, the degree of disenfranchised grief, the involvement of the birth father, and the degree of openness in their adoptions are explored in terms of their impact on the birth mothers' experience of loss. The stories of two birth mothers whose lifestyles were unstable reveal unexpected wisdom as they made adoption plans for their babies. Most of the birth parents' stories are of women for whom I was birth parent counsellor. Some birth parents' stories came to me through Birth Mother's Day.

Part III of this book contains stories of courageous and tenacious adoptive parents for whom I was adoption practitioner. Through the private domestic adoption system, three couples became parents with varying degrees of openness with their children's birth families. Two families became parents through international adoption—a couple adopted from China and then from Korea; and a single woman adopted two children from China against all odds. These adoptions are presently closed. The final story of the book describes a situation in which adoption was wrong for all parties—it did not take place.

The conclusion of the book highlights important issues in adoption: secrecy versus openness, the right of adoptees to know their origins, the right of members of the gay community to adopt, and the shattering of false premises to reveal the truths on which adoption is founded.

The Epilogue, the joyous outcome of having written the First Edition of this book, contains the search and reunion story with family members of my birth father, reflections about him and birth fathers with whom I worked, and a letter of gratitude to my adoptive dad.

Names and circumstances of some individuals have been changed to protect their privacy.

As I documented these stories, I was struck by how so many people in the adoption circle find unique ways to express extravagant, generous love for the others. The people in the following stories provide a shining example of the life-fulfilling possibilities in adoption.

Carol Shipley
Ottawa, Canada

PART ONE

THE ADOPTEE

Chapter One

Blank for Half a Century

Adoption books for children usually begin from the moment the child enters the adoption family. Brief mention is made of the child's birth, then the story is told from the adoptive parent's perspective. For example, Ann Turner's (1990) charming book about a child adopted internationally, begins, "Once I was a picture you held in your hand." And Fred Rogers, of *Mister Roger's Neighborhood*, a revered children's TV show in the late 1960s, writes lovingly, "Your family needed and wanted a child to love and care for, and you needed a family to love and care for you." (1994, 7)

But isn't this Chapter Two of the child's story? Chapter One begins even before the moment of birth, when a child is in the womb. Often, young adopted children don't even realize that they were born the same way as everyone else. However, in recent years, children's enlightened adoption literature has begun to fill the gap. The adoption story, *Did My First Mother Love Me?*, written by Kathryn Ann Miller (1994), affirms the love of a birth mother for her child. And *Rosie's Family* by my colleague Lori Rosove (2001), addresses the thoughts and feelings that an adoption child has for his birth parents.

But there were no children's books at all about adoption when I was growing up in the 1930s. The first chapter of my life would have described the woman to whom I was born and my time with her for the first four months of my life. It was blank for more than half a century.

Even today, adoptees from orphanages in countries like China, have little or no background history about themselves. Operating in extreme secrecy, birth parents dropped their child off at the orphanage gate or the police station entrance. The first chapter of these children may remain blank for their lifetimes.

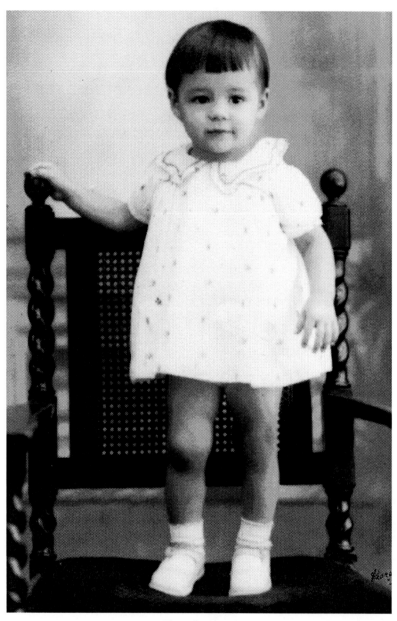

Carol, age 2

Chapter Two

Childhood

But from the moment he knows, his tragedy begins.
— Albert Camus

I was born in Winnipeg on the Canadian prairies in the depths of the Great Depression of the 1930s. The prairies suffered more than any other area of Canada. Two-thirds of the rural population were on relief; a ten-year drought turned the rich prairie soil to dust, sweeping away the hopes and dreams of many farmers. The city of Winnipeg was extremely hard hit. In 1932 its unemployment rate was the second highest in Canada, and the city plunged into debt due to the overwhelming demands for welfare.

I was adopted at the age of four months. Growing up, I had no memory of the first chapter of my life, of my birth, and those first four months spent with my birth mother. I was not even aware that I had spent those early months with her. I don't think that my adoptive parents knew that, either. It was not for over a half century that the missing first chapter would be filled in, when I was reunited at the age of 52 with my birth family.

My adoptive parents, Frank and Dorothy, had "emigrated" from southern Ontario to a small village just outside of Winnipeg. Frank, a thoughtful and kind man, small of stature and short of breath, had moved west to a supposedly better climate for his bronchial asthmatic condition. He found a job as a clerk in the office of the Canada Cement Company in Fort Whyte. The plan was that Dorothy, his fiancée, would join him when he found a job and a place to live. She would come by train, a common mode of transport in those days. Dorothy stepped off the train one bitterly cold January morning in 1930, with Frank right there to greet her. He was 25 and she was 27 years of age. He had already made arrangements for them to be married that afternoon in a big Anglican church in downtown   Winnipeg. In those days, there was no time to be lost—if she was to be with him overnight.

A shy, slim woman with pretty wavy hair and a gentle smile, Dorothy assumed the role of housewife as did all the other wives in Fort Whyte. She and Frank lived in a small house on the highway that cut through the village. Dorothy became terribly lonely for friends and family in far-away Ontario. Westerners were somewhat wary of Easterners. But Mattie, an outgoing woman, lived just a short distance away down the highway. How Dorothy appreciated the warm welcome she received from Mattie, who became one of her dearest friends.

Children were part of the plan when Dorothy and Frank were married. Six years went by, and they had not conceived a child. It was difficult for them to talk to their family doctor about this very personal problem. And so they applied to adopt a baby, requesting a girl. It was the time when an illegitimate child was stigmatized and called a bastard, and the single mother of that child felt lasting shame since everyone knew she had experienced sex before marriage. Few women had the means to raise a child on their own, and fewer still could endure society's condemnation. And so it was that there were many more children than there were couples wanting to adopt them. It was also the time when adoption was viewed as a natural process by which children, especially babies, could be transferred with ease from one set of parents to another.

Dorothy and Frank were very pleased that they were about to become parents. Their good friend, Mattie, had written a letter supporting Dorothy and Frank's application to adopt, and eagerly anticipated my arrival on the scene. I would have been described as a "blue ribbon baby" in that era: a white, healthy, Protestant, almost newborn.

My adoptive parents did not meet my birth mother when they went to the hospital to get me. They were not told that my birth mother had visited me every day in the hospital nursery for the first four months of my life. She had lived in the hospital and worked for the matron. They were not told that my birth mother smiled and cooed as she nursed me and as she laid me on a blanket outside on the grass on warm, sunny afternoons. They were not told that moments before they met me, my birth mother cuddled me in her arms for the last time, and sobbed as though her heart would break. They were told that my birth mother was too young, too poor and too unmarried to raise me. And they were told that I was a very happy baby and always smiling.

Dorothy and Frank brought me home from the hospital to a small house in the village. 'The baby' was unusually quiet and still. I cannot seem to use the first person 'I' to describe myself at this point of entry into my new family. It's as though I am viewing the baby as if she were not me. The abrupt separation from my birth mother created a primal wound, a rift that was deep and wrenching. The dictionary defines the word "rift" as "split asunder by force; to break, as the heart." Abruptly, I was no longer who I had been.

In her book *The Primal Wound*, Nancy Verrier describes it as "a wound which is physical, emotional, psychological and spiritual, a wound which causes pain so profound as to have been described as cellular by those adoptees who allowed themselves to go that deeply into their pain (1993, 10)." It is caused by the separation of the child from his biological mother, "the connection to whom seems mystical, mysterious, spiritual, and everlasting" (1993, 17).

Bonding begins in utero and continues throughout the postnatal bonding period. When this is interrupted by a postnatal separation from the biological mother, the experience of abandonment and loss that results is indelibly imprinted upon the unconscious mind of the child, causing what Verrier calls "the primal wound". My adoptive mother had no idea. Nor did I. I simply know that 'the baby' was mourning the loss of the familiar voices and sounds, smells, touch and smiles of her birth mother and the hospital staff who had cared for her in her first four months of life, and from whom she had been torn away. She withdrew into sleep and unresponsiveness. She was a very sad baby.

I slept so much that my parents often checked the crib to see if I was still breathing. They could not coax me into a smile. One of their friends asked, "Is there something the matter with her?" My parents worried. A Scottish friend who had ten children assessed things this way, "There is nothing the matter with her. She's a dour youngster. All she needs is a bit of loving."

Looking back, I believe this separation created a well-spring of tears deep within me. I didn't cry much growing up, I think because I feared that if I started, I would not be able to stop. And this feeling did not end until I met my birth mother half a century later, and the two segments of my story were linked.

In enlightened adoption practice, the transition from birth home to adoptive home takes place gradually for children older than newborn, so that the trauma of separation is not so wrenching. Yet it is still too often said that babies are unaware of what is taking place, and so are unaffected by a move and a change of care giver. I know from a very deep place that babies take it all in. Marcy Wineman Axness (1998, 15), an adoptee, mother, and writer asserts that in order for adoptive parents to affirm an adoptee's reality, they must bear in mind that their child lost her mother soon after birth. And so even though an adoptive child may be blessed with loving adoptive parents, this blessing was preceded by a profound loss.

My father, Frank, easily expressed his feelings and pride as a father. As I grew older, he nurtured my love of books and was proud of my achievements at school. Although his chronic ill health sapped his strength, he was a faithful employee who was respected for his gentle authority. Every year he helped villagers who were unable to complete their income tax returns because they were illiterate. A man of integrity, he lived his faith by leading us in prayer when someone was ill, such as when Auntie Mattie's elder daughter suffered complications following the birth of her second child. Dad seemed to identify with the shy, stammering man who became King George VI. If the King could overcome his disability by giving speeches to the Commonwealth, Dad could rise to the occasion by conducting church services in the two-room schoolhouse when there was no preacher available. Like the King, Dad's deep and simple commitment to the Christian faith gave him comfort and strength throughout his life (Shawcross 2009). The King included this poem in his Christmas broadcast to the Commonwealth at the outbreak of World War II in 1939. It became Dad's inspiration:

I said to the man who stood at the gate of the year—

"Give me a light that I may travel safely into the unknown."
And he replied,
"Go out into the darkness and put your hand into the hand
of God.
That shall be to you better than light and safer than a known
way."

Entitled *The Gate of the* Year, this poem by M. L. Haskins (1908) has also become my inspiration. Dad was respectful and considerate of Mom and looked to her for emotional support when he was ill. This was difficult for Mom, who tended to be overwhelmed by circumstances that generated strong feelings.

Dorothy was unsure of herself as a new mother. No rituals or acknowledgment existed for forming a family in this way. She and my father were expected to act as if the baby had been born to them. Dorothy was a private person and it was natural for her to want to keep such information to herself. However, what she lacked in confidence, she more than made up for in constancy. She was always there, and I took her for granted. She was not the kind of mother who hugged, played, laughed and sang with her children. To cry was to "go to pieces" and I saw her cry only once in her life, after she slapped me in exasperation over the fuss I was making for the hundredth time about putting on my brown ribbed stockings over my itchy long wool underwear. Her remorse was overwhelming. I think she was afraid of strong feelings, and the cost of this fear was an inability to express her love openly. Yet a hot breakfast was always on the table before school; dollars were set aside in a tea cup so I could take piano lessons; my Brownie uniform was washed and pressed; there was always a birthday cake, and nicely-wrapped presents under the Christmas tree.

Auntie Mattie, officially my godmother, became my second mother. She was the first person in that small prairie community to come and view the new baby, and ever after, to champion this still somewhat questionable way of acquiring a child. In Mattie's eyes, I was wonderful; her unconditional love was unwavering. I think Mom sometimes wished she could be more like Mattie, a warm, open, happy woman. Yet Mom was never possessive or jealous of the attention that Mattie lavished on me.

When I was just over a year old, Mom faced a crisis. My grandmother who was visiting us from Ontario, developed a lump in her breast. Mom consulted Mattie who had had a double mastectomy a few years before. My grandmother would have to be taken back to Ontario by train. Mattie was quick to volunteer to look after me. For three weeks, Mattie and her two daughters fussed over me and played with me. Mattie and I fell in love. The visit was not without incident, however. I had learned to stand up and did so whenever I was put to bed. Over and over and over, Mattie would enter my bedroom and lay me down. Finally, out of patience, she lay me down, tapped my hand and said firmly, "Stay there." Her daughters were shocked and appalled. "Did you slap Carol?" they asked incredulously. Anyway, it worked! Mom had been warned that I might not know her when she returned. How difficult it must have been for her when I was not all that thrilled to see her again. I wonder whether I was expressing passive anger, a reaction to being "abandoned"—to being separated from a mother, once again.

I was special in Mattie's eyes. Even when I was 45 years old, my eyes filled with tears when she flung her arms wide and said, "Oh Carol, it's so wonderful to see you!" I heard the following words on the lips of many who came to Mattie's funeral years later: "She made me feel special." It was her great gift. Secretly, I felt the most special of all.

Auntie Mattie filled me with delight. When Mom took the five-mile monthly shopping trip by train and street car into Winnipeg, I stayed with Mattie. As she held me in her arms, we would gaze at a painting in her living room while she wove a magical fairy tale out of thin air. At an out-of-tune upright piano, she held me on her lap as she played and sang *Pop Goes the Weasel* in a high, sweet voice. When I was about four, I began to pick out tunes on that piano. Mattie said, "You must get her a piano, Dorothy. Carol has a gift for music." (Somehow Mom and Dad found the money to buy one, and so began my lifelong passion for music.) I would climb the ladder into Mattie's attic and delve into an old dress-up trunk filled with costumes, hats, and a World War I bugle. Nothing was too much trouble. It was a world of make-believe, singing and fun with Mattie.

Auntie Mattie thought that things were always better with a nice "cuppa" tea. And her cups of tea were the best in the world! She would sit me down at a tiny table in her kitchen and fill a small red-and-beige striped china cup, reserved just for me, with real tea and all the sugar lumps and cream I wanted. After three or four refills, she would invert the cup, turn it round in its saucer three times for good luck, and tell my fortune in the tea leaves. The fortune was always exciting and positive.

Mattie's unconditional, exuberant love fed my spirit as long as she lived and even now, long after her death. Her loving heart and open home helped a sober, lonely child thrive in a way I could not have otherwise done. Years later, I began to realize that her life had not been without worry and difficulty. She suffered a double mastectomy following a diagnosis of cancer; she feared she might lose her only son who went to war when he was 18; and there were money problems even though her husband earned a good wage. She taught me that attitude and perspective towards one's circumstances are far more important than the circumstances themselves.

Two years after I was adopted, Mom became pregnant. No one was more astonished than she was, except maybe her doctor. Dad was delighted. She experienced morning sickness and, with her lifelong aversion to throwing up, this was a trial. Women did not share stories about pregnancy in those days, nor did they get much prenatal education from their doctors. Mom found childbirth unbearably painful and frightening, and never wanted to experience it again. My new sister, Lois, was a lovely, sweet child with blue eyes and blonde hair that rolled into ringlets when she was a toddler. Our parents were very pleased to have two girls.

I was a slim, tiny child with knobby knees and dark, short, straight hair—one wisp always escaping the barrette. Our family did not have a lot of visitors. When we did, I hid behind the chesterfield, in painful shyness, listening to the grown-ups talking. This was my refuge till I was four. After an hour behind the chesterfield, I would venture forth, begin talking to the guests, and by the end of the visit, be sorry to see them leave.

The small village of Fort Whyte, dominated by the Canada Cement plant, was populated by no more than one hundred families living along the highway. Most of the village men worked in the plant and had subsistence farms. The women were housewives who stayed home to look after their families. Some were not seen from one year's end to the next, except peeping behind their curtains or seated beside their husbands in the family car. Many villagers were peasants from Belgium and Ukraine. A few second-generation men whose parents had come from the United Kingdom seemed to have the best jobs at the plant. I smiled shyly as I made my way around the village. Behind the smile, I was often frightened of the townspeople, especially the men with their gruff exteriors.

No child escapes the teasing of other children. I had no answer for the one who asked, "Hey, how come you have such hairy arms?" I would go home in tears to Mom who did not seem to know how to comfort, strengthen, or help me learn to laugh it off. I saw that such incidents upset her, so I tried to keep my hurts to myself.

Prevailing adoption practice dictated that the adopted child's legal connection with her birth family be severed totally so as to enable adopted children to become legally and in large degree, psychologically the same as children born and raised in non-adoptive families. This was the "as if born" concept in which adoptive parents liked to believe that the child never had any other parents and belonged to them "as if" she were of their own blood. The birth mother pretended "as if" she never had given birth to a child that she relinquished. And the adoptee identified with her adoptive parents "as if" they were her "real" parents. Sealing the adoption records reinforced the concept. The child "for all purposes" became the child of his or her adoptive parents and "for all purposes" ceased to be the child of his or her birth parents. Thus, from the beginning in most western societies, the concept of adoption has been embedded in the myth of rebirth of the child.

Although my parents followed the prevailing adoption practice, they were honest and enlightened parents of the 1930s. They told me my story as soon as I was old enough to understand the words. Sadly, this was all too often not the case for most children in closed adoptions in which original birth records were sealed, no identifying birth family information was passed on to the adoptive parents, and no contact took place between birth families and adoptive families. My story went something like this: "We wanted a baby girl, so we went to a hospital where there were a lot of babies. We looked at them all, and you had a beautiful smile, and we picked you to be our little girl." As any child might do, I assumed that this was the way that people got babies.

It was a lovely story. But why was I so sad? Years later, it was comforting to hear Marlene Gates Howard, my lifelong friend, say "I think you're lucky, Carol. You can be sure that your adoptive parents wanted you." And yet I was eventually to realize that the idealistic concept of the adopted child being a chosen child was not accurate. It was not the adoptive parents who did the choosing, but rather the social worker who matched the child with the adoptive parents. And in the era of today's open adoptions where identifying information is not only shared but an ongoing extended family relationship is formed between birth families and adoptive families, it is the birth parent who chooses the adoptive parents for her unborn child. Looked at another way, no matter how it is softened, a child chosen by adoptive parents is a child unchosen by birth parents.

The reality is that adoptive parents usually try for years to have a child born to them for several heartfelt reasons—for genetic continuity; to have a jointly conceived child as an expression of love for each other; and to have both the psychological and physical experience of pregnancy and childbirth (Johnston 1992). Fertility treatments—the second choice for most couples when biology isn't working for them—was not available until the 1950s—so it was not an option for my parents. The last resort to which a couple turns is adoption. Even preferential adopters, who choose to adopt even though they can give birth, almost always adopt after giving birth to one or two biological children first.

One day when I was about six years old, a chum and I had a spat. She used an effective way to taunt me: "You're adopted. Your mom and dad are not your real parents, you know." I did go home with that one. My parents reacted in surprise and honesty. "Yes dear," they said. "You are adopted. But you know that, don't you? We told you how we got you—at the hospital where there were lots of babies, and we picked you, remember?"

Had you been present at that moment, you would probably have thought that the child accepted this explanation easily. Again, I cannot use the first person pronoun to describe that little girl. Time stood still. It was a *kairos* moment, as the Greeks define it—a supreme moment in which something special happens. It was the first time I had heard the term "adopted". And it was then that I felt different from everyone else: I had not come into my family in the same way that other children had. I became conscious of my woundedness. Albert Camus phrases it eloquently, "But from the moment he knows, his tragedy begins" (1955,122).

What I didn't know then was that my adoption was an open secret in the small village and beyond. It was hush-hush knowledge. I did not ask my parents any more questions about my adoption until I was in my late teens. They did not raise the subject in any kind of open, natural way. They felt it was not anyone's business but our own. They had told me the truth, and what more was there to say? It was a typical closed adoption of that era.

The secret was kept in countless ways. Each incident relating to the secret underscored the feeling that my differentness made me "not as good as" everyone else. A part of me was waif, alone and lonely in the world in spite of having a secure, safe home with parents who loved me. My parents' choice of adoption was not their first choice, and I internalized myself as second-best.

I tanned easily; my dark skin turning a deeper brown. Someone would tease, "Gosh, you're dark. Are you part Indian?" I would smile in discomfort; my parents would say nothing. This happened more than once and I began to wonder if I *was* part Indian. When there was covert racism in the question, it did not feel good. Strangers to the family would physically compare my sister and me—a common approach that adults take to children. They would admire my sister's blue eyes and blonde ringlets, and to me they would say, "Where did you get those big, brown eyes? From your father?" My parents said nothing. The remarks did not feel like compliments, but rather near-exposure of an almost shameful secret. My parents' silence hurt. How was I to know that this was the late '30s when they were advised to keep adoption a secret from the outside world to shield me from the stigma of illegitimacy? There were no follow-up conversations of such incidents, ever.

At age eight, I was a skinny child with a poor appetite. My conscientious adoptive mother said it was time for my annual checkup with our family doctor. Tall, stern Dr. Stirling peered down at me over his glasses and ordered me to take off all my clothes. Cold, naked and seated on the high examining table, I listened to him tell my mother that I was indeed underweight, for which he prescribed a tonic. I hated those nasty-tasting remedies. I remained silent, keeping my embarrassment and humiliation locked inside.

Some years later, when I was 15, I went to see another doctor for a checkup in order to attend Girl Guide camp. This doctor needed some medical history. Was there a history of heart disease, asthma, diabetes, epilepsy, mental illness etc. etc. in my family, he asked. I didn't know how to answer. I knew that my adoptive family's medical history was unrelated to my own, about which I knew absolutely nothing. My adoption was not openly talked about, so heart pounding, I gave him answers "as if born" to my adoptive parents. I felt like a fake.

In my late teens there was need for another checkup. This time it was for a summer job for which I had applied. When this doctor asked for medical history, I blurted out, "I'm adopted". With a slash of his pen, the doctor drew a thick black line diagonally down the form, and printed "*ADOPTED*" alongside of it. I felt stripped naked—different from everyone else, a person without a history, a non-person.

At school I found village children whose birth stories were akin to my own. Maybe children with primal wounds are drawn to each other. We were the ones on the edge. Gordie was an active freckle-faced towhead who was being raised by his maternal grandparents whom he called Mom and Dad. His "Aunt" Kate, who was really his mother, came home often to visit. I noticed what an inordinate interest she had in Gordie. It seemed that everyone but Gordie knew the truth about his origins. An open secret. Gordie was full of imagination as he played games of soldiers at war, threw marbles in the dirt, fashioned guns from pieces of wood, and constructed entire villages in my sandbox. He was a safe, comfortable friend.

Muriel was my age and bigger by a head. Wilful and undisciplined, she wore beautiful clothes and a permanent scowl. She

Dorothy   **Frank**
Lois   **Carol**

lived in the only grand house in the village, as her father was the superintendent of the cement plant. Her big play room was distinctly uninviting, with broken toys and naked dolls tossed about. It was a house full of empty. Muriel had been born to her birth mother in

England, and adopted into the home of her maternal aunt, who, like an English flower, was too delicate for the likes of rough-and-ready Canadians. Muriel's adoptive mother seemed to know nothing about raising children. Muriel was rough. On one too many occasions after she had twirled me around by the neck, I went crying home to my parents. Frustrated, Dad burst out, "Well, just go and give her a good punch!" The light dawned. Next time Muriel advanced, I bent over, head forward, and ran full steam into her stomach! This warranted a complaint from her mother to mine, but Muriel directed her aggression elsewhere from then on. Muriel's origin was an open secret: in the good times it was talked about in the confines of home, and in the rough-and-tumble of children's interactions, it was sometimes tossed out as a way to wound.

Kalfern and her sister arrived suddenly in our village to live in the home of Mrs. T. They were to be her foster children. She scrubbed them with harsh soap and a hard brush in the bath the night they arrived. Nervous, sensitive, and skinny, Kalfern had learning difficulties, which did not endear her to the strict, unyielding, mean Miss Neal, our primary school teacher. Unlike her sister who was lippy and wet the bed and soon moved on to yet another foster home, Kalfern, the compliant one, did what was expected of her. She felt hugely second-best to Mrs. T.'s favourite daughter. Kalfern and I became friends. She told me that she had parents and brothers. "Why can't you live with them?" I asked. Eyes huge and hurting, she told me that her mother had become ill and had been sent to a mental hospital. I had not heard of that kind of illness before. Her father had not been able to look after the children, and they became foster kids. Kalfern said I was very lucky to have such a nice mom. After a few months, Kalfern was sent to another foster home. Her letters told of being treated like hired help—she was expected to shovel animal manure out of the barn. We wrote to each other over the years. Eventually she found permanent foster parents who were kind. Years later, she told me that her mother had never left the mental hospital. She had set fire to herself one day and burned to death. Kalfern matured into a very attractive woman. The stigma of the foster child seems to have stayed deep within Kalfern. She led a home-bound life as she and her husband raised three sons within the predictability and security net of the Canadian Armed Forces. After 70 years, the bond between us remains. Once a year we get together and renew our friendship as we talk of our common past, our lives now, and our future.

Margaret and Doreen, sisters of Cree heritage, came to live in the village each summer with their older sister, who was the wife of a quiet Danish man. During the school year they lived in an Indian residential school a few hundred miles away. They had been taken off the reserve and away from their parents to attend this residential school. They did not talk about their parents, and I didn't ask. Their sister was a silent woman, with no upper teeth, who stayed indoors. On rare occasions she accompanied her husband to town in their car. I was one of the few people in the village who actually saw her. While I waited in the cold back shed off the kitchen for Doreen and Margaret to come out to play, their sister would appear in the kitchen. The girls were allowed to play only in their front yard. I suspect their older sister believed that segregation was the only way to handle things in an all-white community. Her niece lived down the road in a tumble-down shack filled with eight children and a husband who beat her. There was little contact between the two families. Doreen, Margaret, and I would sit in one corner of their front yard, sharing secrets, playing games, and reciting rhymes they had learned at residential school. Once or twice a summer, I would invite them to play at my house across the road. Seeking permission from their older sister was a major undertaking. A couple of times they were allowed to come to my house for one hour. I suspect permission was given because my mother was viewed as a kind and gentle woman. They would leave obediently at the appointed time. Then their summer visits ended. I heard that as young adults, they had moved into Winnipeg. We lost touch. Some years later, I learned that Margaret had died in childbirth with complications related to toxemia. Had she lived in poverty without adequate medical care?

Gordie, Muriel, Kalfern, Doreen, Margaret and me—all of us were children who were not being raised by the mothers who had given birth to us. It was an unspoken bond.

Mom said I didn't really "come out of myself" until I started school. I was a quick learner, and in school, I could prove myself worthy. I was a compliant child; people tell me that I was always pleasant and smiling. This masked my sadness and loneliness and the feeling that I was not the same as everyone else. Since the adoption was not an open subject in my home, the secret was kept from my sister, Lois. As incredible as it may seem, I did not realize this. It was many years later that I began to understand the impact this must have had on my sister's life.

Carol, age 16

Chapter Three

The Teen Years

Ambivalence took root deep within.
— Betty Jean Lifton

In my early teens, thoughts of my birth mother moved from the back burner to the front burner of my mind. A fantasy began to take shape, partly as a result of what had happened to a couple of older girls in the village. Mom's good friend and neighbour, Grace, was troubled about the young man her daughter, Diana, was dating. His employment prospects were dim, and he drank too much. One day Mom told me that Diana was pregnant and would soon be getting married. Mom said, "Diana has broken her mother's heart." Mom was not connecting this situation to that of my birth mother. But I did. It was a heavy message that I took to heart. Is this what an unwanted pregnancy did to a family? Then there was Angela, pregnant, unmarried, and unwilling to hide behind closed doors. As she dared to walk about the community, people were silent and scandalized. Angela kept the baby and eventually married the baby's father. But these hasty marriages did not remove the taint of shame and stigma that followed these women.

My fantasy about my birth mother was of a beautiful, sensitive, poor girl, alone and isolated, who loved me but was unable to keep me. I would take the fantasy just so far, and then uncertainty swept through me. Maybe she never gave me a moment's thought after she gave birth to me. To quote Betty Jean Lifton (1975, 106), "Ambivalence took root within." I had not yet begun to think about my birth father, although I think there was a subconscious connection between him and the romantic fantasies I would weave about boys to whom I was attracted. And there was always one.

The positive birth mother fantasy is written about in the adoption literature. It has been described by women adoptees who participated in a research project I undertook in 1989-90 that focused on their experiences of adoption reunion. And it has been an integral part of my own adoption experience. The fantasy mother is a positive figure—often beautiful, sensitive, spirited, creative, courageous, and always nurturing. There is usually a good reason why she had to give up her baby. Sometimes a fantasy that runs counter to the positive one is the birth mother whom adoptees fear they will find. This one is rejecting, or crude, ugly and demanding, or mentally incompetent and/or very needy. These opposing fantasies serve to explain the ambivalence experienced by adoptees when they consider searching for their birth mother. They tell themselves it may be better to live with the dream than to find reality and be dashed to earth by it. Betty Jean Lifton (1975), an adult adoptee who writes profoundly and insightfully about the adoptee experience, believes that for the adoptee, the birth parents never completely lose the aura of fantasy, both positive and negative, even after adoption reunion.

Time was running out in Fort Whyte for our family. At 49 years of age, my father was on sick leave and would not be returning to work. His asthmatic condition had worsened. He had not the full capacity of even one lung. His body was retaining fluid, and he had congestive heart problems. As well, the Fort Whyte schooling situation for my sister and me required us to make a change. Teachers in the tiny two-room schoolhouse provided schooling as far as Grade 8. So my sister and I began to take the bus to school in the Winnipeg suburb of Fort Garry. Before that, I had joined Girl Guides at the Anglican church our family was attending. This meant that my father drove me the five miles in and out from Fort Whyte to Fort Garry at least once a week. Five miles. Now it's nothing; then it was a gift. My world was expanding, and I was thrilled with the new friends I was making.

I became close friends with Marianne, a girl I had met in Girl Guides and who was in my class at school. I often slept over at her house, talking into the night about boys we had crushes on. One night I shared the secret of my adoption with her, and found that she accepted me without fanfare. Why did I fear that she wouldn't? She shared her own story: the pain as a young child of lying in bed at night, listening to her parents' loud, angry fights. A bitter separation led to a move across the country for her mother and her four children. Marianne told me how shocked her mother had been to have a baby boy born with a hare lip and cleft palate, a congenital deformity for which her mother was totally unprepared. Many operations and reconstructions followed for Marianne's brother Ed. (This experience of Ed's stayed with me when I, an adoptee with no known medical history, began to think of having children of my own. I mistakenly thought it was an inherited defect.) Sharing our family stories gave support to both Marianne and me. And so she became my silent ally when the topic of adoption arose in conversations with teenage friends. My heart would thump with anxiety, and I would fall silent as another classmate's adoption was discussed. When I blurted out the fact of my own adoption, the conversation came to an abrupt halt.

It was not that people were critical of me. They weren't. I didn't fully understand my reaction to a neighbour's comment to Mom that she and Dad were lucky that I had turned out so well. I was furious. I felt demeaned and depersonalized, as though I was a radio that had proven to be a satisfactory purchase. Mom was surprised by my reaction. We did not explore it. I think it struck a nerve because, in fact, I had internalized the importance of doing well, especially in school; in other words, of being a satisfactory product. Betty Jean Lifton (1975) describes it as the adoption bargain internalized by the adoptee—to be a perfect model daughter so the choice that the adoptive parents made will have been worth it.

When the possibility arose for us to move into Fort Garry, I couldn't wait. We found a dear little bungalow, a stone's throw from the church we belonged to and the school I attended. It was the perfect move, and I never looked back. As a self-absorbed teenager, I was not thinking very much about my parents—the big adjustment for my mother, having to leave good friends behind, and my father's worsening illness. My sister and I began attending different schools and developed different sets of friends. We had little in common during this time.

It was the early 1950s, and I began to date in my early teens. Whenever I had a steady boyfriend, I would share the fact of my adoption with him. There wasn't that much to tell because I knew so little. I believe there was a dual motivation: to see if I was acceptable and accepted, and to create an aura of mystery to make me more interesting. None of the boys I dated ever reacted negatively to the fact of my adoption. Why did I fear that they would? Some of them tried to imagine my beginnings. The seeds were being planted that would propel me towards a search for my birth mother.

You might have called me a teen who had it all. To my amazement, I was voted president of the Student Council of our small high school. I was also selected to sit on Eaton's Junior Council, comprising a male and female representative from each high school in the city. This role gave me a part-time job in Eaton's flagship Winnipeg store. My good marks and participation in school life resulted in my being chosen as one of 50 girls to go on an all-expenses -paid trip to Queen Elizabeth II's coronation in 1953, followed by a tour of the British Isles and France. The trip was sponsored by industrialist/philanthropist Garfield Weston. I was also awarded the Governor-General's Academic Medal as the student with the highest grade point aVerage in my high school—Viscount Alexander Collegiate Institute. I took my belief in God seriously, taught Sunday School and loved to wrestle with theological and ethical issues in a teen group encouraged by a progressive minister at the local United Church. I was aiming for the Gold Cord award in Girl Guides but time ran out on me. I continued to take piano lessons from a gifted teacher who imbued me with a deep love of music. I had lots of boyfriends and close girlfriends. Betty Jean Lifton's poetic comment resonates: "As a tree sleeps in winter, so did some part of me stay sleeping even while the rest of me bloomed" (1975, 5).

I was not a bit sure that I deserved it all, nor did I feel confident that I was on solid ground. For example, it was my task, as school president, to make a phone call to a Fort Garry businessman, requesting a financial contribution for the first-ever school year book. I procrastinated as long as I could, and then wrote down what I would say on a piece of paper, so that I wouldn't go blank. I finally dialed the number when my parents were not around to overhear how nervous I was.

After graduating from high school, I went on to take a general Arts course at the University of Manitoba. I was no longer a big fish in a small pond. It was a challenge to be expected to think my own thoughts instead of to learn and regurgitate someone else's views. My steady boyfriend was a Canadian Forces jet pilot stationed in Quebec. We began to think of marriage. The sensible path would have been to stay home, get a job in Winnipeg and earn as much money as I could to continue at university since my two-year bursary was used up. Instead, I went off to work for the summer of 1955 at the Banff Springs Hotel as a chambermaid. I had a marvellously exciting time climbing mountains, soaking in hot springs, exploring brilliant blue-green lakes, and dancing, dancing, dancing the nights away. All of this should have told me that I was not ready to get married, but I was not willing to face it.

After that carefree summer, I returned home to Fort Garry having promised my jet pilot that I would leave Arts and enter the Faculty of Education to become a teacher. Thus, I would have a portable career as I moved from one air force base to another with my husband. Then reality struck me on the morning I was to register for Education. It was if I was on autopilot as I found myself registering for Arts instead. When I told my mother what I had done, horror broke through her usual reserve. She liked my jet pilot very much, and reminded me of my commitment to him. My conscience took over, so next day, I cancelled my registration in Arts and registered for Education. It was a disaster. Almost immediately I fell into a depression. It became so deep that as I tried to smile and be cheerful in my classes, my facial muscles would ache afterwards. I avoided my friends because I could not be myself, and I didn't know what was wrong with me. When friends did come to see me, and I saw the looks of concern and bewilderment on their faces, I wanted them to leave because it was so painful. I felt as though I'd been a fake all my life, and the real me had emerged. In despair, I was a profound disappointment to myself and certainly to those who viewed me as bright and full of promise. I believed that I had not deserved the awards that had come my way in high school, and that I was not capable of genuine love for a man, since I longed to escape the commitment I had made to my jet pilot.

My parents were concerned and sought out the name of a psychiatrist for me to see. I would have none of it. In my eyes, the stigma of being labelled mentally ill was worse than any help I might receive. Things came to a head at Christmas time. My marks in Education were the worst I had ever received. My self-confidence was gone, and the breaking point was near. I was assigned to practice teach in a junior high school class. I was to prepare lessons in Maths and English grammar for a morning's teaching with the supervising class teacher looking on. The night before, anxiety paralyzed me. I could not prepare even one lesson. How could I pull it off? The kids would see right through me. Then it dawned on me that I was not sufficiently mature for the responsibility of teaching children. It was irresponsible of me to continue. I did not even know that I was deeply depressed! I withdrew from the Education program, and stayed alone in my room for two weeks. My jet pilot was understandably having second thoughts, and we agreed to part, which was a huge relief to me.

The depression gradually lifted. Because I didn't know what else to do, I took a general secretarial course at a business school in downtown Winnipeg. Around that time, a new boyfriend, Ken Shipley, began to call and take me out. I know I was not very interesting to be with, but he accepted me just as I was, for which I was very grateful. The business course which was extremely easy for me as I had learned to type 40 words a minute in Grade 6 in my two-room schoolhouse, was somehow therapeutic. Upon its completion, I went to work as a secretary for a professor at the University of Manitoba. It was not at all what I had hoped for myself, but I was doing the best I could. And the specter of depression haunted me. I was easily thrown by upsetting circumstances, and whenever I felt mildly depressed, a chill would go through me as I recalled how awful it had been. I feared it would return full force. And since I had turned down psychiatric help, I did not understand the underlying reasons for it.

Carol and baby son, Dave

Chapter Four

Motherhood

Your children are not your children.
They are the sons and daughters of Life's longing for itself.
They come through you but not from you.
And though they are with you, yet they belong not to you.
— Kahlil Gibran

In my early twenties, Ken Shipley and I were dating steadily. We were becoming serious about each other, and marriage was entering our conversations. We both wanted children. I trusted Ken, had confidence in him, and knew instinctively that he would be a wonderful father. Thoughts of what I thought was Marianne's brother's genetic condition came to me, and I wanted to prepare for any possible conditions my children might inherit from me. I broached the subject with Mom and was both surprised and pleased that she was willing to contact a Manitoba government social worker for me. Once the appointment was set up, it flooded over me how much I wanted to know about my origins. The first chapter of my life would no longer be blank. Riding the bus from the university to the appointment downtown, I found myself telling a priest, whom I barely knew, what I was about to do.

The social worker read from a file, open on her desk. I sat across from her. For the first time, I learned that my birth mother was Ukrainian, that, in her twenties, she had given birth to me and that I had remained in the Grace Hospital nursery in Winnipeg until I was placed for adoption. During that time she had lived in the hospital hostel, visiting with me, and working in the hospital until I left with my new parents when I was four months old. The details were sparse. She was single; she had gone to high school; she had been a "domestic"; and she was good at needlework. Her father, a teacher, had died of an undisclosed cause in his forties; she had one sister, and no one in the family seemingly knew about my birth.

The social worker went on to say that either of two men could have been my birth father: a man of Scottish Canadian ancestry in his late twenties who liked to read and who was musical—in fact, he was the leader of a small orchestra; or a man of English Canadian background, in his early thirties, who had been in the Armed Forces and who had a weak heart. Inheritable medical or genetic conditions, if any, were not recorded.

I was very surprised, even excited, about the Ukrainian part. Many school friends in Fort Whyte were second-generation Ukrainian-Canadians, and I had been very fond of a young man of Ukrainian descent. After twenty years of not knowing, and feeling bewilderingly fake whenever someone asked me about my ethnic background, I knew it at last! What I did with the birth father information was interesting. I chose the musical Scot to be my birth father. I created a fantasy of a dashing, handsome, romantic man who swept my mother off her feet. It is impossible to keep reality separate from fantasy when you are trying to fill in the gaps of your own life story. As many adoptees do, I was weaving the factual information of the social history into my fantasy to make it more beautiful.

During the interview the social worker asked, "Would you like to know your birth mother's name?" There were no laws prohibiting the sharing of such information at that time. Some years later, however, identifying information such as this was considered highly confidential and impossible to obtain. The prevailing attitudes of the times swept over me in that split second. I blurted, "No, I am very happy in my adoptive family, and do not want to know who she is." I was to rue that split-second decision for years. I believe three things caused me to turn down this information: first, adoptees were thought to be ungrateful and disloyal to search for their birth parents, and I did not want to hurt my adoptive parents; second, adoptees who searched were labelled psychologically unstable and socially impaired individuals and I certainly didn't want to take that on; and third, I was just plain scared. What would I find in Pandora's box?

A few years passed. Ken and I were married, and were fortunate to be able to conceive and have children easily. I gave birth to our three children in Grace Hospital where I was born years earlier. Thoughts and feelings for my birth mother overwhelmed me as I lay in my hospital bed having given birth to our first-born son, Kevin, on Christmas Eve. The labour had been long, hard, and slow. At 8 pounds 5 ounces, Kevin was a strong, vigorous baby right from the squishy moment of birth. I was surrounded by loving family members, with congratulatory cards pouring in, and a dozen beautiful, big red roses, symbolizing love, from an ecstatic father-in-law upon the arrival of his first grandson. My joy was boundless as I held my child, the perfect Christmas Eve gift. But... how had it been for my birth mother? Had she been all alone during her labour and delivery? Had anyone visited her following my birth? Now that I had experienced the profound joy and the hard labour that comes with the primal birth experience, I wondered how it had been for her. I felt sadness and compassion for her loss as mother more than I felt my own loss as child.

The years went on, and two more beautiful children were born. The joy as each one entered our lives was profound. Ken and I and the children, Kevin, David, and Jill, moved to Saskatoon when Jill was a small baby. My role as mom to three little ones took my time, energy, and enthusiasm. Even though Ken's salary was a modest one, I was fortunate to be able to stay home with the children, and pursue my goal of a university degree, one class at a time. Beyond that, the future filled me with apprehension. I lived off and on with mild depression and was too easily thrown by circumstances which shook my self-esteem. I had the sense of being in search of... I knew not what.

When Jill was five years old, she began to wish for a little sister at the same time that I felt compelled to adopt a little girl. Somehow our family would not be complete until we did. Before we were married, Ken and I had discussed adoption, agreeing that if we were unable to conceive and have children, that we would adopt. There had been no time to think of adoption until now—the babies had come one after the other. I broached the subject of our adopting, and Ken felt we could not handle it financially. I knew he was right—I was not earning a salary at the time. I dropped the subject.

A year later in 1969 Ken and I had a fanciful discussion about what we'd do if we won the lottery. "Know what I'd do?" I said. "I'd pay off our mortgage, finish the lower level of our house, get a nice camper trailer and a good car. I wouldn't change a thing except to make the life we have easier. And... I'd adopt a little girl." Ken looked thoughtful.

A few weeks later, he said he thought we should open up the subject of adopting a child. He was earning a little more now, having received a recent raise. Several families we knew had adopted Metis children through a Saskatchewan government program called AIM— Adopt Indian Metis. We understood it to be a way for these children to have permanent adoptive homes rather than remaining in foster care throughout their childhoods. The story of adopting Elaine is for another chapter.

Once Elaine, at age three and a half years, was settled into our family, I had to sort out what I wanted to do with the rest of my life. In my early thirties, I was experiencing a classic mid-life crisis. In psychotherapy with Dr. Dave Keegan, I learned that adoption was the base note on which my life song rested. I explored it as far as I could. There wasn't much known about the importance of adoption reunions between adoptees and birth parents, and Dr. Keegan did not urge me to seek a reunion.

On television and in newspapers, I was hearing about individuals in the emotional throes of a reunion and it sounded like a lot of histrionics to me. I wondered what a reunion with my birth mother would have to do with me. I had a life, and a busy one, after all. I had not done any reading on adoption reunion, or adoption in general. I even found it upsetting to hear a psychologist speak about the general impact of adoption on children. It was a loaded issue, and I stayed away from it. But it was always on the back burner of my mind.

Kevin   David Carol Jill Elaine   Ken
1971 at Pike Lake, Saskatchewan

Chapter Five

The Search

It is better to know than not to know.
— Jean Paton

The adoption reunion whoopla continued, and gradually societal attitudes began to change. No longer were adoptees described as ungrateful and maladjusted if they searched for their birth parents. The concept that it was their right to know their roots, their history, the first chapter of their lives, and even to develop a relationship with their birth family was taking hold.

The shift in societal attitudes towards adoption had actually begun to take form in the early '50s. Jean Paton (1954) was the first American adoptee to document the feeling of "genealogical bewilderment". It was a sense of emptiness, of not knowing one's biological origins that adult adoptees experienced. She challenged the prevailing attitudes that a birth mother who gives up a child and never searches was considered to be acting out of integrity, and that an adoptee who searches is committing an act of disloyalty towards her adoptive parents. However, I was completely unaware of this wave of liberalization spreading through the world of adoption. Even if I had known about it, I was not yet ready to open my own Pandora's box of adoption.

Jean Paton maintained that no adoptees under 60 years of age should say they have completed their attitude about their adoption. She also maintained that the type of birth-parent image an adoptee carries in her head is important because it influences behaviour. I am convinced that an adoptee's attitude about her adoption ought to remain open to new insights for one's lifetime.

Adoptees that Paton studied spoke of their loneliness and a feeling of not really belonging anywhere. Seeking a birth family for the sense of security that they were missing and discovering that the birth family could not provide it resulted in a greater loss than before. In spite of the disillusioning experience that knowing often is, Paton believed it was easier to make an adjustment to a known situation than to one that was not known. In other words, *it is better to know than not to know* (1954, 128). Jean Paton liberalized the adoption climate so that adoptees felt freer to speak the truth about their adoption and reunion experiences.

The turbulent '60s and early '70s were periods of new militancy for many minority groups. The climate was more receptive to what another American adoptee had to say about adoption, search, and reunion. Florence Fisher, who has been called the Betty Friedan of the adoptee liberation movement, described the adoptee's problem of unknown origin. Fisher said:

> Fear and the unknown are inextricably linked. To give birth [to a child of one's own] is to establish the hereditary link. It forces you to think back about your own heritage. The adoptee goes back only into himself. Beyond that there is a wall. And it is the fear of what is behind that wall... that causes all the mischief (1973, 15).

Fisher also pointed out that "the search" signified ingratitude, rejection and pain for many people who could not imagine that it might bring happiness and relief to all concerned.

As Ken and I raised our four children, I took university classes, one at a time. As my self-confidence rose, I would put my big toe into volunteer social work that came my way. I became a board member of Anetawikit, a small group home for young women who were making an adoption plan for their unborn children. As a hands-on board member, I met and talked with a number of these birth mothers. On the surface, I was trying my hand at social work. Subconsciously, I was checking out whether these women loved their babies. And each one did—unconditionally. My search for my own birth mother had begun.

It was 1980. Ken and I and our four children had just returned to Canada after more than two years of living and working in Botswana in southern Africa, and we settled in Ottawa rather than returning to Saskatchewan to live. The only permanent job in Ottawa that came my way was at the Children's Aid Society (CAS), working with children at risk in their families of origin and with children in foster care. Adoption was a stone's throw away from this work. I was drawn to working in adoption since it provided insecure, traumatized children with permanence. I knew instinctively, however, that I could not do adoption work. As Adoptee, I had too many unanswered questions and too much unresolved pain. My CAS unit supervisor sensed this and suggested that I place my name on the Adoption Disclosure Register in Manitoba to indicate my interest in connecting with my birth mother. I did so and was informed that there could be no reunion because my birth mother was not registered. This was how a passive registry worked: if adoptee and birth mother both registered, there could be a reunion; if the birth mother did not register, the Adoption Disclosure staff would not actively search for her to see if she wanted contact with her child. The liberalization of laws controlling access to sealed records, which had begun in the mid-1970s had not yet altered the adoption disclosure policies and practice in Manitoba.

But what did it mean that my birth mother had not registered? One never really knows and one speculates... was it that she wasn't interested, or that she was ill, or worse, that she was dead? Then I heard about a volunteer organization named Parent Finders that lends support to adoptees and birth parents who want to find each other. I attended a meeting and was put off by the militancy and anger of the speakers. They were unequivocal in recommending a reunion for everyone, and intolerant of those who were hesitant. Those seeking reunions seemed desperate and unfulfilled, and those who had had successful reunions were tearful and glowing. I backed away. However, I got some tips on how to conduct a search of my own. I learned that my birth family name might be on my Adoption Order which I had never seen. And yet, I backed away. Would finding my birth family make any real difference to my sense of self, to who I was? My ambivalence slowed my process.

Years later, I read an article by Lois Melina in the *Adopted Child* newsletter of November 1998, which gave explanation to what I was going through:

For adoptees the process of searching seems to have a distinct character. Whether the search is something the adoptee has always planned or something precipitated by a life event, it often begins haltingly, as though the act of actually searching must be re-evaluated once the process is started.... Throughout the process, the adoptee may take another look at her original motivation. If the adoptee feels close to her adoptive parents and good about her adoption, she may ask herself questions like: How will my sense of self be different if I learn more about my origins—aren't I the same person whether I know or not? Why do I want to stir up unknown waters if I love my [adoptive] family and generally feel good about myself?

Melina noted that answering such questions and dealing with the feelings they engender, takes the adoptee time. This is actually the preparation for the search. It readies the self for what the adoptee instinctively knows will be an upheaval.

So the adoptee may take two steps toward the search and one step back; proceeding into the unknown and retreating into the familiar. The pace is her own. It may be shaped in part by the amount of time or resources she has to devote to it and by the support she receives from friends and family. It is certainly shaped by her emotional readiness. It is also driven by an awareness that if she waits too long, it may be too late to find what she is seeking....

Melina maintained that even when adoptees ready themselves for the unknown, there is often a difference between the abstract idea of what they might find and the reality. The searching and the finding unleashes emotions in ways no one can fully prepare for (1998, 1).

I drew away. And then came a big breakthrough. One day while visiting Mom in Belleville, I took the plunge and broached the subject of adoption in a general way. Mom said she wondered if I ever thought of searching. I said, almost without expression, that it had crossed my mind, and I wondered if she had my Adoption Order. "Yes, I do, dear. I think it's in the strong box in my closet. Would you like me to look for it?" I acted calm; I could hardly breathe. Another *kairos* moment. She was so willing. Why had I waited so long? There, on the Adoption Order, was my original name: Carol Lynn Bachinski changed to Carol Ann Bowyer. As soon as I could, I shared this news with Marianne, my dear friend from high school, who was convinced that I had a right to know my origins. As amazing luck would have it, she was now a nursing instructor at the Grace Hospital in Winnipeg, where I had been born. "Why not come to Winnipeg," she asked," and we'll find a way into the hospital medical records on a Sunday morning when the regular staff is off for the weekend." A private-eye search was under way.

I flew to Winnipeg from Ottawa, and one hour later, found myself in Marianne's office at the Grace, where I donned a white lab coat, clasped a clipboard, and listened, unbelieving, as she conceived out of thin air a research project that the two of us were undertaking. It would be a study of the link between oxygen deprivation at birth and mental retardation. One of the infants whose file we wanted to find was Carol Bachinski's (mine)! We entered the Medical Records Department where Marianne, with aplomb, introduced us both. I just stood there, speechless and sweating. Soon we were riffling through the filing boxes of babies born in 1936, the year of my birth. There were very few cards for that year, and mine was not one of them. The medical librarian thought there had been a fire many years before, and some of the files had been destroyed. So near, and yet so far. To console ourselves somehow, we looked at more recent cards of babies, Kevin, David, and Jill, born to Carol Shipley. No oxygen deprivation there!

While in Winnipeg, I met with a social worker in Adoption Disclosure to obtain an updated written social history. Parent Finders had advised me to ask for an updated history every few years in the hope of obtaining a few more tidbits of information each time. The social worker was pleasant but unwilling to go beyond the law to provide anything but non-identifying information. I wanted to snatch the file out of her hands. Florence Fisher described how she had felt when people refused to give her information about her past: "I held back a great emotional scream inside me" (1973, 81). That was it... a great emotional scream held inside me. I was a client and an enraged one. It was my right to know. Did they think I would handle the information like an insensitive clod? As a future social worker, that feeling of powerlessness stayed with me as I strove to connect and to empathize with my clients.

As for sealing of the records, this very act perpetuated the stigma of illegitimacy rather than removing it. Where else in society is such secrecy condoned? Fisher stated that the practice of [closed] adoption consigns a child to lifelong anonymity. It was psychiatrist Robert Lifton's contention, as quoted in Lifton (1975, 248) that the need for origins is more basic to a person than sex drive, and that a gap in one's sense of identity contributes to a sense of distance from people . Studies by professionals like Freud and Erikson confirmed that "knowledge of one's hereditary background is a necessary part of identity formation and that any interference with the process of linking with the past is likely to result in identity confusion" (Lifton 1975, 65-66).

For the remainder of the Winnipeg visit, I pored through Henderson's Directories in the city library, tracking Bachinskis. But when women change their names upon marriage, they disappear from the pages of history. It was plain bad luck that my birth mother had no brothers.

I decided to phone a few Bachinskis from the phone book, anyway. I retreated into one of the bedrooms in Marianne's home where there was a phone. With a shaking hand, I copied down names and phone numbers of five Bachinskis. Then I sat, concocting a story about filling in the branches on my family tree, even writing down the words. I couldn't do it. I would dial the first few numbers of the phone number on the paper, then hang up, and try again, and again, and again. It seemed like an hour before I made the first cold call. There were no promising leads, but one of the families I phoned sounded nice, so I decided to visit them. A retired man named Mike Bachinski and his wife lived in St. Boniface. I found their small bungalow, and had my sunglasses on as I rang their doorbell. I was invited in. I kept my sunglasses on. Was that to lessen my feeling of exposure and make it easier to lie to these people? But as soon as I was seated in their living room, I could not keep up the family tree story pretense. I blurted out the truth—that I was searching for my birth mother. Their words were kind and gentle. They said, "We wish we *were* related to you. We hope you find her." They asked me to let them know if and when I did. Behind my sunglasses, tears streamed down my cheeks. I was an orphan—the lost lamb who had strayed from the fold.

I retreated from this raw experience. But I did continue to gather information from the Adoption Disclosure people in Manitoba, who sent the following page of my social history. As I read, I reacted:

Her birth mother was in her early twenties when she was born, a single young woman of Ukrainian nationality and Protestant faith." *[But why did my birth mother switch from the Catholic faith of her parents to the Protestant faith, I wondered. Not for many years would I know that the answer lay in my grandmother marrying a Swedish Protestant after the death of my grandfather.]* She was of medium height and build, with brown hair and brown eyes. Her health was good; and other than her having had an appendectomy [*this was new information*], there were no illnesses, diseases or health problems listed.

Her birth mother's family consisted of her parents and one older sister. The parents were both stated as being of Ukrainian nationality and Roman Catholic faith. Her mother was in her early forties at the time of the birth. Her father had died at the age of 40. He had been a school teacher. *[Why had he died so young? A later letter phrased it as, "there was some confusion as to the cause of his death." Suicide as the cause of his death came to my mind, which was later proven to be right. Adoptees do so much with a veiled comment.]*

The birth mother completed Grade 10—Art, Spelling and English were her best subjects. Then she went to work as a domestic. Unfortunately, there is no available information concerning the birth father or his family. *[Technically true, but there were descriptions of two possible birth fathers in the file, as I had learned earlier.]*

The information states that Mrs. Shipley's general health and development after placement were good, and there is no indication of any serious problems. She seemed to be a particularly happy baby. *[But they never knew what a sober baby I became—one who never smiled and slept all the time, and a child who didn't really "come out of herself" until she started school.]*

Grains of sand dropping through an hourglass. What a way to form an identity! Information like a birth mother's favourite school subjects seem insignificant to people who can go to their mother anytime and ask her. But I couldn't. I wove a lot around that piece of information. I had never been good in Art; in fact, in Grade 2, my teacher had failed me in Art with a mark of 48—the only failure in my school history. My report card read, "Carol is a good little worker. She must improve in Art." And with that singular lack of encouragement, I never did. But I was a good speller and pretty good in English, as my birth mother was. Where did my passion for music come from? And my left-handedness?

A colleague at Children's Aid whose private passion was helping people find each other encouraged me to place ads in newspapers and was willing to be the contact person. I assumed, wrongly as it turned out, that my birth mother had grown up in rural Manitoba and moved into Winnipeg when she left school. So I placed ads in rural Manitoba weekly newspapers as well as the Winnipeg Free Press. If only I had placed ads in Saskatchewan weeklies and monthly ads in the Free Press, I would have found her years before I did. She herself would not necessarily see such an ad, but I was to learn later that her daughter-in-law read them regularly. So near, and yet so far... My ad read: "Bachinski—searching for a female in her seventies. If Carol, February 4, 1936, means something to you, phone collect. Ask for Carol 613 233 3028." I got one reply from a man who thought I was looking for one (a man, that is!) Again, I felt exposed, even violated, and I did not try again.

In the throes of my reunion some years later, I learned that many more female adoptees search than male adoptees. The ratio is about 80:20 (Sachdev 1989, 3). Is this because women have a genetic concern for the children they will bring into the world? Is it because women have emotional courage that fuels them to seek after the truth of origin, no matter how painful, and that they have an intense desire to undo the trauma of separation and abandonment? Is it because, as Jung is quoted by Lifton, the desire to be reunited with the mother is the desire to be reborn through her (1975, 154)? Is it because women who have faced the primal intensity of bearing a child are more willing to face the intensity of a reunion/rebirth experience? Is it because women assume the major role in honoring and preserving family connections and relationships? Is it because women are less prepared than men to live with the half-truth of adoption all their lives, that they seek the missing pieces in their quest for integration in order to understand the meaning of the whole of their lives? Or is it because it is socially acceptable for women to express feelings and vulnerability? These are good questions for a research study.

As for the timing of the search, it is often the anticipation of a major life event, such as wanting to bear a child that sparks it. Often it is the reaction to a major event such as the birth of one's first child or the reaction to a loss in life, such as the death of the adoptive mother that prompts adoptees to begin their search. For others it is simply a sense of readiness, a sense that time is running out, a longing to fill the emptiness, to banish the bewilderment and alienation, or the conviction of the "right to know".

Robert Andersen, adoptee and psychiatrist, tells us:

> The emotional component is by far the most important part of the search: the wish to undo the trauma of the separation. The hope is that the wound caused by the separation can be healed, thereby providing a more authentic base for living life (1988, 19).

In the throes of the search, I knew this only dimly if at all. Now I know it in every fibre of my being.

Chapter Six

Found!

I've found her! I've found her! I've found her!

In 1986, I received a letter from the Manitoba Department of Social Services, Adoption Disclosure Division, informing me that new provincial legislation would enable them to search actively for my birth mother. It was now an Active Registry for adoptees, rather than a passive one. But... I had to wait my turn. Since the inception of the Registry in 1981, 300 adoptees had registered and were waiting. Sounded like forever. Then in July of 1987, a registered letter arrived stating that they were beginning a one-year search for my birth mother. All through that year I heard nothing. Feelings of cynicism and hopelessness overwhelmed me. I was sure she was dead. The following year, in July of 1988, I flew with Ken to Winnipeg to attend the 35th reunion of my high school. My heart was in the past that morning as I was about to meet old friends. I remember thinking, "Why not give the Adoption Disclosure Registry people a call? They probably haven't done a thing for me in the past year, but there's no harm in asking."

Here is how I remember the phone call:

> I am Carol Shipley, an adoptee, born in February of 1936. You are conducting a search on my behalf for my birth mother. Donna Dixon: Just a moment, please. [*long pause*] We've found her!
> Me: Oh my gosh! I thought she was dead!
> Donna Dixon: No, she is very much alive. We have tried to phone her, but she hasn't answered. We will not write her a letter because of confidentiality. We will contact you as soon as we have talked to her.

Feelings of jubilation, incredulity and fearlessness swept over me. Euphoria was taking over.

The next morning I called Donna back, asking if I should stay on in Winnipeg to meet her. Donna let me down gently, saying that things did not happen that quickly. If my birth mother agreed to have contact with me, she had to come to their office to sign a consent form. What would happen if she said no, I wondered. Would I have a chance to write to her to try to persuade her? Donna said that would be possible, as she explained that contact takes many forms—anything from an exchange of information to meeting face-to-face.

It was totally fitting that I took this awesome news to my high school reunion. Marianne, my lifelong ally, rejoiced with me, and I was eager to share this news with Allan, a classmate, who was also an adoptee. He protested that he was not interested in a reunion, but before he left Winnipeg, he phoned to ask for Donna Dixon's phone number. *So* many of us say we are not interested—that it has nothing to do with our lives. Yet it has *everything* to do with them.

Upon my return to Ottawa, I talked things over with Ken who was unfailingly supportive and steady. One evening as we walked along the Rideau Canal near our home, I reviewed every possible scenario I could imagine about who she was. What would be her story? Was she a woman who had been a victim of any number of awful circumstances? Did she have Alzheimer's disease? Was she an alcoholic? Did she have a major mental disorder? Was she in a nursing home? Was she thoroughly unlikeable? Would she slam the door in my face and refuse to see me? Was she very emotionally needy and would she attempt to enmesh me in her life? Did she have values diametrically opposed to my own? All my life I'd encountered women such as these and I was trying to brutally prepare myself for the worst.

Ken listened quietly and replied, "Carol, there's one scenario you haven't mentioned. Maybe she has a Ph.D in Psychology and is a psychotherapist!" No, that hadn't crossed my mind. I felt ready now for anything and anyone. I was on the cliff's edge.

One weekend I was on retreat at a lake cottage with staff (of which I was one) and residents from Martha's, a group home for women who were formerly homeless. I was deeply moved by the tender support and shared anticipation that many of the residents and staff expressed to me that weekend. I swam out about half a mile to a big rock in the lake. As I swam, I sang all the way out and all the way back, "I've found her, I've found her, I've found her, I've found her!" Even a month before, I had no idea that such powerful, primal feelings lay within. One adoptee describes this anticipation as, "It's as if I'd arrived home... I would know who I was."

A week later, I received a notice that a registered letter was awaiting me at the Post Office. It said that my birth mother had been in to sign the consent form and wanted to meet me. I sat in my car, letter open in my lap, tears rolling down my cheeks onto the letter. Fifty-two years—a lifetime of waiting. Wild stallions couldn't hold me back now.

I learned that my birth mother would be linked up with a social worker in Winnipeg, and I would be assigned a social worker at the Children's Aid in Ottawa. I really *had* become a client. I learned that I would have to wait my turn in the lineup of reunion-seekers. But I couldn't wait. I would use whatever influence I had to speed things up. Joyce Ireland, my former supervisor at Children's Aid, placed a call to the supervisor of Ontario's Adoption Disclosure Unit in Toronto. Within a few days, I was assigned a social worker. When I met with her, my intention was to convince her that I was well-adjusted and stable and would handle a reunion well. It was the same old stuff of thirty years before—the adoptee having to prove herself in order to find out who she was. This social worker had surprising news. The social worker in Winnipeg, assigned to my birth mother, claimed he knew me from earlier days in Saskatoon. What a stroke of luck to have Scott McDonald in on this! Supportive in every way, he wrote this note to me: "By the time you receive this, I will have told your birth mother how fortunate she is. She has a kind of bubbly energy I'm sure you will find familiar."

I finally knew her first name: *Vera*, such a wonderfully Ukrainian name. I knew that she was 74 years old, that she lived in Winnipeg, that she had been married, and was now on her own. For the first time in my life, I felt I had a strong voice. I decided to write Vera a letter and send her a picture, in the hope that she would do the same. Then Scott McDonald phoned, describing her as "a delight of a mom— lively, a vital ball of energy." He said she painted in oils, that she was living independently in an apartment building for seniors, and that she had a son younger than I *[I'd always wanted a brother]* who was very protective of her. Then Scott asked something for which I will be forever grateful: "How do you want to do this, Carol?" He handed power to me—the client. I told him that I'd like Vera's address and phone number. "Her phone number will have to come directly from her," he said, but he gave me her address. I could think and talk of nothing else. Obsession. My friends and family were happy and a little worried for me. Euphoria and obsession are, by definition, extreme states of being.

Scott suggested to Vera that she write to me. And her little letter, with a return address, enclosed a small photo of herself. I could not get enough of looking at this neat, compact, smiling woman who was my birth mother. Her letter crossed mine in the mail. She tried to explain why she could not keep me. She was proud that she had a son who had been married for many years, and two granddaughters, one of whom was especially good to her. It was a once-in-a-lifetime experience to write to Vera, telling her in well-chosen words who I was, where I grew up, and about my life and family. It had been a very good life. I was proud to tell her that I had done well in school *[funny how important it is to tell a mother that]*, and in fact, was returning to school to begin a Master's program in Social Work at Carleton University in a month's time. Those of us who have been clients usually have strong opinions of social workers, both negative and positive. How would she take the news that I was a social worker?

The phone call came next. As if it were a perfectly ordinary occurrence, I phoned her on a Sunday morning in August of 1988. It felt as though we knew each other from some faraway place long ago. I don't know what we said to each other, and it didn't really matter— maybe things like, "How have you been?" and "Thanks for the letter and picture", that I would come to meet her in early September, and that she had vacationed in Cuba recently. She sounded warm and bright. The rhythm and cadence of her voice matched my own. She told me of her father who had died when she was 3, that he was a homesteader in Saskatchewan who had had a mental breakdown. She told me that shortly after leaving the hospital where I was born, she married a man just out of military service. He had a young daughter. She soon found out that he was handy with his fists. Vera pulled no punches. She would fill in the gaps in my history, I was sure of that. She spoke of her son who had worked for the City of Winnipeg for many years, and of his two beautiful teen-age daughters. She was proud of her granddaughters. One had aspirations to be an Olympic-level swimmer.

Remembering details of my social history I'd received many years back, I asked her about her interest in needlework. Her story was life-giving. "In the hospital I had no money to buy you anything pretty, so I cut down an old blouse of mine, and sewed you a dress by hand. I embroidered the bodice and crocheted around the hem. Then you were the prettiest baby in the nursery and so lively. That's why it was heartbreaking to give you up." She had made the dress for me to wear the day I was to leave the hospital with my new parents. It didn't happen. I didn't wear the dress, and so, as a child, I never saw the love that went into the making of it. Is it any wonder that I feel so strongly that adoptees and birth family members should meet and share their stories instead of reading dry facts on the page of a social history?

Vera was a seamstress. She told me that over the years, as she sewed alone at her machine, she often thought of me. "Did she get a nice home? Are they being good to her?" she asked no one. Her heart ached when she would read a newspaper story of some foster or adopted child who had been mistreated. I told her that my parents were happy with me, and that they had kept my name—Carol. "To me, your name was a song," she said.

Vera spoke of her full-sister, Jennie, who was dead, of her half-brother, Orville, and her half-sister, Rose, from the marriage of her mother to her stepfather. Rose lived in a small town on the St. Lawrence River, an hour away from Ottawa. One of Rose's daughters was a nurse in Cornwall; the other daughter lived a few kilometres away from me in Ottawa! Vera was worried about her son who had recently suffered a slight stroke.

Vera recounted her reaction to the phone call when she learned I was searching for her. She thought that the social worker had said, "This is the government." And she'd said to herself, "What the hell have I done now?"

Vera began to tell the story of her pregnancy, and her "confinement." After she had made her way to the Salvation Army hostel, through the help of a friend, the Matron announced to her one day, "There's a lady here who wants to see you. She says she's your aunt." Vera's reply was "No way, I'm not seeing Aunt Jean. She has no children of her own, and she'll want to raise my baby, and I won't let her. There's no love there, and she's bad-tempered."

Then she told me the goodbye story. One day the matron came to her, saying that the new parents had arrived to take her baby, and that it was time to say goodbye to me. How she did that, I'll never know. She spoke of sobbing in the matron's arms afterwards. She could not stop. Vera had nursed me every day for four months. The loss was too great to bear. Even in the midst of extreme grief, she thought of what a tough job the matron had, holding heart-broken girls like her in her arms. My question of whether my birth mother had loved me was answered ten-fold.

When I shared the goodbye story with my friend, Marianne, her voice broke as she said, "That was like cutting off both her arms." Sorosky et al. (1978, 56) write about the experience this way:

> Birth parents are assured that relinquishment of their child will be a resolution to their problem and the experience will be forgotten; yet their continued pain, for some like a 'psychological amputation' and mourning, to which no one listens, tells them otherwise.

Two hours of conversation flew by. I was falling in love with a lively "with-it" woman who was willing to share her life story. I couldn't wait to meet her.

Vera and Carol

Chapter Seven

Reunion with Vera

Unrivalled ecstasy

It was September of 1988. Three days after I began my studies in the School of Social Work as a *very* mature student, I flew to Winnipeg to spend five days with Vera. It was essential to me that I go alone. Many adoptees go it alone, anticipating that the emotions they will experience will be so intense that there will be no reserve for relating to anyone else. I packed carefully to make sure that the clothes and jewellery I wore would make me look my best. I sat on the plane, quite unable to take it in. It was almost like going to meet a lover. I was to read later in the research of Sorosky, Baran and Pannor (1978, 161) that, in fact, the majority of reunion experiences reveal a romantic emotional content that is unrivalled in the most imaginative fiction. One adoptee told me that the first meal she shared with her birth mother had the ambience of a new lovers' tryst. There was also the discomfort of being in unknown emotional territory for which there was no social etiquette guide.

As I came down the escalator in the Winnipeg airport, I spotted her: a compact woman in a white leather jacket with an older Scott McDonald, her social worker and my friend from Saskatoon days. Vera's eyes were warm and brown, her hair was brown, and she was smiling. Scott said, "Hi Carol," and to Vera, "Yes, here she is." I think she and I hugged each other, then stood back, hands on each other's shoulders, and drank each other in. We smiled, and laughed, and stared. Unbelievable—after fifty-two years of not knowing. I learned that Wayne, her son and my half-brother, was waiting for us in the airport coffee shop. We headed over there. Scott said goodbye and assured me that I could call him at home any time over the next few days. Wonderful backup. I wasn't much thinking of Wayne in all of this; yet I knew he would need to check me out to be sure his mother was safe with me. He was a short, stocky man with dark hair like mine and a great smile. He looked like the movie actor, Danny DeVito. He drove us back to Vera's small, neat two-room (kitchen and bedsitting room) apartment in the early evening, and he did not leave until 5 in the morning. What I didn't know then was that Wayne had always looked out for his mother—so no way would he allow a long-lost daughter to enter her life and hurt her in any way. But I felt an unbearable need to spend time alone with Vera. What if Wayne spent every waking hour with us? I might be seeking Scott's intervention more quickly than I'd anticipated.

They were amazed when I told them about my efforts to find Vera over the years. I spoke of having registered to find her, but that Vera's name was not in the Adoption Disclosure Register. She didn't seem to know anything about the Register. She said, "They told me that when I gave you up, it was forever—that I would never see you again." It came to me that she did not feel entitled to register. She spoke of how hard it was to give me up, and compassion for her loss (not my own) flooded through me. I went over to where she was sitting to kiss and hug her. And then she looked up at me in wonder, "How did I get such a wonderful daughter?" she asked.

Wayne described how lively his mom used to be. He said he wished I could have known her years ago. I protested, "She seems pretty lively right now." But he pressed on. "The lithium she takes has levelled her out a lot," he said. Vera hung her head. It was a moment of crisis for me that I buried. I had worked at Martha's with women who had bipolar disorder and were on lithium. I knew then that Vera likely had a major psychiatric illness. How I wish that Wayne hadn't dropped that bombshell on me thirty minutes into the reunion. How I wish that Vera had not experienced shame when he dropped it.

I remember trying to make a point about Vera's situation—that she had no choice but to place me for adoption, and that in another era, we might never have been separated. Wayne cut me off. "There will be no talk of that," he said. I was confused. What had I said that was unacceptable? He was on high alert for anything I might say that would upset his mother. I sensed how important it was to get to know him. He was an important person in Vera's life and a devoted son.

That night—morning, actually—I lay down on a mattress on the floor of the bed-sitting room, and tried to sleep. She was just a few feet away from me, sleeping quietly, on a single bed. I stared at her bare arm—it was shaped just like mine. Next morning I saw the outline of her breasts under her nightie—they were shaped like mine. I looked at her thick big toes, shaped like mine, and her hands, like mine, and the olive colour of her skin, like mine. Never before had I seen myself reflected in another woman. It's an earth-shaking aspect of reunion. When you grow up with people all around you who resemble you, you take it for granted and experience it in a subconscious way. When you don't grow up with it, you don't know what you are missing, but you know that something is.

The discovery of people to whom one is biologically related, after a lifetime, produces an ecstasy that is unrivalled. Integral to this is seeing oneself physically in another person for the first time. Adoptees describe it as a miracle experience, a moment of staggering significance. One adoptee told me, "I was looking at everything about her—her face, her hair, her ears, how she moved her hands, how she walked. I couldn't get enough of taking her in." Another said:

> I can look at this person and think, I got blood! You have no idea what it did for me.... It brought me back to life, is what it did. To try and explain the feelings you go through upon meeting someone you belong to... There are no words to describe it.

Yet another described her feelings upon giving birth to her first son, "To finally have someone, my own flesh and blood... It was magnificent." While all mothers feel something like this at the moment of giving birth, there seems to be a special intensity to the feelings of an adoptee mother who has not had those flesh connections ever before.   Vera looked after me as though I were years younger. She made my breakfast very capably in her small kitchen. She hauled out albums and pictures of her childhood, and of Wayne in his childhood. She was telling me my story. At one point she seemed to realize that there was nothing I did not want to know. She left nothing out. She had lived her life as a risk-taker who did not count the cost. I suppose I was somewhat of a risk-taker myself, or I wouldn't have been staying in her apartment just after we'd met. There was a strange sense that I knew her in some intimate way, but she *was* a stranger.

Vera shared her family history that I had waited half a lifetime to hear. Her handsome father, Joseph Bachinski, had been an officer in the Prussian army in the late 1800s. He had immigrated to Canada and married Kate Tesluk. Kate gave birth to two daughters, Jennie and Vera. They homesteaded on stony, scrubby land in the Canora area of Saskatchewan. To make ends meet, Joseph did the books for the Doukhobors, a Christian sect of Russian immigrants who lived in the area, and he also taught school. The respect he earned from others in the community is reflected in this first person account by a Ukrainian pioneer from *Land of Pain Land of Promise:*

> Since there were several literate people in our community, they used to get together at our home on the long winter evenings, to read the papers and discuss their contents. Many a sunrise found these men, though weary from the previous day's hard toil, going without a wink of sleep to forge a happier lot for themselves and their children.
>
> Those sleepless nights were not spent in vain. In 1904-05, thanks to the efforts of our pioneer fathers, a small but beautiful school was built. Its first teacher was the scholarly and patriotic Ukrainian, the late Joseph Bachinski (Piniuta 1978, 74).

For all the immigrant Ukrainians of the prairies, life was full of hardship, discrimination, and back-breaking work that never ended. Myrna Kostash, in her book *All of Baba's Children,* reports that the discrimination experienced by Ukrainians living on the prairies ranged from the Anglo-Saxon's expressions of "undisguised and unapologetic prejudice" to regarding Ukrainians as inferiors, saying, "We are prepared to treat them with fairness and civility; we are not prepared to be bossed by them." (1977, 39). "Bohunk", the contemptuous epithet commonly used to label the Ukrainian, led Kostash to raise the question, "The Ukrainian as nigger?" (1977, 40)

Joseph was prone to deep depression. Tragedy struck when Joseph and his family were visiting relatives in rural Manitoba. Joseph took his own life during that visit. My hunch that he had committed suicide had been correct. Vera's mother, returned with her daughters to the farm in Canora with no means of support. Before long, she married a Swede who owned a big house. From then on, Vera's childhood was not a happy one. She was "the black sheep"— not favoured like her older sister Jennie. She feared and disliked her stepfather who would spit on the floor if she or her sister spoke Ukrainian in the house.

Vera shared some harsh memories with me. She told of a Canora woman who used a coat hanger to give women abortions. These women were desperate to stop having children. Her sister, married to an abusive man who constantly made her pregnant, had her insides ruined from such botched abortions.

On the bright side, Vera generously gave me several lovely photos of herself taken through the years. When I admired something—a brooch, a scarf—it was mine.

She seemed to know I would want to know about my birth father, and talked quite freely about him. She had enjoyed his company, especially going to dances with him in the Rainbow Ballroom. His name was Wilf Noble, and he had lived in a boarding house a few streets away from her. He was not the Scot who was leader of a small dance orchestra around whom I had woven a fantasy. Wilf was a handsome man who looked a little like the "gangster" actor, George Raft, she said. She had not experienced sex till he came along, and she enjoyed it from then on. After my birth, she seemed to recall that Wilf came to see me at the hospital, but she never saw him again after that. He had been married, and separated probably, and she thought that he had a couple of other children.

Following my birth, the hospital matron encouraged Vera to consider becoming a nurse. She could see that Vera was smart and had potential. But Vera had no money, and no one offered her any. Could there have been a way? At any rate, after leaving the hospital, she was married within the year to Jim Harris. Her mother was not happy with Vera's choice. Soon after the wedding, Jim mistreated Vera , and she came to believe that he had married her to look after his three-year-old daughter. Vera and the child did not bond. How could they? Vera had just lost her beloved baby, with no heart for accepting someone else's child. She endured Jim's abuse and continued to work as a domestic.

Wayne was born in 1939, the only child of this marriage. Jim spent his time drinking and womanizing, and leaving her and the children to fend for themselves. When he did come around, he mistreated her. When Jim asked her for money to cover the cost of an abortion for his girlfriend, it was the last straw. Vera left her husband and returned home with Wayne to her mother's farm in Canora, Saskatchewan.

During the five days of the reunion, there were playful times. Instinctively we went back in time and I became Vera's little girl. My treat of all treats, as a child, was to stop with my parents at the Dutch Maid Ice Cream shop on Osborne Street, where my sister Lois and I would choose a cone from 21 different flavours. "Let's go," Vera said, "the Dutch Maid is just around the corner." So off we went; I chose a lime sherbet cone, and she paid. Fun. There were times, too, when I visualized crawling up onto her lap, and snuggling into her while she rocked and cuddled me. But I didn't go that far.

I was curious about the downtown area where she and Wilf had lived when they were dating. "Could you find the houses?" I asked. As we cruised slowly up and down streets in my rented car, she found her old rooming house and guessed at the one he had lived in. Fun.

We drove to Fort Whyte, five miles out of the city, where I had lived from my babyhood to early teens. I showed her our company house, so shabby and small in the light of today. The old concrete sidewalk that extended the length of the company houses and separated from the highway by a wide, deep ditch was still there. I thought of how much kids can do on a strip of sidewalk: hopscotch, skipping rope, and bouncing ball. Across the highway was a free-standing garage behind the big house where the cement company superintendent and his family lived. It was the perfect setting to play the exciting Anti-Anti-I-Over game where kids on one side would throw the ball over the roof, and if a kid caught it on the other side, he would run around and touch a kid with the ball on the opposing side. I looked at the spots where the old swing that Dad had erected had been, where the tiny vegetable garden had been, and where the sandbox-playhouse had been. I remembered the kissing that went on in the playhouse behind cardboard walls. I remembered going off into the bushes behind the house where people had discarded their junk, and dragging cupboards and old dishes back to furnish the playhouse. My mother certainly disapproved of us grubbing around in garbage, but she didn't stop us once it was in the playhouse.

I wanted Vera to know all about my life as it had been. And this was my first disappointment. She didn't ask questions or seem much interested. Was it too painful for her to know about all that she had missed of my childhood? That thought didn't occur to me at the time.

I learned about Vera's mental breakdowns. In Brandon Mental Hospital she remembered being strapped down to receive shock treatments. I wondered if this was the reason for her adamant refusal to wear a seat belt in my car. Feelings of shame and low self-worth were surely the outcome of these experiences. Wayne remembered how a breakdown would begin: she would be unable to sleep; she would start to clean the house relentlessly; her handwriting would get bigger and bigger as her irritability increased. He came home one day from school to find her gone; the landlady took him in until a relative came for him. How overwhelmingly difficult that must have been for a small boy. He lived without her for as long as a year sometimes, on the Saskatchewan farm with his grandmother, aunt and uncle. He loved trailing after his uncle and so began a lifelong, affectionate, teasing friendship between them. And it was there, I think, that his deep feelings of insecurity and a strong need to control took root.

There was a kind of reversal of roles in Vera and Wayne's relationship. It was not difficult to imagine how it could have happened. Wayne had cared for and assumed responsibility for his mother for a very long time. It was almost like watching a married couple with the dominating husband checking his submissive wife on her poor table manners, "Don't talk with your mouth full, Mom! How many times do I have to tell you?" And she would hang her head and take his criticism.

She spoke of the lovers she had had over the years. Being in the company of men pleased her, and made her feel young, attractive, and happy. But she was always "the other woman". The one she'd loved the most was married to "a woman who wouldn't give him any sex, and a man has to have sex!" He would invite her to spend a few days with him, and they would travel together and stay in a nice hotel in a faraway city. This man asked her to move to be closer to him. She talked it over with Wayne who pointed out that she would be far away from her only family, and that she would be with a lover, not a husband. She stayed put. When this man became ill with Lou Gehrig's disease, he asked his wife to send for her. Vera did not go. "How could I come between a man and his wife?" she said. I didn't follow her logic, but I did understand her reluctance to go to her lover's deathbed in such circumstances. I was pleased that she had had sexual relationships with men who made her happy, but very sad that she had lost out on a loving, legitimate relationship that would have given her status and a sense of self-worth. My illegitimacy, her abusive marriage, and her hidden affairs were all part of the picture of Vera, "the other woman".

Vera's middle name was "Resourceful." She had always worked: at a dry cleaners, as a domestic, and as a nurses' aide for private patients. She was proud of herself that she had taken a course to qualify for the latter. She was frugal—some would say tight—with her money. But she managed to stretch it. She was just great at making something out of nothing. She could always alter a piece of clothing to make it fit. She always looked nice but would often refuse to buy something new for a special occasion, preferring to make something over that was already in her closet. When she was in her late 60s, she taught herself to paint in oils. Her artwork was often copied from a nice picture. It was good enough to hang on the office walls of the dentist for whom she babysat. My birth mother was talented—I admired the stitchery and embroidery that graced the walls of her apartment.

Vera introduced me as "my daughter" to a couple of her women friends in the apartment block. That was lovely for me. She had told them about my existence, and they welcomed me.

It was a whirlwind. I felt an extreme sense of urgency to learn as much as I could as quickly as I could, because I feared that at any moment, the door might slam shut in my face. It had been shut for half a century. I became more and more strung out with the intensity of the experience and the lack of sleep.

One of the seven core issues of adoption experienced by the majority of adoption triad members—birth parents, adoptive parents, and adoptees—is the fear of rejection. The other core issues are loss, guilt and shame, grief, identity, intimacy, and control (Melina 1990). One way that many adoptees handle their sense of rejection is by becoming a people pleaser—holding back an honest reaction in order to sense what people want to hear. I had long ago mastered the art.

One afternoon Wayne invited me out for a drive. He talked about life with his mother. It hadn't been easy. If she stopped her meds, she went into a round of ceaseless, unending activity. He had watched over her all these years and would continue to do so. That was his job, not mine. It was as though I was one of the family, as though I hadn't had and didn't have a life, and he was filling me in on the life I should or would have had. It was very strange—as though I'd been waiting in the wings for fifty years. Yet I also knew that I'd lived a full life during those fifty years.

We stopped by a cemetery. We were due back at Vera's apartment for the Ukrainian dinner that I had requested. I was to meet the rest of the family: Sue, Wayne's wife, their two daughters and their boyfriends. As we sat in his car, Wayne told me a story. In this cemetery was the grave of Vera's child, his younger sister. It seemed that Vera had had a child with a man with whom she was not living. She had tried to care for Wayne and for the toddler. The two-year-old child had been ill for days. Vera left for her days' work, leaving the child in the care of a babysitter. The babysitter became increasingly concerned about how sick the child was, and called Vera home from work. Vera tried to give the child a bottle, but the child choked on the milk, and died in Vera's arms. The baby's name was Carol Lynn. I went cold. Vera had named this child after me, the child she had lost through adoption. Until I had entered the picture a month ago, Wayne had had no idea that his mother had named this child after me. We grieved together silently for our mother's profound loss.

I was in emotional overload. It was time to head back to Vera's apartment for dinner. Vera was bustling about. There was no place to change for the occasion except in the bathroom. Depleted in every way, I lay prostrate on the bathroom floor for a few stolen minutes. The guests were gathering, and I walked out, smiling, to meet them. The women in the family were very beautiful and friendly. Pictures

Carol   **Wayne**

September, 1988

were taken at every turn. I felt very young—like the little girl who had returned after a long time away. Family members were curious and interested in me. The meal was delicious. Vera had made a big effort, and it had turned out well.

A trip to Grand Beach on Lake Winnipeg, north of the city, was planned for the next day. It was a favourite place of Wayne's and, as it happened, a place I had loved as a child when Mom and Dad would rent a cottage down the path from Auntie Mattie and her brood. Wayne sought some time alone with me. I wasn't sure that Vera was pleased about that. Did she think he would talk critically about her? We strolled along the wonderfully familiar beach, and I sensed that perhaps Wayne was attracted to me. I'll admit I was uneasy. His behaviour was faultless. Rather, he shared his feelings as a brother would—his unhappiness with his workplace, his lack of friends, and how distant he felt from his daughters. He had raised his daughters to be seen and not heard. He had told them what to do and think instead of listening to them. Now they were turning away from him as young adults, and he wished that things could be better between them. Sue was obviously close to her girls. From my reading of literature on adoption reunion, I learned that feelings of genetic sexual attraction are fairly common in reunions, and something to guard against. A birth mother may feel attracted to the son who looks exactly like the birth father that she hasn't seen in years. In fact, people with a poor sense of boundaries and a high degree of neediness may find themselves in bed together.

Vera shared the family tragedies on the last evening of the reunion. She spoke more about my grandfather's death. He had hung himself in the basement of his wife's parents' home where the family had gathered to visit. Vera's paternal uncle had also taken his own life. Deep, dark, depressive feelings coursed through the souls of the Bachinskis. Her mother had forever mourned the loss of her husband. She would be out barefoot in the garden, weeding, Vera said. "Why aren't you wearing shoes?" Vera asked her. Her mother replied, "I am closer to him [your father] and to God this way." Powerful and primal. I would have liked to have met my grandmother, Theodora Tesluk. I asked Vera about the death of the second Carol Lynn. "That must have been terrible for you to have your little girl die in your arms." She replied that it had been a relief, that it was too much for her to raise two children. I was shocked by how much she had blunted her feelings. Wayne later told me that he was convinced that the emotional and financial load of raising two children was beyond her.

After the most intense five days of my life, I left for home with a lifetime of information, stories, impressions, and reactions. Vera told me that our meeting had lifted a big weight off her shoulders—just to know that I had had a good life. I learned later that most birth mothers do not want the confidentiality promised to them years before. They feel a sense of relief and a diminished sense of guilt if they are able to share with the adoptee the reason for his or her relinquishment. But I knew that I could not share with her the ways in which adoption had wounded me. I'm not sure that very many adoptees can. If, after going through the agony of loss, why would a birth mother want to learn years later that her child suffered from the loss of identity, from not knowing that she'd been loved by her first mother, that she was sensitive to rejection, that she often felt "not as good as" even though she'd been raised in a stable, loving adoptive home? Many adoptees, including myself, must do their own processing. The adoptee does not have a voice at the time of the adoption placement, nor can she speak up to the birth mother, at the time of adoption reunion, for fear of hurting her. The adoptee goes through life not wanting to hurt others, and in so doing, buries her own hurt. Who wants to know about the adoptee's wounds? Does the adoptive family? Do adoption social workers? Those who work in adoption know that an adopted child has so much more to gain than a foster child who lacks security and permanence. The truth about adoption lies in the paradox that everyone stands to gain from an adoption and everyone stands to lose.

I sent Vera a dozen long-stemmed red roses when I left, thrilled that I could finally express my love to her in this way. Twenty-eight years earlier, roses sent by my father-in-law had filled my hospital room following the birth of his first grandson. That was the first time I felt compassion for her loss as mother. Full circle. Maybe my gesture had more meaning for me than for her. Maybe spending that kind of money on flowers was not part of her lifestyle and made her uncomfortable. In any case, she never spoke of them. But in those early days I wanted to shower her with gifts—things she had always wanted. The reunion had taken place. The unfolding would begin.

Mom, Carol and Vera

Mom and Vera

Chapter Eight

Reunion Aftermath

Whether the outcome of the reunion fulfills fantasies is not so important as the fact that it gives the adoptee, finally, a feeling of wholeness.
—Sorosky et al.

Following the first stage of my reunion, I had a major life task to do. I had lost my birth family identity through adoption and had borrowed the identity of my adoptive family. Now the challenge was to sort it out.

Later in the fall of 1988, Vera flew to Ottawa to meet Ken and the children. It was probably as overwhelming for her to meet my family as it had been for me to meet hers. She was kind to Elaine and responded well to her quiet manner. She did not connect as well to Jill's zany, fun-filled spirit. She seemed to like Dave, Kev and Ken, the men of the family. The children were amazed at the physical similarities between Vera and me: our hand gestures when we spoke— even the way we stirred soup! I took her over to Martha's where I had worked and introduced her to some of the women who were so interested in my reunion story. I bought tickets to a Rita MacNeil concert, thinking she would enjoy that. Rita, who died in 2013, was the much-loved singer from Nova Scotia who sings from her heart. At first Vera turned me down, and then agreed to go. She enjoyed "the big girl's" singing.

I assumed Vera would be as interested in my life as I was in hers. I hauled out my photo albums so we could immerse ourselves, but she was not interested. Why not? I hid my hurt. I showed a video of an interview I had conducted with my friend and social work student, Jan, who is disabled and uses a wheelchair. The content touched on Jan's personal relationship with her boyfriend. Vera erupted angrily, saying that people like her shouldn't be talking about such things; people like her should be kept hidden away from people who find it upsetting to see them. I was stunned. We tried a singsong—the kids sang and I played the piano. She walked away and went to sit in the living room. Music seemed to irritate her. She complained about how big our house was and how long it took me to put together a meal. Our lifestyle must have made her uncomfortable. Maybe she felt that she didn't belong. I buried these comments and incidents, not yet ready to face up to them.

Wayne visited us several months later. He had taken off twenty pounds and looked jaunty in a peaked cap. But he, too, was ill at ease. His attempts at humour didn't come off. I knocked myself out making a nice dinner to which the kids had been invited to meet him. In hindsight, I think he would have been more comfortable in a less formal buffet-style setting. After dinner he said, "Boy, I'm glad that's over." I sensed he was nervous and unsure of himself, but the comment hurt. He was not interested in the activities I suggested. He had brought along photo albums of vacations he and Sue had taken. I became impatient with his long, detailed descriptions of each and every picture. At one point, I asked him about a picture on the adjoining page. "Don't interrupt," he barked. "I am not there yet. Wait till we get to that page." I was really turned off.

The younger daughter of Vera's half-sister lived in Ottawa, not far from us. Joanie was Wayne's cousin and mine as well, and I had never met her. Without an advance phone call, we drove to her house, and rang her doorbell. She had no idea who I was. He was having fun, springing a surprise (me) on his cousin. Much later, Joanie told me what went through her mind on the doorstep, "You bugger! You've got a new woman, and I *liked* Sue." As for me, I hardly knew what I was feeling. Like Exhibit A? Joanie seemed nice, and I hoped to get to know her. She was married, with one daughter in high school.

Wayne enjoyed talking to Ken about home repairs. They were both skilled at fixing things. We were pleased when he offered to fix a door handle. I invited Wayne to go cycling with me, but he made excuses. I realized that Ken's bike was much too big for him since Ken was eight inches taller. So I offered Wayne my bike, and I rode Ken's, which was miles too big for me. Riding behind me, Wayne laughed at my efforts to reach the peddles, my butt sliding from one side of the seat to the other. I didn't find it funny.

A few months later, I made another trip to Winnipeg to visit Vera. This time I hoped to spend a little more time getting to know Sue and Wayne, and less time with Vera. But Sue wasn't around much, although at one point, she asked me, "I was just wondering, when something bothers you, do you go up the wall? And do you get depressed like Wayne and Vera do?" My answer was yes, and she nodded knowingly—as though this confirmed the behaviours that ran in the family. I felt scared and pushed the fear to the back burner of my mind.

One evening Vera invited a few of her friends over—Charlotte, Evie, and Stan. Stan was retired from the Army and from his job as a security guard. I noticed his watery eyes, his red face, his slurred speech, and his wasted body. He arrived at the party drunk, weeping as he repeated over and over what a wonderful thing it was that Vera and I had reunited after all these years. He lived in a nearby apartment, where he sat day after day, drinking and smoking. He was also racist, and save for Charlotte, they all went on about Indians staggering around the streets of Winnipeg, and how they should be back on the reserves where they came from. I said nothing. Charlotte and I made eye contact, and she could see that I was upset. Stan went into a coughing, choking fit, gasping for breath. I was terrified that he was going to die.

I sat frozen in horror. These were Vera's friends! My honeymoon with Vera was over. I had believed Vera was interested and accepting of people from other lands and cultures. I recalled an earlier private conversation with Charlotte, a member of the United Church like myself, about how pleased we were that our church was now affirming of gays and lesbians. My hunch was that Charlotte was a lesbian, a truth about her life that she could never have shared with Vera, who would have been cruel and intolerant. But what did I expect of an elderly woman, anyway? The tearing down of the Vera whom I had idealized had begun. When everyone had gone home, Vera summed it up, "Well, that was a nice evening—getting a bunch of friends together to meet you." She had thought it was just fine.

There was one more incident. While I was staying with Vera, the phone rang at 8:30 one morning. Vera answered to hear that it was a wrong number. She blasted the woman who had called: "What's the idea of calling so early? You have no right to disturb my sleep!" I was aghast. Where was this irrational, unreasonable rage springing from? Then it hit me—eventually I would be on the receiving end of that rage. I would not escape it. I might be the Perfect Daughter now, but it would not last. I was frightened and upset. I went very, very quiet.

Vera's generosity emerged before I left to return to Ottawa. I had been admiring sweaters embroidered with flowers that were in the windows of all the women's clothing shops. She offered to make one for me. We bought an inexpensive black sweater, and I chose a picture of roses from her picture collection. She got right to work, and adapted the design, embroidering the roses onto the sweater. She must have worked non-stop, because the sweater arrived in the mail in Ottawa two weeks later. It was beautiful and I loved it.

I was back again in Ottawa and the School of Social Work. This time, despair and depression hit me big time. I did not know that adoption reunions are encounters of elemental intensity, which create unprecedented emotional issues in the lives of adoptees. Nor did I know that researchers had termed reunion a beginning, not an end—of sorting out a unique relationship for which there are no social guidelines. It's a period that Betty Jean Lifton refers to as "the aftermath" of reunion.

I was out of touch with what was happening to me and tried to mask it. It was a deep depression similar to the one I had experienced in my late teens, and I was very scared. The difference in me was so striking that friends and professors were noticing and questioning. I felt so foolish. I had been on a mountaintop of euphoria for a long time. I had felt that there was nothing I could not do, now that I had met my birth mother, and knew my roots and myself. But now I was in a desert of despair. I returned to Suzanne Robinson, my trusted therapist, and we talked about my mother's manic depression. My fear was that I was bipolar like my mother. In fact, I was convinced of it. Suzanne was just as convinced that I was not, but arranged for me to see a psychiatrist with the credentials to provide a diagnosis that would convince me. I *was* relieved when he confirmed that I was not bipolar. I do believe, however, that I have the potential to be. But because of the stability and security of a good home, my ups and downs are more likely to be related to pre-menstrual tensions and the day-to-day blows to my self-esteem.

The despair continued. My friends Delia and Jane were there for me, as was Ken and my therapist. I came to realize that I was mourning the loss of my idealized mother. The grieving took time. Other children get used to their parents' strengths and shortcomings over a lifetime of the normal stages of development. I was trying to make an immediate adjustment, and I could not do it. The unprocessed issues were overwhelming: sorting out an identity with the new essential pieces of the puzzle, healing the emotional wounds caused by rejection, loss and abandonment, and reframing my feelings of love and belonging to my adoptive family. Much later, and after reading adoption literature voraciously, I realized that, on a conscious level, I was glad that I had searched and found my birth mother; yet, on an unconscious level, I was devastated. I felt deeply ashamed that I could not seem to accept Vera just as she was. After all, she had been wounded by her experiences and in her own way, was doing the best she could. I did not know that arriving at acceptance takes its own time.

At a later stage, I learned much from adoptees who participated in my Master's thesis research project on reunion. One experienced a second rejection when she found a birth mother whose "lifetime of guilt had taken up permanent residence in her soul" as a result of the conception of her child. The adoptee did not benefit emotionally in any way from the reunion with her birth mother. Yet she felt deep compassion for the utter devastation of her birth mother's experience. It was a formidable task for her to reshape the fantasy mother who fought to get her child back into the sad, submissive woman who lived in life's shadows. As Betty Jean Lifton writes, "The task ahead was to integrate the experience into my present life and carve out a new self distinct from the one society had assigned me" (1975, 269).

The next step in the unfolding was Vera's second visit to Ottawa. It resulted in one of the best parts of the reunion—the willingness on the part of my two mothers to meet each other. I sensed all along that if they met, it would bring healing into the experience. I would have understood reluctance on the part of either or both of them, but when they both agreed to meet each other, my heart soared. Vera said, "After all, I want to thank her for looking after you all these years." And Mom said, "Yes, I think I would like to meet her, dear."

Vera and I drove the three hours to Belleville, and rang the buzzer for Mom's apartment. As we walked up the hallway together, Mom was waiting and smiling at her open door as she always was. Later she told me that as she watched us walk together up the hallway, she said to herself, "Ah, yes, that's Carol's mother all right." Even the way we walked was similar. How do genes work, anyway?

We sat down for tea. Mom had laid out her prettiest fine china tea cups, and lemon loaf slices on a floral china plate. Vera admired Mom's eleventh-floor apartment overlooking the Bay of Quinte. They liked each other immediately—these women who had led such diametrically different lives. Was that because neither of them put on airs, and that Vera sensed immediately that Mom simply accepted her as she was? I wished I could be a fly on the wall. It was just three women having tea together in an apartment in Belleville. But what a momentous tea!

It was close to Mother's Day and Vera presented Mom with a gorgeous ruby-red gloxinia plant. Rarely had I seen Mom's face so radiant, as she thanked Vera for this gift. Vera said, "I've thought of you a lot over the years." And Mom replied, "I've thought of you, too. It must have been so hard for you not knowing where or how she was."

I couldn't believe it! I knew how often I'd thought of Vera over the years, but I had no idea that my two mothers were also thinking and wondering about each other. For whose protection had we been kept apart? Vera said, "The saddest day of my life when I said goodbye to Carol was the happiest day of your life." [*I thought, what an utterly beautiful thing to say!]* Then she lightened it up with, "Of course you were the one who got to change the diapers!"

I decided to leave them on their own for a bit, and walked downstairs, marveling at the courage, honesty, and generosity of these two women—Vera who was 75, and had battled mental health issues her entire life, and Mom, so reserved, who was 86 years of age. Vera was at her finest. I will never forget the gratitude she expressed to Mom. And if Mom felt threatened in any way by Vera, she did not show it. She had never uttered a word of resentment that I had reunited with Vera.

After returning to Ottawa, I drove Vera to a town on the St. Lawrence to meet with her half-sister, my Aunt Rose, her husband, Cooke, and their daughter, Pat. Joanie, their younger daughter—my birth cousin to whom Wayne had introduced me in Ottawa, came too. Rose was interested and welcoming—a mature, stable and respected member of her small community. Unlike Vera, she did not come at life from a black sheep persona. She volunteered at the town museum; she gave classes in needlework; and she had a close relationship with the two daughters she had raised. I felt cautious, but thought I might be able to check things out with her if difficulties arose. Cooke seemed a needy man who constantly declared his love for Rose and cried easily, as he endured the unrelenting pain of shingles. Rose said little. She stood by her man, and engaged in neighbourhood activities when she could. Their daughter, Joanie was easy to be with. She was married to a rather anti-social man, and was close to her teenage daughter. Their older daughter Pat enjoyed her life of teaching and vacationing with a good friend. I was pleased that the reunion was continuing, and I was meeting extended family members. It felt more relaxed and natural, compared to the intensity of the earlier stages of reunion. They were good people, and easy to visit with. They shared stories and family photos of a younger Vera, some of which I took home.

Because I had to return to Ottawa the next day, Vera offered to take the bus back to Ottawa in two days' time. I took this at face value. Little did I know that this was totally against my birth family's sense of how guests should be treated. Our family's way was to enable guests to be as independent as possible. Rose doubted that Vera could get on the bus, and get off in Ottawa! So she drove her to Ottawa. They must have shared some criticisms of me. I heard later that Vera had not been impressed that I did not rise to get her breakfast and that Ken pointed her in the direction of the toaster and coffee pot. I was treating her like "family", as I define it, and it was not to her liking. She became rather silent. I didn't know what was wrong, but neither did I ask.

The kids came over—our youngest daughter, Elaine, was not among them—and we relaxed with drinks. Vera had bought a bottle of sherry and had too many sips. The subject of Indians on the streets of

Winnipeg came up. She bad-mouthed their drunkenness and their filthy habits in hotels. We went quiet. Then I said, "But Vera, Elaine is Indian. And there are reasons why Indians behave in big cities as they do." She said, "Oh, I didn't mean *her*." I was aghast. Later, when the kids and I talked it over, I could see that they were not as upset as I was. They knew that many parents, and kids too, for that matter, have racist attitudes, and that you can't take them all on. But this was my *mother* talking this way! The next morning, she offered a veiled apology. "Sometimes I talk too much." I had to face the truth that my mother had racist attitudes. And I was to learn later that my brother did, too. It is a common pattern that people who are themselves targets of discrimination and oppression often treat other target groups in a similar manner. Ukrainians on the prairies have certainly had their share of insults and discriminatory policies to deal with.

In the summer of 1989, I completed the birth family meetings. Ken and I flew to Saskatoon, and then drove to Canora where we met Vera and Wayne, who had driven from Winnipeg. We met in a Canora restaurant with Uncle Orville, Vera's half-brother. He was friendly and affectionate with everyone, including me. I sensed his innate kindness and liked him very much. Before leaving the restaurant, Wayne took me aside to warn me not to tell anyone I met on the streets or in the shops who I was. Vera was not prepared to have the people of Canora know about me. My re-entry into her life, and especially coming to the village where she grew up, had stirred up old feelings of shame and secrecy in her. My existence was the reason for her shame and her need to be secretive. I felt the wound, for which I was totally unprepared.

We drove out to Orville's summer cabin. Ken and I felt very welcomed as we played horseshoes, and sat around, wondering when supper was coming. Orville's wife Ethel, between smokes, was getting there. Wendy, their daughter, who had lived rough for some time, came along. Wayne told jokes that were not funny. Vera was sullen. After supper Wayne, Vera, Ken, and I headed back to the house in town, where we were to sleep. Wayne and Vera were snappish. I was very uneasy.

In the morning when I came into the kitchen, I asked Vera where the coffee mugs were and she snapped, "Right in front of you, if you'd open your eyes." Something was wrong. Her rage was directed at me, just as I'd feared would happen. I was emotionally unsafe. Apparently I had done the wrong thing by accepting Ethel's invitation to breakfast. It was not Vera and Wayne's preference. But how was I to know the family dynamics? The plan changed, and we all met together in a restaurant with Vera and Wayne paying. It was not a bad plan at all, but why hadn't they spoken up?

Ken thought that I already had the best out of the reunion—my history, the circumstances of the adoption—and that trying to have an ongoing relationship with Wayne and Vera was asking for heartache. He did not want to see me hurt over and over again. He was pinning his hopes on the benefit of the reunion itself, not on a continuing relationship. In the research of both Triseliotis (1973) and Sorosky (1978), parties to a reunion considered the reunion successful and fulfilling in that it allowed them to get on with their lives even when there was a very limited ongoing relationship afterwards. I would sort it out for myself.

Two more incidents caused further strain between my birth family and myself. I had given Vera a copy of my thesis Adoption Reunion and After: Women Adoptees' Experience (Shipley 1990) which was part of the requirements for my Master's degree. It was a study by a woman adoptee, about women adoptees, for women adoptees. I interviewed four women adoptees in depth about the issues that adoption reunion raised for them, and how they strived to integrate these issues into their lives. And I reviewed the adoption literature in Canada from its beginning to the present. I was proud of the work I'd done. It brought me to an intellectual as well as an emotional understanding of what I had experienced. The experience of the women I interviewed closely paralleled my own and helped me integrate my own reunion experience into my life. Vera reacted angrily to my thesis. "Nothing but adoption, adoption, adoption," she said. It had been a mistake to give her a copy. It was not on her wavelength at all.

In our annual Christmas newsletter of 1989, my biggest news was the reunion with Vera. I told our good friends and family of having met my birth mother, of how it had been the most significant thing I'd ever done, and how the meeting of my two mothers had been a healing experience for all of us. Vera was furious. She did not like me using the term "birth mother" and she did not like me calling the tea party with Mom a "healing" experience. At last... we're having a fight, I thought. We would work it through and in so doing, understand each other better. I tried to explain to no avail. We were on different wavelengths. I could not reach her. She must have felt exposed or judged or both. She continued to write to me, but the letters were angry, even mean. I checked the problem out with Aunt Rose, Vera's sister who pretty much agreed with Vera. The gap of misunderstanding was wide. Ken urged me again to cut off the communication altogether. I had gained so much from the reunion, but now it was time to end the hurt. I couldn't do it. I wanted so much to make it right again. After a year, it occurred to me that a full-scale apology from me was the only way. I said I was very sorry I had written about her in the newsletter and that I had upset her. Vera accepted that, and I knew then that my expectations of her had been way out of line. If there was to be a relationship, things would have to be on her terms or not at all.

In spite of these hurts and disappointments, I will always be grateful for Vera's generosity in sharing her story and mine. It allowed me to feel complete, to take wing by knowing my roots. Adoptees need to know their genealogical background in order to attain "rootedness", a dimension that some experts believe adoptees lack. Obtaining background information is a fundamental way of redressing this lack of rootedness. Florence Fisher, an adoptee pioneer, says,

> How can those secure in the knowledge of who their natural parents are tell me how I should think and feel, when they have never felt or thought the same ambiguity, longing and emptiness? When you know, it means nothing. When you don't know, it means your life. (1973, 112)

Some adoptees fear that they will lose the piece (or is it peace?) in adoption reunion that makes them feel complete. I do not fear this, nor do I fear that depression will ever again be my life companion. I feel overwhelmingly indebted to Vera for my life in all its fullness.

Lois, Mom, and Carol

Chapter Nine

Adoptive Family Bonds

No one told me you were adopted.
— Lois

I was beginning to feel more affection for my adoptive mother and sister than I had ever felt before. My heart was now open to them. It was no longer important to me that my spirit was not quite like theirs. They were quietly reliable women, loving in their own way. They did not play head games, or fight dirty. I could now appreciate that I had grown up in a family that, while it did not express a great deal of affirmation and encouragement, equally, it did not stand in the way of pursuing my dreams. Dad had been proud of my academic accomplishments, and if he had lived, would have encouraged my ongoing academic work. Mom's prevailing anxiety was that everyone have a job and it didn't much matter what the job was. This came out of her own experience—a father who had never financially supported his wife and four children. I was beginning to understand. I could see that Lois understood Mom better than I did in some instances. She accepted Mom the way she was, and didn't waste emotional energy getting frustrated and angry for what Mom wasn't able to give or do.

In my search for Vera, I had not told Mom what was going on. And I did not tell her when, at last, Vera and I made contact. But when I returned from the five-day reunion in Winnipeg, the elation was such that, if I could, I would have advertised on a huge billboard in front of the Peace Tower or hired a hot air balloonist to run a message, "I've found my birth mother!" Now that I had met Vera, I could not wait to talk to Mom. To my amazement, Ken was not supportive of the idea. And when I asked the kids, they agreed with Ken. I was indignant. What was the matter with finally telling the truth about my life? Ken got through to me when he asked, "Who is the telling for, your Mom or yourself?" I knew the answer. The honeymoon euphoria was so high at the time that it would have been hurtful for Mom to hear me rave about how perfect Vera was.

After I had come down from the mountain peak, I checked with Lois about how she thought Mom would take the news. To my surprise, she thought Mom would handle it very well. Why had I not told her at the beginning of my search? I seemed to have had no idea how she would react. Could it be that the issue is so close to adoptees that they cannot predict how their adoptive parents will react? Lois was quite right. When I finally told Mom, she said, "I think that is lovely for you, dear. And I am sure that it has made Vera happy, too. She must have wondered about you all these years."

Mom was picking up on how happy I was to be at home on the prairies again. She asked if, some day, I might want to return to live in Manitoba or Saskatchewan. At the time she asked, I thought I would. Implicitly, this would have meant a move farther away from her. She expressed no resentment whatsoever.

She had never resented my strong connection with Auntie Mattie, either. This was at some cost to her self-esteem, I know. She was becoming very special to me as the veil dropped from my eyes, and I recognized her unconditional, unselfish love for me. She would have agreed with me when I say that our relationship deepened and strengthened after I met Vera. Her unselfish love deepened our relationship. It was the kind of love described in the Bible's New Testament as part of Paul's letter to the Corinthians:

> Love is patient and kind; it is not jealous or conceited or proud; love is not ill-mannered or selfish or irritable; love does not keep a record of wrongs; love is not happy with evil, but is happy with the truth. Love never gives up; and its faith, hope and patience never fail (1 Corinthians 13: 4-7, *Good News Bible).*

Sorosky, Baran and Pannor (1978: 192) write: "... if one statement can be made unequivocally, it is that a primary benefit of the reunion experience is the strengthening of the adoptive family relationship." There is recognition that the adoptive parents are the true "psychological parents" (1978: 196) to whom the adoptee feels closer and more intimately connected. And this is exactly what happened to me.

I began to review my sisterhood with Lois, wondering why we had not connected well in our growing-up years. Her interests had differed from mine; she had the difficulty of following in her older sister's footsteps in school where she took the brunt of an insensitive teacher's abusive ways. She learned to play with her pals and do her own thing. Since the reunion, we have shared our sadness at the absence of occasions when Mom would sweep us into her arms to comfort us. There were none. If we fell and skinned our knee, Mom would be upset and show a kind of helplessness about what to do. Our needs brought out her feelings of inadequacy around nurturing. Dad could do it better.

A few months after my reunion, I asked Lois what it was like growing up with a sister who was adopted. Her reply staggered me, "I didn't know you were adopted, Carol. No one told me." I couldn't believe it! It seems that one day when Lois was around sixteen, someone asked her, "Which one of you Bowyer girls is the adopted one?" She went home, and learned from Mom that it was me, and that the reason she hadn't been told was because our parents were afraid she would tease me about it. She recalled how I had been allowed to tease her through the years, but she had never been allowed to retaliate. Surely not knowing this important truth about our family, which was known by people in the community and by the rest of us in the family, must have hurt Lois, and affected her sense of belonging in the family. I am amazed she didn't resent me forever. It helped me to understand why there was very little closeness between us over the years.

As Mom was nearing the end of her life, Lois and I had lots of opportunity to share memories, both good and not-so-good. It brought us close and changed us both. I had always felt that there was something lacking in me, in that I could not feel as deep a love for my adoptive family as I did for my friends, my husband, and my children. Meeting Vera changed all that. An adoptee told me that she believes she held herself apart from her adoptive family and, to a large extent, created a feeling of difference. She didn't look for the commonalities and the links. She had no way of knowing that until she found her birth mother. Her experience resonated with me. I had been too quick to see and experience the differences in how feelings were expressed, in achieving academically, in pursuing my passion for music.

The core of the depression—sometimes mild, sometimes deep—that plagued me over the years was based primarily on a sense of abandonment and feelings of low self-esteem. I had difficulties with the rough-and-tumble of life. I tried to be a people-pleaser, but was dismayed by the label. Friends would tell me that I had strong, sometimes negative, reactions to situations, yet I would not voice them. I held back, kept things in, and smiled a lot. After Vera, things began to sort themselves out. I was no longer depressed. Blue—yes; sad—yes; but depressed—no. More than twenty years of depression-free living. My husband can confirm it. I am out there and more real than I have ever been. I get into more open disagreements with colleagues, family members, and friends. The fear of rejection has receded, and the people-pleaser label no longer fits. I'm tougher and more grounded. Finally, I am living my own life.

Elaine, age 6

Chapter Ten

The Story of Elaine

The best lives are lived where difference is cherished.
— Mark Haddon

There were the obvious reasons for adopting a little girl: we knew we could accept children by birth and by adoption; many children already in the world needed homes; we wanted a girl, a sister for Jill, close to Jill's age; we felt a deep respect for Indian people. And there were the reasons I was not so conscious of: I felt compelled to adopt a little girl, like me. I thought that as an adoptive mom, I would have the compassion and understanding to love and nurture her because I had lived her experience. I think I was looking for an exquisite connection with this little child. I thought I would be able to provide the empathy and nurturing that Mom was unable to give me, because I would *understand effortlessly.* Little did I know I was on dangerous ground. The child would be her own little person, with a unique temperament and way of coping with the traumas that had befallen her. She was not *me.*

I placed the call to the Adopt Indian Metis Centre (AIM) which had been set up by Saskatchewan Social Services to place children of Native ancestry in permanent adoptive homes rather than leaving them to the impermanence of foster care. A few of our white liberal friends in Saskatoon had already adopted children of Native ancestry. It seemed a loving and exciting way to bring another child into our family.

I introduced the fact of my own adoption to the social worker to assure her that one of my motivations was my own happy, successful adoption. The adoption home study consisted of several interviews with our social worker, focusing on Ken's and my childhoods, our marriage, our children and our parenting, and our attitude towards people of races other than our own, specifically Native peoples. Social workers educated us about the adoption of older children who were traumatized by life. Their frustration lay with the underlying attitudes of parents who wanted to adopt these children. "We'll be fine," they would say, unwilling to face probable future challenges. We were cautioned that little was known about how Native children adopted into white families would handle adolescence. Much later we learned that, within the demoralized and scattered Native community, there was no agency to place their children for adoption in Native families. And the only two Native families who applied to AIM to adopt these children withdrew from the process.

And yet we wondered if it was the best thing to do for a Native child. A Native child raised by white parents would lose her heritage, her customs, and her traditions—those aspects of life that would enable her to be fully herself. As Native-positive as we might be as her white parents, we could not raise a Native child authentically in her own culture. We attended a lecture by a renowned Saskatoon psychiatrist on the subject. I heard her say, "These children need their basic needs met: nutritious food, a warm bed, opportunities to learn, and parents who will nurture them and love them and keep them safe. They cannot wait. They need these needs met right now." We knew, too, that self-worth is not dependent solely on culture, but also on their need to be loved and valued—a need that knows no colour. We were also aware that Native children spent years bouncing from one foster home to another, without having the chance to bond with anyone or to learn who they are. And so while we believed that culture/race was of great importance, we did not feel it should necessarily trump all other considerations.

The year was 1969. We moved forward into the adoption home study process.

Kevin, age 10, David, age 8, and Jill, age 6, were in on the adoption plan from the start. They were particularly dear when our social worker made a home visit to meet them. Taffy, our Siamese mama cat had just had kittens. The children shared with our social worker an explicit description of how kittens are born.

We were approved, and then we waited. After a few weeks, I phoned. Our social worker said, "Yes, there is a little girl available, and she is healthy, except that her legs are very bowed." My heart sank as I thought how difficult it would be for this little girl to be the sister of Jill, who had the graceful body and posture of a dancer. We turned her down. Years later, when I became an adoption practitioner, I would note that almost every adoptive applicant, in filling in their "range of acceptance", feels guilty when they say "no" to a child with some limitation or disability. I assure them that there is another set of parents out there who is just right for that child.

Then our social worker phoned us:

> We have another healthy little Metis girl of Cree ancestry who is three, and has been in her present foster home for a year. Her name is Elaine. She was apprehended when she was two, was placed in a foster home near her first home, and then moved to a foster home farther away because her birth mother knew where she was, and it was feared that she might try to get her back. Elaine is the baby of a group of siblings, most of whom are in foster care. Her left knee turns into the other, and she falls a lot, but a specialist who examined her, reports that she does not have a hip problem.

Yes, we were all very interested. Our social worker wrote a loving, gentle social history which she titled "The Story of Elaine".

We travelled with our social worker to Prince Albert, 100 miles away, to meet Elaine. And likewise, Elaine travelled about 100 miles from her foster home in the village of Leoville to the Child and Family Services offices in Prince Albert. After talking things over with our social worker, it was decided that our children would be participants in the meeting. We thought it would be easier on Elaine to have children there to play with, and important for Jill, David, and Kevin to play a full part in this adoption. We brought gifts—a Dr. Seuss alphabet book and a little doll.

Elaine's child care worker gave us a typed sheet detailing Elaine's daily routine, the foods she liked and a description of her personality. It stated that she ate three heaping bowls of porridge for breakfast!

We were ushered into the visiting room where we awaited Elaine's arrival. The door opened and there she was! A tiny, serious, fine-featured little girl, with darting black eyes and thin, short, black hair, her little hands nervously fingering her pink lace dress, handmade from what I guessed had been a bridesmaid's dress. The dress was small enough to fit a large doll. She wore tiny tan moccasin slippers and carried a teddy. Her tummy was distended, and her arms and legs were thin. The children moved forward to say "hello" and gave her the presents. When the Dr. Seuss book was opened, Elaine tried very hard to put correct names to the pictures, looking to me for approval. I teared up, overcome that such a small child would know that her big task was to please these total strangers, so that they would want to take her home with them. She was a dear, stressed little girl, and we all fell in love with her. She came back to the motel room with us, and the children opened their hearts to her, just playing and having fun. Next morning, we told our social worker that we would simply like to return home and begin our lives with Elaine.

Once in Saskatoon, Elaine tried to be helpful and do everything correctly. At the lunch table, a drop of soup spilled onto Elaine's plate under the bowl, *not* even on the tablecloth! She pointed out to me this "bad" thing she had done. At bedtime, she dropped off to sleep—like turning the knob on a radio to "Off". Jill recalls Elaine's morning routine. As the day dawned, her eyes would pop open, and she'd get dressed, strapping her favorite new shiny red Mary Jane shoes usually on the wrong feet. *Ka-klack-ka-klack-ka-klack-ka-klack-ka-klack* down the hall past her sleeping family. I'd call out, "Elaine, it's too early to get up, dear. Take off your shoes and go back to bed." And back to bed she would go. Thirty seconds later—*click-clack,click-clack-click-clack-click-clack.* "Elaaaine!" Ken called this time. *Klackity-klackity-klackity-klackity-klackity.* Another thirty seconds later—*click-a-clack, click-a-clack, click-a-clack.* This time I yelled, "eLAINE!!" *Klackity-klackity-klackity-klackity-klackity—click-a-clack.* "ELAINE!!" Ken and I yelled together. *"Klack, klack, klack, klack—click.* She was all set to go down stairs to set the table for breakfast! My heart ached for her. She was only three years old.

The honeymoon didn't last. I noticed crayon scribbles on the walls, and whole rolls of toilet paper in the toilet bowl. She had a stubborn streak, refusing to get into the car for an outing. Once when we had an important appointment and she would not cooperate, I unceremoniously scooped her up under one arm, and dumped her into the back seat of the car where her brothers and sister were waiting.

Elaine's survival skills were excellent. For years—not days, weeks or months—her eyes darted anxiously about as the serving dishes of food were passed around at mealtime. Why did it never occur to me to lessen her anxiety by dishing out her food first? I found a bun behind the plates stacked in the china cabinet. All but one cookie would be gone from an almost-full bag, but she could not admit that she'd eaten them. If I'd known then what I know now, I would have told myself that a child who steals or hoards food usually has sound emotional reasons for doing so. Then I might have provided her with food so that she would experience me as provider. I could even have provided her with a fanny pack and kept it stocked with snacks. Apparently, that usually quickly ends hoarding and stealing of food (Becker-Weidman, 2001). On outings, she was often the first to notice a landmark. Once when we were hopelessly lost, she pointed out a store, and we knew we were on the right street, after all.

She would run to meet friends and family who came to visit, sometimes giving them a hug, wanting them to like her. And they did! The very first time she met Ken's parents, she climbed onto their laps, and told them she loved them. They were *impressed.* She soon knew the neighbours from one end of the street to the other. Everyone liked Elaine. She often asked them for candies and cookies, but of course we didn't know that till much later. If she had been naughty at home, she would head off to Mary's house down the street to soak up Mary's kindness and affection. Months later, I felt that she could just as easily have lived with any family who was good to her as stay with us. We did not understand that this was an important survival skill that she had developed—the giving of indiscriminate affection. How else does an insecure little child make sure that her needs are met, except to be nice to *all* the adults around her? It was later, rather than sooner, before this behaviour abated.

I became impatient for a stronger connection with Elaine. But impatience does not give birth to connection. I know now that it caused her to freeze inside. I think she feared that impatience would turn to anger or hitting. One morning as Ken was putting on his trousers, he reached out to tickle Elaine on the tummy with a loop of his belt. She bolted from the master bedroom, ran to her own room, and shut the door. Fear/flight reaction. We knew in that moment that she must have been strapped with a belt in one of her foster homes. If Ken had simply tickled her tummy with his fingers, she would have squealed with delight at the familiar, gentle roughhousing. So much had happened to Elaine, and she did not hold the missing pieces of the puzzle. They were locked up tight inside her. It didn't work to try to get her to talk about her feelings. Sometimes I would guess her feelings and she would burst into tears because I had got it right, and then I would hug her. This was surely developing attachment, and yet I still wanted her to be able to share verbally.

She grew and she grew and she grew—10 inches and 25 pounds in one year! Each time she put on her pants, they were too short. Her hair grew in strong and thick. The warts which had covered her hands and to which I dutifully applied Compound W, magically disappeared. Good nutrition and emotional security were making a difference to her physical health and development.

Elaine had a short attention span. Children's TV programs did not interest her for more than a few seconds, nor did children's story books. We were sure she had not been read to. Her speech and comprehension were that of a one-year-old rather than an almost four-year-old. Over time, this made the difference very marked between her and her very verbal older siblings. She would tune out of dinner table conversations because she couldn't follow. This became a habit that did not bring us closer to her. She loved her father's physical affection, the roughhousing and the gentle teasing. My natural inclination is to talk. If I had only known then that 93 per cent of all communication is non-verbal, I could have curbed my unrealistic expectations, and expressed my affection for her in whatever ways she could accept.

About a year later, I heard her humming as she played in her room. Until then I had concluded that she was not interested in music or in singing. But what did she have to sing or hum about, until she began to feel some sense of security? As she was turning four, we took a long family vacation by car to Ontario to proudly introduce her to all my relatives in and around Belleville. Throughout the trip, she wailed every night. It was the first time she had had nightmares, and it was difficult to comfort her. One night as Elaine sobbed in Ken's arms, he whispered, "Are you worried that you're never going to see your pretty house again? You know, we're going back; we're just here for a little while." The nightmares ceased. A few weeks later, as we drove onto our street in Saskatoon, she began to bounce up and down in the back seat, saying, "My pitty house, my pitty house!" To her, the long car ride must surely have meant another move. The nightmares did not return.

Aboriginal people were not accepted by all the neighbours. Elaine's association with us helped, but did not guarantee her complete acceptance. A few said something like, "I think it's great that you adopted her. I don't think I could do what you are doing," or "What a lucky girl she is—to have the life she has now." It was "friendly" racism, and I recognized it by the squirmy way it made us feel. A stranger made a blatant comment that I couldn't believe I was hearing: something about our "chocolate bunny". These comments elevated us to the role of rescuing a child from an inferior life, and implied a great social responsibility on our part as adoptive parents. There was no recognition of what the child had lost or what the adoptive parents had gained. The comment about being unable to do what we were doing sounded complimentary but it came across as negative. It reflected the prevailing societal attitude that biological parenthood is superior to parenting by adoption. H. David Kirk would say that adoptive parents are role handicapped (1984, 31-32).

We didn't think to ask Elaine what happened when she wasn't with us. Would she have been able to tell us? Sadly, she absorbed the negative attitudes of the dominant culture towards Natives, in spite of our efforts to draw her attention to the positive things that were happening on some Indian reserves. As she grew older, she seemed uncomfortable and would sometimes answer, "Don't forget; I'm half-white, too." We tried to keep her in touch with her heritage. Several of the children of the Saskatoon Open School that our girls attended were Native children adopted by white families. (The Saskatoon Open School was a two-classroom unit within the Saskatoon Public School system—the parents volunteered in the multi-grade classrooms. The regular curriculum was followed in the mornings; group research, presentations and the social aspects of learning were emphasized in the afternoons). There was some connection for Elaine there. Years later, the Native children in our Open School told us that when they entered a convenience store near the school, they were watched much more closely than the white children. In the Perreault and Vance anthology, *Writing the Circle: Native Women of Western Canada* , Jenine Dumont (1993, 40) writes:

> When I was thirty-five and my last child was a precocious two-year-old, we stopped in a small northern Alberta town to buy something at a drugstore. My son was touching things, etc. When I went to the counter to pay for my purchase, the clerk looked through me with disdain and I got this terribly chilled feeling. It's a feeling that I cannot describe. It comes when you know that someone dislikes you because of your race. I thought I had come to terms with my Native blood. Maybe I have, but other people have not.

Did something like this happen to Elaine?

Elaine accompanied one of the Open School mothers and her daughter, both Cree, to the Native Friendship Centre in Saskatoon. An elder took Elaine under his wing. But Elaine became uncomfortable with him and didn't want to go anymore. The elder had apparently told her that she was "lost", and I don't think she liked the feelings that went with that. As Elaine's white parents, we did not feel that welcome at the Friendship Centre. Now many years later, our Native son-in-law, Vinny, arranges pow-wows and other events at Odawa Friendship Centre in Ottawa where he works. He and Elaine often invite us to attend events. We feel very welcomed, as do other white people who attend. Trust between Natives and whites has grown and times have changed for the better.

In the late '70s, Ken and I were interested in a posting overseas. We finally found one that suited a family with four children—a shared job as Field Staff Officers for CUSO, an international development organization that placed Canadians in short-term job placements in countries where they were most needed. The country was Botswana, in sub-Saharan Africa. Elaine was 11 years old. We arrived in Botswana's capital city of Gaborone on January 1, 1978, and eventually settled into a three-bedroom bungalow quite close to the primary school Elaine would be attending.

The school system was patterned after a British rote system of learning, which was easier than what Elaine had been used to, and she brought home good marks. Elaine had reached puberty earlier than most girls her age, and she looked older than the other children at school. And so it was that, Elaine, along with Jill who was 14, fell in with the teenage crowd. It was a rather exciting group of young people from many diverse backgrounds. Their parents were expatriates from Norway, Sweden, Germany, the United Kingdom, the United States, South Africa, Zimbabwe, and Canada. I was curious and interested in this rainbow of heritage, but Elaine was not. She was happy to fit into a group where colour did not matter. When kids would try to guess what her background was—Egyptian, South American, Chinese, she would smile and say nothing. Although she fit in colour-wise, she could not keep up with these older kids, and must have often felt overwhelmed.

The President of Botswana was Sir Seretse Khama, a highly respected chief of the Bamangwato tribe. He had studied law in England, where he met and married a white girl named Ruth Wilson, creating one of the biggest political scandals in Africa. Theirs was a powerful love story. Lady Ruth and Sir Seretse had four children. Their twin boys were part of the teenage crowd. Elaine became friends with Tony, one of the twins. Like everything else, she did not publicize this friendship until we were saying a final farewell at the train station where she and Tony exchanged tearful hugs. I tend to think that their connection was partly their mixed-race backgrounds. To our astonishment, she mentioned that she had sometimes visited Tony at State House, and that on one visit when she was in some difficulty, she had borrowed a tampon from Lady Ruth's boudoir!

When we returned to Canada—Ottawa in fact—two years later, Elaine began attending public school. By then, she was a silent, depressed girl of 14 who took up with the kids who experimented with street drugs and too much alcohol. She and I could not communicate. Attempts at conversation ended in too much "conversation" from me, and none from her. She tuned me out. In fact, she had a remarkable ability to dissociate from my "sermon" by doing math problems as I went on and on. She was lost, and she was lost to us, for certain. Jill was able to keep the sisterly connection, but she assumed a surrogate parent role and the responsibility weighed too heavily on her. Yet Elaine graduated from high school, tried a few short-term jobs, and had a steady boyfriend. Years went by, and while we thought she had kicked her abuse of alcohol and drugs, she had not. She was uncommunicative and hostile and we were at our wits' end. I withdrew from the parenting role, recognizing that Ken's straightforward matter-of-fact style worked best. We were encouraged by a counsellor to claim our parental authority. The bottom line for us was that Elaine must sleep at home. When we underlined that bottom line, she was gone within days. It was awful, and it was a relief. We were not in direct contact for a long time, but through Jill, we always knew where Elaine was, even if her living situation was far from good.

Elaine had a gift for reaching out to counsellors who could help her. She applied to a community college to study Early Childhood Education, was accepted, and moved away from Ottawa. In spite of her ongoing relationship with an abusive boyfriend (another thing we did not know), and her addiction to drugs and alcohol, she completed the two-year course. It was not difficult for her to find work in day care centres, and she had a lovely, gentle way of caring for toddlers.

On one of my trips to the prairies, I dropped in to the provincial Adoption Disclosure Unit in Regina to enquire how Elaine might obtain a social history. A non-identifying social history was soon mailed to her. It noted that her birth mother had been inquiring as to her whereabouts and would like to meet her. Elaine did not appear to take this well. She showed no interest in pursuing it. (But I realize now she was having a *kairos* moment, when time stands still—similar to when Mom shared my Adoption Order with me.)

Elaine started to move closer to her heritage when she obtained a treaty number and was able to get a treaty card which identified her as a treaty Indian when she used it to purchase things. Then she became engaged to her boyfriend. Our hearts sank, as we did our best to welcome him into the family. He was a very closed person, and we observed no enthusiasm on his part about marrying Elaine. She went through hell, we believe, and lost a lot of weight. Eventually, she called off the wedding, returned home for a few days, got a job in Ottawa, and started seeing a counsellor to deal with the abuse from her fiancé, which she subsequently told us about. And sometime after that, she got clean and sober. Remarkable achievements, all of them.

She began to test the waters of the Native community in Ottawa, attending pow-wows, and joining the baseball team. There was considerable interest within the Aboriginal community in this beautiful new Cree girl who seemed to have come out of nowhere. Elaine had been in touch with the chief of the Peter Ballantyne Indian Reserve, Pelican Narrows, Saskatchewan, where she was registered. Just before her 30th birthday, she announced that she was planning a trip to that reserve in northern Saskatchewan to learn more about her Native heritage. I had come through my own reunion some years before, and had somewhat tempered my conviction that every adoptee should seek reunion. But I remained very convinced of the riches to be gained in learning who you were, no matter how emotionally difficult the process was. Elaine was having none of it. She stated categorically that she was not going to her reserve to find her birth family. She was going to learn about her heritage!

We figured that it would probably take about half an hour on the reserve to find someone she was related to. She already knew that McDonald was her birth family name. She planned to fly to Flin Flon, rent a car, and drive to the reserve, arriving at night. I knew she would not take kindly to a suggestion from me that she arrive in daylight. What did I know about reserves, anyway? I contacted my dear friend, Lynne, who worked with the Aboriginal Head Start program and knew the northern Saskatchewan communities. Lynne gently suggested to Elaine that she arrive on the reserve next morning. She also offered to drive to the Peter Ballantyne Reserve from Regina, a 10-hour drive for the weekend, just to be around in case Elaine ran into difficulties. I was overwhelmed by her generosity. I prepared a small scrapbook which I titled "The Story of Elaine" just as our social worker had done those many years ago when we adopted Elaine. I included that first story of Elaine, along with photos, *just in case* Elaine did find her family. She was pleased to put it in her knapsack.

Elaine settled into a cabin at Pelican Narrows on the reserve and made her way to a little restaurant for breakfast. The waitress, who took her order, asked, "Who are you?" When Elaine mentioned her birth family name, the waitress said, "Well, I am your aunt." She told Elaine that her birth mother and older sister lived in Denare Beach, a small village off the reserve about 100 kilometres away. "Do you want to meet them?" she asked.

Elaine phoned us. She was sitting in the restaurant, smoking and shaking, waiting for her birth mother and sister, Cherie, to arrive. When Elaine met her sister, Cherie exclaimed, "We've been waiting for you for 25 years!" There is no remark that is more healing, more accepting, more welcoming than that. She went back with them to Denare Beach. Her sister was the eldest of four—the one who had looked after the baby (Elaine) when their mother was not there. Elaine was the last one of the family to return, they said. They assumed she had stayed in Leoville, Saskatchewan. They were so happy to welcome her back. The others had been either adopted or fostered, some of them by abusive families. Her eldest brother had been raised by his grandparents, and was now a Mountie in a northern Saskatchewan post. Her sister Marion was coordinator of Aboriginal Services in Prince Albert. She had spent some time in jail for killing someone, and is a recovering alcoholic. She warned Elaine about their mother: "Just you wait, she can be cold and unfeeling." Her sister Doreen was the most badly affected by their mother's drinking—she had severe fetal alcohol syndrome with the resulting life problems. Then there were five other boys, living not far from Denare. One brother was in Saskatoon, training to be a lawyer. Another brother named Paul, who'd been adopted, was in the penitentiary for break-and-enter and armed robbery. Sometime later, he began writing to Elaine—she called him her "pen Paul."

Lynne called us from the restaurant where Elaine met her family, describing them as open and generous. Elaine's aunt asked Lynne to tell us "not to worry, we won't try to take her away from you. We just needed to know after all these years that she's OK." Lynne described the whole experience as a miracle. She thought we had every reason to be proud of Elaine: her family could see how good she is with

114

children, that she has a good education, that she's lived in Africa. Lynne thought that Elaine's return was healing for the whole community.

Elaine phoned again the next day. In her unique way, she said, "Would you like to speak to Jean?" "Who's Jean?" I asked. "My mother." she said. Jean took the phone and sounded shy, "I never thought I'd be talking to you," she said. We agreed that our daughter, Elaine, was a lovely young woman, and we were both proud of her. We chuckled about Elaine's unique way of packing her knapsack—throw everything in and zip it up! As I spoke with Jean, there were echoes of my two mothers having tea together, and sharing their loving thoughts and feelings about me, their daughter. Then Cherie came on the phone, saying she thought Elaine had been lucky to get a family like ours. She said, "Thank you for taking care of my sister." That was so wonderful to hear. We hope some day to meet these dear members of Elaine's birth family.

I have a beautiful image of Elaine's reunion. Elaine and her mother are sitting on the couch, holding hands, and saying little. The welcome was everything. Elaine learned that her mother had started having babies at a young age. Elaine's grandparents felt shame about this, and banished her mother to the woods to live with her four small daughters in a shack. Isn't this something like sending a pregnant teen to a church-based home for unwed mothers? Shame is never a good basis for doing anything. Jean drank heavily and liked to be with Elaine's father from Buffalo Narrows. She sometimes left the children for long periods with Cherie, age eleven, in charge. Word of the children's plight got to the child welfare authorities; and one day, Elaine, age two, was apprehended in their mother's absence. Elaine told Cherie of a recurring dream she had had all her life: she was standing up in the back seat of a car, sobbing, and looking out the back window at children running after the car. Cherie said, "That was no dream. That is exactly what happened. Me and Marion were running after the car that took you away."

Word got around that Elaine was home, and in the space of a few days, about 50 of the 300 relatives in the area came from near and far to meet her. Meeting her grandparents, who celebrated their 65th wedding anniversary in 2011, was very special for her.

The unfolding of the momentous experience of reunion with her birth family began for Elaine. Equally momentous was the embracing of her Aboriginal heritage. And for me, it was the completion of a circle: adoptee adopts a child/adoptee finds birth family/adopted child finds birth family. Elaine admitted that she had been preparing for her reunion for three years—that she would take out the letter from the Saskatchewan Adoption Disclosure authorities about her mother wanting to find her, read it, put it away, and then take it out again. She had not been ready until now.

Elaine now knew who she was, and where she had come from, and she entered more fully into the life of the Native community in Ottawa. She began to date Aboriginal men, and after one very tragic relationship that did not work out, she and Vinny Kicknosway, who is Potawatami, started to see each other. Vinny was older than she was by more than fifteen years, and was well respected as the Healing and Wellness coordinator at Odawa Friendship Centre, where he had worked for many years. Elaine joined a drumming circle, and began to learn the songs of her people. Soon she was leading the circle. She had found her powerful, hauntingly beautiful voice that came from deep within her soul. I had to remind myself that this was the little girl who had had no interest in music and could not carry a tune! She took the skills and gifts she had with children in mainstream day care, and began to use them in the Native community. She was asked to set up a day care for children of Inuit background who lived in Ottawa; she worked in women's shelters, primarily with the children; she worked with teens in difficulty on the streets and in the jails; she led women's groups to honor and teach traditional practices. And she returned each year to northern Saskatchewan to participate in an annual Sundance ceremony and to visit her birth family.

We knew that Elaine very much hoped to have a child, but it appeared this was not to be. Then, to her amazement, she became pregnant at age 36. She found a compassionate Native physician who diagnosed her high-risk pregnancy and followed her closely. Elaine had pre-eclampsia, a condition where there is risk of the umbilical cord tearing away from the uterine wall, accompanied by high blood pressure and edema. She gained 80 pounds. Our fears were compounded by the SARS epidemic which was sweeping through Ontario hospitals at the time. In the labour room, Elaine's beloved elder, Karen, smudged her in spite of the raised eyebrows of the nursing staff. But the labour contractions would not begin, and so the decision was taken to deliver the baby by C-section. Vinny gowned up and accompanied Elaine into the delivery room, while Karen and I waited in the labour room. Baby boy, Theland Gardner, arrived safely to his father's great joy. Elaine was too groggy and frightened to rejoice till later. Karen took the baby in her arms, set his tiny feet on the floor to be welcomed by Mother Earth, and smudged the baby with sweetgrass. Theland's name was given to him by Vinny who created it from two words: The land. Gardner, his second name, is the surname of Elaine's deceased birth father. A powerful birth experience.

Elaine

Elaine and Vinny had become role models for healthy living in the Ottawa Aboriginal community. Vinny had been married and was on very good terms with his first wife and their two sons. Elaine had come close to marrying twice in the past. I sensed that she longed to be married, but had reconciled to a happy common-law partnership with Vinny, and to parenting Theland with him.

One day she phoned to arrange a visit with Ken and me. She and Vinny had something important to tell us. Vinny broke the news. His divorce to his first wife had become final, and over the time that he and Elaine had been together, he realized that he loved her deeply, and that he wanted to marry her in a traditional pipe ceremony. We could see that Elaine was thrilled. A marriage to Vinny fulfilled our hopes and dreams for Elaine. Vinny was a man whose eyes shone with goodness and kindness, and who worked tirelessly for and with his people. He had successfully fought his own demon—alcohol—and had been in recovery for many years. It was an impressive achievement.

We knew nothing about a Pipe Ceremony. We soon learned that, for Native peoples, there is no more sacred ritual for connecting the physical and spiritual world. The pipe is a link between earth and sky. The two main parts of the pipe, the red clay pipestone bowl and the wooden stem, have symbolic value. Joining the two parts is a metaphor for the union of Mother Earth and her creatures. The pipestone bowl or cup is considered female, and the wooden stem is male. When they join together, it is akin to the male joining with the female. Tobacco, brought by those who request the ceremony (in this case Elaine and Vinny) and blessed through prayer, is burned in the pipe.

It is unimaginable for Native Canadians to break their word after smoking the sacred pipe in the pipe ceremony. The pipe is the vehicle for carrying their word up to the Creator, and in return, a blessing descends from the Creator to the individuals smoking it. The commitment made is to the Creator, and cannot be broken. And so there is no divorce for two people following a pipe ceremony. The pipe carrier is usually the official who performs the ceremony. Aaron, a respected elder and long-time friend of Elaine and Vinny, was their pipe carrier. His job was to ensure that the couple was very serious about the commitment they were making. The bride and the groom dress in traditional Native wedding regalia, usually made by hand, and everyone is invited by word of mouth to the wedding. The wedding is a time of celebration during which there is feasting, visiting, and a "giveaway," through which the married couple provide many gifts, with each guest choosing what they want.

Elaine and Vinny chose to be married at Minwaashin Lodge, the Aboriginal Women's Support Centre in Ottawa, where Elaine coordinated the Sacred Child Program. It was the perfect setting for a December wedding. Aaron's partner, Sylvie, helped Elaine and Vinny organize the event.

We assembled in the big room at the Lodge. Many of Vinny's and Elaine's friends and family members in the Aboriginal community were invited, as were all of us in Elaine's adoptive family. Her dad and I were thrilled that each of Elaine's siblings, their partners and their children were able to come—the McGarity-Shipleys: Kevin, his wife Carol, their children Ellen, Michael, Jonathan, and Olivia; the Urban Shipleys: Dave, his wife Ruth, their children Rachel and Ben; Jill and her then husband, Marc Gallant; as well as Elaine's cousin, Erinne White; our close friend, Lynne Robertson, an evaluation analyst for Aboriginal Head Start; and Elaine's proud godmother, Thelma Howard, who journeyed from Saskatoon for the occasion. There were 17 of us.

A royal blue carpet of indigenous design graced the centre of the room. Elaine looked beautiful in a white faux leather skirt with brilliant turquoise blue cape, beaded moccasins, a beaded white sash and beaded hair clip in her long, black braid. She carried a beaded cloth bag which had been passed on to her through Ken's parents, who treasured this bag given to them by Natives of their farm district in Manitoba. In this way, Elaine was honoring both her families. Vinny wore white pants, a black shirt with a ribbon band, and moccasins. Theland, too, was dressed in fine Aboriginal regalia. Aaron, who had a humorous and compelling presence, explained the significance of the ceremony to us all and led the couple through it. It is disrespectful of Native culture, in fact, forbidden, to describe in writing some parts of the ceremony in which Elaine and Vinny were involved. These aspects of the ceremony are sacred, and known only by the couple and the pipe carrier. Elaine and Vinny smoked the pipe and then it was passed to everyone in the room. Each person could freely choose to smoke it, or to touch it reverently (which some of the children did), and pass it on.

The traditional part of the feast included moose stew and Three Sisters' Soup which consists of a wonderful combination of corn, beans, and squash traditionally grown and eaten by many Native peoples. Ritual was experienced through the quiet, measured pace of the entire event, as the guests respectfully took their turns helping themselves to the food.

Ken and I had made arrangements, with Elaine's blessing, for a quilt to be created by the Nahua women of Tlamacazapa, Mexico, whom we had come to know and support in recent years through our friend, Susan Smith, whom we had met years before in Botswana. The quilt was a woven design in earth tones with overlaid African print intended to represent the years that Elaine spent in Africa. As Ken and I presented the quilt to Elaine and Vinny, I recited a poem I had adapted from *A Grateful Heart:*

> May the Creator like a mother eagle spread wings of her love and protection over you this day and forever.
> May your lives be like wildflowers growing freely in the beauty and joy of every day.

The giveaway that followed was great fun. Ken and I, as elders, were first up. We both chose toques which we popped onto our heads, to the amusement of all.

The pipe ceremony was a time of coming together, of rejoicing, and of healing the rifts we had earlier experienced. It was a powerful cultural and family experience.

As of this writing, Theland is ten years old and has been taught the traditional beliefs and practices as they are known to his parents. He loves to go to pow wows, dancing and drumming with the big guys and with his mother. His rhythm is steady and strong; his dancing is creative and compelling. He and his mother are sought after in Ottawa and cities and towns nearby to sing, dance, and drum at special events, community festivals, and sometimes even on Parliament Hill for Canada Day. Elaine and Theland are gifted. It is not always easy to straddle two worlds—the mainstream Ottawa community and the Aboriginal community—or to integrate them. We are proud of Elaine

—her accomplishments, the way she has overcome some major life challenges, her loving, attentive mothering of Theland, and her commitment to Vinny. Elaine fully embraces her traditional First Nations culture which means that sometimes we see very little of her, and then we miss her. The hostility she might have felt towards us as the family who took her away from her people as a toddler seems to be disappearing. Since becoming a mother to Theland and a wife to Vinny, she has gained in confidence, in grace, and in expressing who she is more fully than at any time in her life. We love her forever.

Chapter Eleven

Saying Goodbye to My Mothers

A Love Letter to My Mom

Do not go gentle into that good night
Old age should burn and rave at close of day
Rage, rage against the dying of the light.
— Dylan Thomas

My darling Mom,

That quote from Dylan Thomas' poem published way back in 1952 does not describe you, does it? You did indeed go gentle into that good night, and I often wished you could have raged against the dying of the light. It might have eased your struggle if you had complained, even a little.

Where do I begin, Mom? I could start in 1988 when I was in the throes of *Vera*, when it became clear that meeting her and knowing *finally* who I was, helped me to grow up and treasure who you are, and what you mean to me.

Or, I could start in 1980 when we moved to Ontario following our two years in Botswana. (By then you had lived in Belleville for a decade, having left Winnipeg to move "home again"). It was good fortune that we were just three hours apart and could have frequent visits. At first you made more trips than I did, taking the Voyageur bus, staying a few days with the kids, Ken, and me before you headed back. Those were the days when you did all your own shopping. And what a shopper you were! It was never too much trouble for you to trudge around from store to store, finding just the right card for a friend's birthday, or picking up a can of salmon on sale (it had to be red sockeye), or buying the perfect slip. You walked everywhere—from your apartment on Belleville's west side to the downtown area to do your banking, and to pick up "a bit of ham for a change." You kept up a correspondence with your friends and the children of friends in

Winnipeg, your grandchildren, and always, your special daughter, Lois. What faithful correspondents you two were—writing each other weekly for years about your "doings". You toured by bus with friends to Maine and Vermont to see the fall colours.

Colour was important to you: the colour of paint, of carpet. Things had to match. You chose your dresses well, often in a becoming floral design in pretty pastel colours. You knew that the rich jewel tones suited me, not you. I cannot count the times you helped me pick out an outfit that suited, as we trudged from store to store. You were always pleased when I found a dress that excited me.

You liked to wear beads to match your dress, partly because you were self-conscious about your neck, which you described as scrawny. I don't suppose anyone else thought so, but you did. Your pretty white hair was always beautifully curled around your ears. You were also self-conscious about your ears, which stuck out a bit, but we never noticed. It was very important to you to have George style your hair. He was helpful and kind to you as you became less steady on your feet. People commented on how nice you always looked. It was a sad day for you when you could no longer go to George's shop.

Your apartment overlooking the Bay of Quinte and the Bay Bridge was the nicest place you ever lived in, you said. It was always neat and immaculate, with pretty things about. Once a chair or plant found its place, it stayed there. You were not one for shifting things around, and trying new arrangements. You would settle on a certain way of doing things, and that was how you liked it. Your bed was made with the sheets and blankets loose around the bottom so your feet were free to move. Your bread had to be fresh, white, crusty, and unsliced. Your tea was made with boiling water poured into a hotted pot over a Mother Tucker tea bag, and steeped only for a few minutes so it wouldn't be too strong. You drank it from a pretty cup (how you hated those heavy mugs of mine!) with 1/4 teaspoon of sugar, no less and no more.

You were about to have a birthday, and I decided to write you a special letter about how much you meant to me. So often we hold back on such an expression while our loved one is alive, only to say it at the funeral. I didn't want that to happen. I wrote that I knew it wasn't easy for you to be openly expressive, but that I treasured your quiet, unfailing, constant love. I gave examples from childhood and beyond of your constancy, and told you how lucky I was to have a mother like you. You phoned after you received my letter to say that you'd always wished you could have been more like Mattie, who so freely expressed affection. I told you I loved you just as you were, and that I wanted no other mother but you.

Some time later, I re-read Robert Munsch's *Love You Forever* (1986), the tender children's story about the enduring nature of love and how it crosses the generations. Guided by my intuition, I mailed it to you. You phoned to say it had moved you to tears. My Mom—I'd seen you cry only once in my life. A tender, poignant moment.

As the years went on, you stopped making trips to California to see Lois and to Ottawa to see us. That was a loss. I continued visiting you in Belleville every two or three months, and then more often. It became harder for you to shop on your own and to cook for yourself. You became afraid to use your oven, in case you became unsteady and couldn't lift a hot pan onto the counter. You were so impressed when your grandson Kevin suggested you turn the oven off, open the door, and wait till the pan cooled before you lifted it out. When I came for a weekend, I would launch into a cooking/baking frenzy in your kitchen —chicken, beef stew, blueberry pie, lemon loaf... ah, the lemon loaf that you enjoyed to the end when everything else had lost its taste. Then I came to realize that it heightened your anxiety to have me banging around in your kitchen after your peaceful, quiet weeks of being alone—doing things your way. So I would cook at home, and haul it down in a rented car. I thought that would give us more time to talk and visit, Mom, but you were never a big talker. You were task-oriented; after all, you couldn't do many of the tasks yourself anymore. Choosing a birthday card took too much energy, so I would pre-select a few cards from the display and bring them over to you, seated on your walker. Then you would choose one. I was sad when you didn't want to look for a new dress for spring. You didn't have the energy. Lois and I would try to find a blouse or a housecoat that we thought you would like. About half the time we got it right. Lois more often than I. She had a better sense of what suited you.

We realized that your phone was no longer adequate. It had a funny way of not sitting in the cradle properly, so that it was actually *off* the hook when it looked *on*. One night I tried to phone you for hours—just a busy-busy-busy signal. You had fallen a couple of times that year—easy falls that didn't injure you when your knees collapsed and you slid to the floor. They must have frightened you, though, but you were never one to express such fears. When I couldn't reach you that night, I phoned Mavis Kirk down the hall from you, and asked her to knock on your door. You were flustered and embarrassed by that, so we decided to get you a new phone. I did a scouting trip to the phone shop in the Quinte Mall. A nice clerk recommended a phone with a portable receiver that you could carry around in your walker, and a quick dial system to call friends and family. We both went to the shop to buy it. The clerk watched as you came in pushing your walker. Although it was a short walk from the car to inside the mall, it took every ounce of your strength. I weep now thinking of how hard you tried to keep on keeping on. We never talked about it much, Mom, did we?

Money loomed large in your life, Mom. You were the one in your marriage who "kept the books", who figured out if there were enough dollars for my music theory lessons, on top of piano lessons. Music lessons were all a bit of a mystery to you. But you always found the money. I didn't wonder then, but I wonder now what you sacrificed to do it. Dad was proud that he'd been able to buy stocks and bonds for you in your old age. How grieved he would have been to know that there was not enough money for you to move into a retirement residence (the usual move before a nursing home). You knew that Lois and I would have to contribute monthly once you began spending your capital, and for you, that was unthinkable. You stayed where you were, in your lovely apartment, year after year after year. The prevailing wisdom is that seniors should remain independent for as long as they can, and that children and community services should enable that to happen. That is what we did, but I suspect that if you had had the money, you would have moved to a retirement residence where the responsibility of day-to-day living did not rest entirely on your shoulders.

Your pervasive anxiety became a daily problem. Pushing your walker, you found it hard to simply enter the waiting room of your doctor's office. You knew that people noticed how old you were. Before you moved to the nursing home of your choice at the age of 94, you had pretty well stopped going out. Community supports were in place, but they were not able to stem the tide of your anxiety. Each morning you would have one of your "spells", as you called them. You would finish your breakfast, take your pill (valium), sit in your favourite platform rocker, complete a word puzzle, and wait for the anxiety to begin, and then fade. For a while I wondered if the valium was actually increasing your anxiety and spoke to your doctor. He began to monitor your intake—not that you *ever* took more than you needed—and then he decided to take you off it altogether. You felt as though you were falling apart without it. I found it unbelievable that he took this action, knowing that you would undoubtedly experience symptoms of withdrawal, and I told him so politely in a letter.

Mom, as you became weaker and less able to do for yourself, we reached out into the community for help. Your first helper, Joan, had been cleaning and tidying your apartment for several years. You liked having her around. Sometimes you wished she wasn't so rushed, but she kept to a busy schedule. She offered to do more—to take you shopping and to the doctor and to George's—after which you got together for coffee and a doughnut. You were a woman of simple pleasures. When you could no longer go out to shop, Joan cooked and shopped for you. She thought you should have a little Christmas tree, which she brought and decorated, when you no longer had the strength to bother. Your next helper—Harold, the director of Community Care, took a special interest in you by taking you to the bank and to the doctor—later you entrusted him to withdraw money for you. How happy you were for him when he and his wife had a child after years of being childless! Maybe you remembered what it was like for you and Dad before you adopted me. Kevin teased you about gadding about with Harold which brought a laugh. When you were no longer able to take a bath, you protested that a sponge bath was adequate. A bath lady from a service agency turned out to be a disaster. She made you stand naked and self-conscious in the bathroom, and whipped you in and out of the tub, scrubbing you vigorously in nothing flat. You were humiliated and exhausted for days. After that, it was difficult to persuade you to try another bath lady. Your next helper, June, was perfect in her respectful, encouraging ways. She dusted, vacuumed, and even made muffins. She would shake her head in disbelief that you placed the baking dishes and the ingredients on the counter before she came, so that all she had to do was measure, mix and bake. And finally, Hazel, "the church lady" visited you every other week for five years. A lady like you were, she was a godsend. You found her prayers and her presence a great comfort, especially when the minister came to bring Communion to you. She suited you to a "T" for tenderness.

You loved visits from your niece Eva, and her husband, Harry. They made it easy with their open, affectionate, down-to-earth chatter. They loved you and you knew it. You and your friend, Frances were a team for a while—going shopping, going for lunch. Then it all became too much for you and for her. After that, she faithfully phoned you each morning and evening. These phone calls kept you in touch with the world outside, but demanded more energy than you had. Frances was more of a talker than a listener, and her well-meaning advice was not what you needed. You could not find a way to shorten her 40-minute daily phone calls. It was also important to Leah, your sister-in-law, to keep in touch. When you were still out and about, you visited Leah for tea. Later, it became too stressful. I took over the visiting of Leah, as did Lois when she came to visit from California. Lois and I became your proxies for the friends and family members you could no longer see.

You never wanted to be a bother to anyone, Mom. You were always so happy to see me when I walked through the door of your apartment with my suitcase for yet another weekend. But never, ever did you phone ahead and say, "Oh, Carol, when are you coming down? It would be so nice to see you. I've been a bit lonely." A typical example of your thoughtfulness and courage took place fifteen years before you died. You did not want Lois and me to have to contend with the cost and arrangements for your funeral. So you and I visited Thomson's Funeral Home. You chose your favourite hymns for the service. You picked out the casket, simple and moderately priced. And you paid for it all, then and there. How satisfied you would have been the morning you died to learn that Thomson's had wisely invested that money paid in advance, and that there was to be a refund! You would have been pleased that we used the refund to pay the hotel bill for all your darling grandchildren and their families who came to the service. Your would have been pleased to know that Lois and I each received several thousand dollars from your estate which we wisely invested by your example. We both wish, though, that you had kicked up your heels a little more than you did. But maybe you at least wiggled your toes—on your bus trips, at your euchre games, and during your visits to your beloved cousin Evelyn in Toronto.

I experienced your thoughtfulness in choosing a nursing home. You and I visited the Placement Coordination Services lady to learn how the system worked. Your top choice of nursing homes was Westgate Lodge. Lois and I were not faced with making the decision for a mother who was resistant to a move. You made it so much easier when that time came.

The last days in your Palmer Road apartment were very difficult. The carpal tunnel pain in your wrist was excruciating. I always thought you had a very low pain threshold, but people have told me that carpal tunnel is very, very painful. A splint seemed to help at first—painkillers weren't really the answer. Your doctor proposed that you see a specialist about having surgery to deaden the nerve and the pain. It was a very low moment when you couldn't decide what to do. You were exhausted, and sad, and in pain—we both knew it was time for you to move. I was so *grateful* that we were able to make that decision together. The Placement people were contacted. They informed us that there was a bed in your top-choice nursing home. I wondered how a bed had become available so quickly. (You had likely been assessed "high risk" because you were living on your own.)

As you tried to get into bed that night, you were not able to lift your legs. I lifted them for you, pulled the covers over, stroked your forehead, and told you I loved you. Then, in a most unforgettable way, you looked up at me and said, "Oh Carol, you are such a blessing. What would I have done without you?" I will love you forever for that, Mom. All those years of not having a strong sense of belonging were erased by those few words. Although she would not understand it, Vera played a big part in giving you and me our ten best years together—it is never too late. I have an unforgettable image of you from that last night in your apartment. Sleeping on your living room couch, I was wakened by a slight, worn-out, silent lady in her cotton nightie, heading for the bathroom in the wee hours, pushing her walker with all the strength she could muster, *doing the best she could.*

You were given 24 hours in which to decide to take the bed at Westgate Lodge and move there. It was too rushed, and you felt overwhelmed. We decided to slow it down a day, and pay the difference. I am still angry at the inflexibility of a system that would charge an elderly lady $100 to hold a bed. How could a woman of 94 just pick up and move in 24 hours? You needed time to sort through your things in the home you'd lived in for twenty years.

Quiet and sad on that drive from your apartment to the nursing home, neither of us shed a tear. You had been assigned a bed in Room 9, a large, square, plain room with three other ladies. I was shocked at the small amount of space you would have. You even had to share your corner with another woman whose belongings were in a cupboard in your corner of the room. A lovely, big window overlooked Dundas Street and a park. One friendly roommate, Evelyn, seemed pleased to see you.

After Carolyn, the charge nurse, helped you get settled, we were invited down to the common room for an afternoon of live old-time music. But I was overwhelmed by the people all around me—frail, trembling, mumbling, staring blankly, many in wheelchairs, and almost all women. I sat beside you, listening to the music, with tears streaming from my eyes. I would soon have to leave to catch my train back to Ottawa. Shortly after I left, you made your way by walker to the dining room. As you went by Carolyn's desk, you "went to pieces", as you would say it. "Going to pieces" was probably something you had done no more than twice in your lifetime. Carolyn comforted you. You told me later that you had felt abandoned. I felt that I had abandoned you. Sad, powerful stuff.

It was a rough beginning. That weekend, one of your roommates became very ill and died right there in your room. It traumatized you. You were offered her bed soon after— now you had a better view of the world outside your window.

Your wrist continued to cause great discomfort and pain. I worried about you having surgery at your age, but anything was better than what you were going through. At the Outpatients' Department of Belleville General Hospital, surgery was performed. You took it in stride, returned to the nursing home with a bandage on your wrist, and were able to eat your supper with a knife and fork that evening, which thoroughly impressed your table mates!

You surprised us, Mom, by settling in to the Westgate routine. You attended Resident Council meetings, and spoke up about one or two issues. You attended entertainment events, and enjoyed visits from the regulars, like Bert and Nellie, who began to include you on their rounds. Bert and Nellie were Catholic, and I don't suppose you'd ever before been close to people who were Catholic. It's never too late. You didn't like the food much, nor did many of the other residents. How could the kitchen staff satisfy the residents who were mostly women and who had cooked for themselves, in their own way, their entire lives? Complaining about the food was a common bond. When a resident said she liked the food, the rest of you were in disbelief.

A series of roommates in Room 9 brought you to a low ebb. You handled Pat's aggressive dementia by not engaging with her. Eleanor's confusion was a source of tension as she disrobed in the middle of the day and dressed in the middle of the night. One night you wakened to find her staring at you over your bed. Very unnerving. Susan, with Parkinson's' disease, had all her mental faculties, was sweet and considerate, even though sad and depressed at times. But her tremors and shaking worsened in the evenings and into the night. Evelyn had begun to act like the Queen Bee, invading your space with her huge motorized easy chair— it was becoming a safety issue for you.

You were not sleeping well and you were losing ground. A bed in the newer wing was offered to you, but we were not made fully aware of the kind of person your roommate was. Doris O was 101 years of age, and if she had ever had social graces, she was long past having any interest in using them. She complained that your walker was on her side of the room, that your fan blew onto her side of the room, that your roses smelled up her side of the room, that your light was on in the early evening when she wanted to sleep. Again you did not engage, but it was very difficult. Nurses would tell you what a pleasant woman she had once been, but after her 100th birthday, it had gone downhill. You and I reminded each other that she couldn't live forever. If it became intolerable, we would speak to the powers-that-be. Then one day you left a message on our telephone answering machine. You said, "Hello, Carol. I have some good news. Doris just died." It *was* good news, of course, but I wonder if you ever knew what you actually said! Jacqueline became your new roommate. The two of you were well suited—neither of you engaged with the other. It was the closest thing to a private room you would have.

1999 was the year you ever so slowly left us. I was in Bermuda in late January, unaware that the nurse in charge at Westgate Lodge had contacted Ken, wondering if I should be called to come home. You had had a bad turn, and they weren't sure you would rally. Maybe it was difficult to have me so far away, but if so, you either kept such fears to yourself, or were barely conscious of them. Were you afraid of what you would do if some accident befell me? One thing was sure—you would not have wanted to interfere in any way with my chance for a nice holiday. *So many people loved you, Mom.* Even at the end, new people told me that they loved you, that there should be more like you, that you were a true *lady.* It was decided not to call me home, and you rallied.

In your final year, I visited Belleville more often as your strength waned: every two weeks at first, then every ten days, then weekly, and finally I came and stayed for a daily vigil.

You didn't want to engage with others anymore—you were just so tired. Activities in the nursing home were no longer of interest. You spent your days rocking back and forth in your chair, looking out the window, no longer able to do your word puzzles. Yet you continued to trudge down to the dining room for meals. When that became too much, the nurses encouraged you to walk to the dining room, and get a ride on your walker seat back to your room. You always did the best you could. I think there was a tug-of-war being waged within you: the pull to try to do your best, to walk a little, to keep your clothes and your Room 37 "world" organized, and to eat a bit of your meal; and the opposite pull to let go, just sit, and wait for the end. You had lost your appetite for food and for life, hadn't you, Mom?

You were nearing the end of your 97th year. Visits from friends and family kept you going. Your grandson Dave sent you faxes from

Wisconsin addressed to *My Grandma*. You loved your grandson Kevin's visits with his wife, Carol, faithful and caring, and with the grandchildren from Kingston. Love carried you along in the land of the living for a while longer.

You hung on to life. Receiving some guidance from a palliative care doctor in Ottawa, I talked to you about letting go. Taking your hand in mine, I said:

> Mom, I love you so, and I will miss you very much when you are not with us anymore. But we will be OK and we will carry on after you go—Lois and I and the rest of your family who love you so much. And I am absolutely certain that you will have comfort and peace at the last.

Two weeks before you died, your 97th birthday was memorable. You had been moved to the infirmary, which Lois said was the private room you had always longed for. Elaine, Jill, and I drove down from Ottawa. There were lots of birthday cards for you—the lady who never forgot birthdays. The staff had already been in to sing *Happy Birthday.* The songs of my friend Pat Mayberry were playing quietly in the background. I moved in close to tell you that Jill, Elaine, and I were here for your birthday. When I turned to say a word to the girls, one of the nurses saw a tear rolling down your cheek. You were unable to speak, but you knew we were there. The girls each spoke their love to you privately; I stroked your head, and put your favorite apricot hand cream on your dear hands, which moved no longer. A nurse came in every half hour to turn you from one side to another. One nurse brought in a doughnut dressing, which she'd specially created for the bedsore on your hip. Clarice, in the room across the hall, created some "diversion" by yelling "Help!" throughout the day, until Grace wheeled her off. Grace asked if there was room in our car to take Clarice back to Ottawa for a couple of weeks! So funny, so trusting, so supportive. Air seeping through the window of your room sounded like a sick cow—that provided black comic relief. When it was time to leave, it was very sad for your granddaughters. The end was near.

For the next two weeks, we were in constant touch by telephone with the staff and with you. When I phoned, a nurse would place the receiver to your ear, and I did the talking. Your breathing was slowing and stopping for short spells. The nurses phoned me to come. I was so grateful to Ken for driving me the three hours to get to your bedside, hoping I would be in time. Well, there you were, with Lizzie holding your hand, music softly playing, and your favorite prayer on the wall:

> O Lord, support us all the day long of this troublous life, until the shadows lengthen, and the evening comes, the busy world is hushed, the fever of life is over, and our work is done. Then Lord, in thy mercy, grant us safe lodging, a holy rest, and peace at the last, through Jesus Christ our Lord. Amen.
>
> —The Book of Common Prayer—Anglican

One morning I arrived early because I couldn't sleep. Your night table had been transformed into an altar by the night nurse. On the table was a yellow rose, your favourite flower, in a clear glass vase; the photo of Lois, you, and me taken at the Rochester reunion where you met your darling great-granddaughters, Rachel and Ellen, for the first time; your prayer/hymn book from which I sang "Unto the hills around do I lift up my longing eyes", and recited the Twenty-third Psalm to you.

Lois phoned every day. It was so difficult for her to be far away. She and her husband, Rich decided to come. It was a great comfort to have them, and to have Ken holding the fort so capably at home. You lingered. Your pulse and breathing would slow... and then become more regular. The nurses were amazed that you were still with us. We kept the vigil. We began to plan your funeral. Your dying seemed to go on forever. The night before you died, I put it all into God's hands, feeling a sense of peace and strength that I could continue no matter how long it was. Lois was feeling desperate about work commitments, not knowing how long she would be away. I woke just before 6 on the morning of November 19, 1999. Then the phone rang. It was Ann from Westgate Lodge. Ann, who had been such a bright spark when you were in Room 9. She said you had died while she was on her break. That was your way, Mom, to die alone and quietly, to be a bother to no one. Lois, Rich, and I came over, and sat with you a while in your peaceful room. Nurses and staff came in to pay their respects. You were one of their beloved. Lois and I love you forever, Mom.

Sharing your last year with you, Mom, was a deep honour. I've always believed that dying is part of living, but didn't know it in my heart. Your dying taught me about how to live. I think the meaning of life is all about living with an open heart in a gentle, undemanding, faithful, passionate, forever way. A tall order, and one that will challenge me to the end of *my* days.

I have one big regret about the funeral. While I wanted to pay tribute to you during the service, Lois did not feel she would be able to. I sensed that Rich would have been willing, but I did not pick up on the cues. Neither of them spoke about Rich's willingness, and so it was not until their Christmas newsletter one month later, that Rich shared a loving tribute to you.

People who loved you came to your funeral. Kevin and Carol decided to bring their three children to the visitation and funeral. When four-year-old Mikey walked up to where you lay in an open casket, he called back to his older sister, "Elly, it's not scary; Elly, it's OK". Their little brother Jonathan, age two, coming down with the flu, provided the basics by throwing up on the carpet. I was about to rush out to find water and a cloth, then thought better of it. It was not my job today. Kevin, in his farewell "talk" to you at your funeral, said, "Grandma, more than many other people I know, you understood the importance of being with the people you loved." I spoke as well. Elaine sang and drummed a song for your journey. Elaine's presence brought both laughter and tears. There was laughter because Elaine asked the funeral director if he had an oven. Nonplussed, his mind went to cremation, but what Elaine wanted was a stove oven to warm her drum! Two men told me that they wept as Elaine's song went deep into their souls. We sang your favourite hymn "Abide with Me," and the beautiful "We Shall Go Out with Hope of Resurrection" (Boyce-Tillmann 1996) to the tune of the familiar Londonderry Air. Lois and I felt very close as we planned, stood by and supported each other. It was an unusually warm November day as we gathered in the cemetery to see your casket lowered into the family burial plot in Thomasburg Cemetery to join your mother, brother, and sister-in-law.

The certainty of fully belonging, of knowing deep within that you were my mom, the circumstances of my life, and the maturity of years allowed me to care for you in your dying in a way that I had been unable to do when Dad died. I am deeply grateful, Mom.

Deep Thanks to Mama Vera

Why not go out on a limb? Isn't that where the fruit is?
— Will Rogers

In her late 80s, Vera was in trouble. She was having more difficulty going back and forth the several blocks for her groceries, shuffling behind her walker. Wayne looked in on her every day, knowing that she could not manage on her own much longer. She fell and broke her hip, and was hospitalized. Mental health problems soon set in. She became angry and bitter and was losing touch with reality. So she was transferred to the psychiatric wing of the rehabilitation hospital. It must have been a horrifying reminder of all the past times she'd been hospitalized. Wayne knew she would not be going home again, and arranged a transfer to a nursing home.

I was visiting in Winnipeg on the day Vera was to move, and I offered to help Wayne with the packing up. I stayed overnight with him, and in the morning, I called down to him from the second floor hallway with an innocuous question, something about stripping the sheets from the bed. "If you want to speak to me, come downstairs. Do not shout at me from up there!" he blasted. I was outraged and muttered an "f--- you." To my regret, it was loud enough for him to hear. When I came downstairs, he was livid with rage at my insulting words, so angry that I did not feel safe. I apologized, but stood my ground. I told him that I had not liked his tone—it was disrespectful and abusive. He became teary-eyed and remorseful as he told me of his struggle to manage his anger. I could see that he thought that everything was smoothed over between us. But the incident stayed with me. I could never predict when he would explode. Would it be wiser to discontinue contact with him?

When we arrived at the hospital, Vera was sitting in her room, silent and sullen. It was not clear if she knew who I was. Wayne had brought big, black garbage bags to pack up her things. This made my heart sink, but I did not comment. I asked Vera if I could help her pack, and she grudgingly agreed that I could. I was shocked and nervous, and I ached for her. I lifted one outfit from the hanger in the closet, and she burst out, "That's not mine. Leave it there." "But whose would it be but hers?" I asked myself, but decided not to question.

A young male psychiatric nurse stopped to say goodbye, as Vera slumped in her wheelchair near the nurses' desk. "Well, V," he said, taking her hand in his and smiling at her, "It's been quite a ride, hasn't it?" Basking in the attention of a young man, she smiled back at him. She did not pick up on the double entendre in his words.

A friendly, Filipina nurse escorted us to Wayne's car. As she and I carried Vera's bags, we exchanged pleasantries about her length of time in Canada. Suddenly, Vera exploded, "Will you two keep quiet!" I froze and went silent. Her outburst seemed to have come out of nowhere, but when we were in the car, she turned to me and said, "Why were you talking to that dark woman? I can't stand her." Racism again. I felt sick. Vera's anxiety about moving to an unknown place must have been unbearable. Her life as an independent woman supported by Wayne, cozy in her seniors' apartment, and with enough money for occasional trips to interesting resorts and to meet her daily needs, was over. I did not dare to break through her hostility to her sadness and pain.

After settling in, Vera began to have difficulties getting along with her roommate and was rude to the nursing home staff. She was given a room of her own. *A room of her own* evokes peace, quiet, beauty and rejuvenation. Not so for Vera. Her dementia progressed, and she spent more and more time alone in her room, helped by a mechanical lift to the toilet and into the bath. Sometimes she would look up at Wayne and say, "Why am I still here? I wish I was dead." But she hung on.

Wayne was not happy with the care his mother was getting, and frequently complained to the staff that they were lazy. A few of them were good to his mother, but he found it hard to single them out. "I know I shouldn't, but I put them all in the same boat," he said. He wasn't a popular visitor, and over the next four years, he began to visit less and less often. Finding it unbearable to see his mother living out her last days this way, he longed for it to be over for her and for himself.

When I visited Vera for the last time, she looked old and tiny, lying in her bed. As Wayne fed her, she did not speak except when he asked her a question. Then she would burst out loudly with a "yes" or a "no" or "no more". It was a perfect summer's day, so we wheeled Vera down to the small garden area in front of the nursing home. Her eyes widened with pleasure as she looked up at the vines of bright flowers spilling over the urns. She had not lost her eye for beauty. Then, pointing at me, Wayne said, "Do you know who this is, Mom?" "No," she shouted. "She's my sister. She's your baby girl, Carol," he said. "Do you remember her?" "Yes," she answered. "You have two of us to hug you today," I said. Our eyes, brimming with tears, met above Vera's head, as she sat in her wheelchair. A last moment to treasure.

On my 74th birthday in February 2010, Vera was in my thoughts. I was the same age she was when we found each other after more than half a century. Wayne phoned to wish me happy birthday, he's faithful that way, and to say that things were much the same with his mother. She seemed to be living forever. But five days later, there was a second phone call from Wayne. "It's the phone call you've been expecting," he said. That morning he'd received a call that Vera's blood pressure had dropped and her pulse had slowed. She'd been taken by ambulance to the hospital where she remained semi-conscious, her breathing laboured, with longer and longer pauses between breaths. Wayne was with his mother for her last few hours, and Sherri joined him to be with her grandmother for her last few minutes. Wayne almost couldn't admit it, but he was relieved that the struggle was over. "She's finally at peace," he said. "The nursing home can no longer neglect her." The hospital staff had been kind and considerate and he was grateful. Wayne had no history with them.

I was touched that Wayne had let me know. He said it would be a very small funeral. None of Vera's relatives from Ontario or Saskatchewan would be attending. His mom had no friends left in Winnipeg, and he was not intending to write an obituary for the newspaper because he feared that telemarketers and the like would read it and bother him. I talked with Ken about my need to attend Vera's funeral to honour what she'd meant to me, and for a sense of completion. I called Wayne back. "I'd very much like to come to the funeral, Wayne," I said. "What do you think?" "I wouldn't recommend it," he said. This unnerved me, and I didn't ask him to explain. I repeated again that I'd like to come, and he said he'd let me know what day the funeral would be.

Next day I realized that to get reduced airfare to Winnipeg, I'd have to book a flight immediately and hope that the date of the funeral would fall between Thursday and Monday (she'd died the previous Tuesday). If I purchased it immediately, I would be able to get a reduced rate ticket. So I did that. I phoned Wayne to tell him of my plans to arrive Thursday and leave Monday, and ask if he knew yet when the funeral would be. He blew up. "I am very busy with many phone calls to make. I am in a vacuum. I have not contacted the funeral home, and I have no idea when the funeral will be. *When I know, I will phone you!"*

It was a shocking shift from the tone of the previous night's phone call. I was beginning to feel like "other," a persona non grata. Next day Wayne left a message on our voice mail. In a pleasant voice he said, "The funeral will be Tuesday." But that was the day after I planned to return home! I was torn with doubt, hurt, and confusion. Was this his way of keeping me away?

Conversations with Ken, Kevin, and my dear friend Fran, with whom I planned to stay while in Winnipeg, were a great help to me. I resolved to keep my mind and heart open, not assume the worst, but to go to Winnipeg with the intention of trying to learn the truth about how Wayne felt. If I learned that he did not want me at the funeral, then, as Fran suggested, I could find other ways while in Winnipeg to honour Vera's memory. In fact, I did carry out one of these ideas by visiting and leaving a donation with my beloved goddaughter, Kathy Strachan, the executive director of Villa Rosa, a haven for young single mothers and their children till they are ready to set forth on their own.

At the suggestion of our friend John Standing, I contacted the staff person at the funeral home who had met with Wayne to arrange Vera's funeral. I hoped to find out why the funeral was not being held Friday,

Saturday or Monday. I learned that the funeral home was fully booked for the Friday, that Saturday would require Wayne to pay an extra weekend burial fee, and that Monday was Louis Riel Day, a provincial holiday, when the cemetery would not be operating. I had my explanation for a Tuesday funeral.

In a phone call to Wayne, he apologized for being "short" with me in that earlier phone call. Then I asked him if he thought it a good idea that I would try to change my return ticket so I could attend the Tuesday funeral. He seemed incredulous, exclaiming that he thought that was why I had come to Winnipeg! He did not remember that I had told him of my Thursday arrival and my Monday departure, in the phone call from Ottawa. He said he had a lot on his mind, and he had no interest in hearing that I got a good price on a plane ticket. Then I told him that I wasn't sure that he wanted me at the funeral. He said, "Of course I do. I like you. I want you there. And I'll share the cost of changing your ticket!" So then I gently asked what he had meant by his earlier comment that he wouldn't recommend my coming. He said that he meant that her life was over, and that it was not worth the effort or the cost of attending a funeral for her. But he continued to reassure me that he wanted me there, and that Vera had paid for a limousine to transport family members to and from the funeral home and cemetery, as her last "hurrah". In fact, Vera had pre-paid her entire funeral costs (just as Mom had). Then he invited me to ride with Sue and him in the limo. There really was no doubt in my mind now that I was welcome at Vera's funeral. But as the outsider, I had been very unsure of myself. Wayne outlined a very short funeral service during which he and his daughter, Sherri , would say a few words, followed by "The Lord's Prayer." Then he asked if I would like to say a few words at the service as well. I was very touched.

I spent the rest of the day changing the day of my flight back to Ottawa. The results couldn't have been better. I was welcome at the funeral, and the extra charge for changing my flight dropped from $158 to $7.55! The support of dear friends saw me through. We shared dinners, laughter, and good talks together.

Two days before the funeral, Wayne and Sue invited me for coffee at their place. Wayne hung up my coat, while I stood, a little unsure, purse on my shoulder, at the entrance to the living room. Then he barked, "Put your purse down. Put it down! Why do women hold onto their purses? Do they think someone's going to steal them?" Again, this seemed to come out of nowhere. I was incredulous, but this time I was ready. I stepped toward him, and facing him up close, I said quietly, but firmly, "Wayne, I'm not going to do this. Stop it right now." And he did! Then I went over and sat on the couch, digging my reading glasses out of the purse in case I needed them. Later, I asked Sue if she thought he was more easily upset than usual because of his Mom's death. "Yes, he's more touchy than usual," she said. "But he's a control freak. He's always like this." I tried to remember that I should not take his outbursts personally.

Wayne talked to me about his childhood with Vera. They had lived in downtown Winnipeg rooming houses, often in one room on the third floor, where the poorest of the tenants lived. The landlord would spot a vulnerable single woman and try to get her to go to bed with him. When Vera refused, they'd be evicted. I thought this was more information than a little boy needed to know. From the time he was almost too young to remember, his Mom had "nervous breakdowns". Sometimes he'd come home from school and she'd be gone. If the landlady was a kindly person, she'd watch over Wayne and give him his meals. A precarious, insecure existence. When Vera was admitted to Brandon Psychiatric Hospital for a whole year, Wayne went to live with his grandmother on the farm in Saskatchewan. I recalled that Vera had told me about the horrors of the psych hospital, waking up after a long time of being "out of it". "I was lying in my own shit," she said.

I had known that Vera was diagnosed with bipolar disorder, but Wayne and Sue were sure that she had schizophrenia as well. When an episode was coming on, she began talking to people who weren't there, and was sometimes convinced that voices from the television were telling her things. Wayne learned to read the signs of oncoming illness: her handwriting became huge, and she stayed up all night—cleaning, cleaning, cleaning.

He recalled an incident when he was about 12 years old. He saw the signs of his mother's approaching episode, and he knew he had to get her to the hospital as quickly as possible, so she could get the treatment she needed and get back home sooner. He headed down the street to a pay phone and called the police. Explaining the situation as best as he could, in his 12-year-old way, he asked for help. The officer said, "You mean, you're trying to send your mother to the loony bin?" His eyes filling with tears, Wayne turned to me and said, "If only you had been there with me! I was so alone, with no one to turn to." My compassion for him was mingled with gratitude that I'd been spared his life of insecurity, poverty, instability and the deep emotional wounds he bore from his childhood.

Wayne says that he does not hold his mother accountable for her illnesses and her many hospitalizations. She did the best she could. He had lived through the fear, the confusion, and the abandonment as a result of her illness and absences. Yet he did not blame her.

I did some research on schizophrenia. I tried to imagine what my life might have been if I, the older sister, had been raised by a mother with the dual diagnosis of bipolar disorder and schizophrenia.

The six-day period in Winnipeg for Vera's funeral was similar in length and intensity to the 1988 reunion with Vera. This time, though, I was staying with a dear friend who listened, advised, and understood. Emotional and physical fatigue crept up on me. Depending on the previous day's events, I would sleep well one night and awaken at 3:30 a.m. the next.

The day of the funeral dawned, and I kept my expectations in check. I had bought a deep pink azalea plant and was pleased to see a variety of floral sprays and bouquets decorating the front of the chapel. It was fitting for a woman who, in her lifetime, had loved and painted vibrantly coloured flowers. Two pictures of Vera had been placed on the casket—a beautiful Vera in her 40s, smiling delightedly into the camera, and another Vera in her early 80s, sitting in her apartment surrounded by her artwork. Fifteen of us assembled in the front pews of the chapel. Harvey Cooper, a former Anglican priest and friend of Wayne, made some opening remarks. Then Wayne spoke movingly and emotionally about his mom. The following excerpts are taken from his talk:

> Mom was a Saskatchewan farm girl born in 1913 on a small homestead in Saskatchewan. She walked to school, milked cows

and got water from the well.... After moving to Winnipeg in her teens, she worked hard to make ends meet. She was a provider, wage earner, advisor, problem solver, protector, mentor, defender, advocate, seamstress, confidante, and honest friend. She was 'My Mom'... For ten years following the 1950 flood, we lived on every street in this immediate area.

During a Christmas trip with my wife and children to Barbados in the late 1970s, a bond was created between Mom and her granddaughters that would be special for the rest of her life.

Norma, Mom's stepdaughter, initiated contact in the late 1960s. I now had a sister. When Carol initiated contact with Mom in 1988, it was met with Mom's anxious desire, strength, and compassion. Mom's humility and willingness allowed Carol and me to discover each other's existence. Now I had two sisters. Mom took on a renewed pride in having three children to talk about.

Then Wayne invited me to come forward. I chose to speak directly to Vera, sometimes touching her casket as I did so. My talk is verbatim, as follows:

Dear Vera, I am deeply grateful to you. You gave me the gift of life and then you did one of the most difficult things a mother can ever do. You said goodbye to me and let me go. We were separated from each other for more than half a century.

When we met again in 1988, you were 74 years old (the same age I am today), and I was 52. As I got to know you, I saw that you had the soul of an artist and a poet. You began to paint in oils in your late 60s.

On one of our visits, you gave me a painting of a candle, glowing in the dark. "This is for you," you said. And then you said, "This is the light that guided you in your search for me; the light of hope that never went out that one day you would find me; and now that we have found each other, the light is brightly shining."

Doesn't that sound like a poet?

I pay special tribute today to you, Wayne, and to you, Sue, and to Sherri and Michelle. You supported Vera through the ups and downs of her life. You were a loving, loyal son, Wayne.

Goodbye, Mama Vera.

I recognize that these words to Vera, though shorter in length given the circumstances, are as direct, intimate and love-filled as the words in my letter to Dorothy, my adoptive mother.

It was Sherri's turn. She had dearly loved her grandmother. Sherri described how she shared Vera's sense of fun, and she read a loving letter from her sister, Michelle, who could not be in attendance. The following are excerpts from Sherri's talk:

Grandma, you were the epitome of a strong, independent woman. You were a true survivor of everything that came your way. There is pretty much nothing that you didn't endure in your lifetime.

Grandma, you were very proud of your work. It was a personal victory every single time you completed a job, even if it was simply hemming a dress or cuffing! There's nothing you couldn't do: knit, crochet, tailor, sew, needle point, cook, dance, swim.

Grandma, you were interested in home remedies and economical beauty remedies. You would make your own soap by cooking many leftover bars together.... You were absolutely delighted when you discovered that WD40 can also be used for sore joints. You were a connoisseur of fine wines and liqueurs. You loved having a glass of your homemade dandelion wine with friends, or with Michelle and me. I was amazed the first time that I saw your ingenuity in a very large bucket under your bathroom counter, fermenting. People would ask you why you picked so many dandelions in the empty lots around your neighbourhood!

Grandma, you were in your 70s when one day you went to the doctor and asked for The Pill. The doctor was quite confused and thought he had heard you wrong. You explained, "You know those pills young women take so that they don't get pregnant."

The doctor responded, "The Pill—whatever for at your age?" You further explained that The Pill, when ground up, is supposed to be excellent for house plants. Needless to say, the doctor did not provide you with a prescription!

Grandma, you had style and flare. You relished the compliments and assumptions that others made about your age. Most often people assumed that you were at least 15 to 20 years younger than you were. You loved to dance. You even created a great dance move that Michelle and I coined "The Grandma Shuffle." Anyone who knew you knew that you tended to shuffle everywhere you went.

Grandma, you passed with the knowledge that your perseverance, independence, humour, and love for travel will be passed on through Michelle and me to your four great-grandchildren.

You will always be in our hearts, Grandma. We love you.

I loved these wonderful stories told by Wayne and Sherri about my life-filled exuberant risk-taking birth mother. Will Rogers' old saying came to me, "Why not go out on a limb? Isn't that where the fruit is?" (Carter 2005). Wayne had organized a simple, love-filled service for our mother. I was proud of him.

I felt supported and strengthened at the funeral by my friends, John, Coralie, and Fran, who were all warmly welcomed by Wayne. Two Marys made a strong impression on me. The first Mary and I are distantly related since she is the mother-in-law of my birth niece, Sherri. She is a Ojibway woman in her 70s with a beautifully open face and friendly smile who grew up on an Indian reserve in northern Manitoba in a happy, stable home till she was five years old. Then she was abruptly placed in a residential school nearby, and allowed to return home only in the summers. Her parents were allowed to visit her once a month in a room crowded with other children and their families. Since Mary wanted to continue her education, she and her father met with a high school principal who said, "We don't have any Indians registered in this school, and we're not about to have one." They tried another high school farther away, where Mary was accepted, but she became desperately lonely and dropped out. Mary went on to marry and have seven children. She resumed her education along the way and became the principal of the first Aboriginal high school in Winnipeg. An impressive, strong woman.

The second Mary hired Vera about 25 years ago to babysit her four sons. Mary and her eldest son described Vera as fun-loving and adventurous as she took the boys to playgrounds where they swam in outdoor pools. Mary was very appreciative of Vera's contribution to her sons' lives. When her husband, a dentist, learned about Vera's artistic talents, he asked her to paint pictures on canvas of her early farm life in Saskatchewan, which he hung on the walls of his office reception area. They are still there.

At the cemetery, Wayne's friend Harvey Cooper offered a prayer and then invited each of us to come forward for a ritual sprinkling of earth on the casket. He and I were invited back to Wayne and Sue's for coffee and conversation. Harvey drew my attention to the framed colour photographs on the sideboard: Wayne and I at the 1988 reunion in Winnipeg; and Vera and me, taken a year later in Ottawa. I had sent these photos to Vera at the nursing home several years earlier. Harvey was drawing my attention to Wayne's acceptance of me as his sister and Vera's daughter. The photos were now in *his* home.

In Barbara Coloroso's book *Extraordinary Evil: A Brief History of Genocide,* an unlikely source at first glance, I found something to ponder: "We are sisters and brothers of one another whether we like it or not, and each one of us is a precious individual" (2007, 196). Coloroso speaks of forgiveness, not as an act of will, but as "heart business"—the voice of the heart that speaks in the presence of the soul. Forgiveness is not something you do for the person who has harmed or hurt you, but it is a gift to oneself—so that you will not be bound up in revenge or hatred. It is to help us hold onto our 'caring selves'. In the same book, I love Archbishop Desmond Tutu's explanation of the African concept of *ubuntu:* "I am me only because you are you; my humanity is caught up in your humanity. If I dehumanize you, I am inexorably dehumanized. Concern for the other is the best form of self-interest" (Coloroso 2007, 212).

My forgiveness of the hurts that Vera inflicted on Wayne and me and others in her life springs from the deep hurts that she endured. It enhances my love for her and enables me to let her go. And what of Wayne's outbursts that I have endured with such difficulty? I have struggled with resentment and outrage; I have tried in vain to find various ways of interacting with him so there aren't any outbursts; I have overreacted with indignation and disrespect in turn; I have not tried hard enough to understand. He, too, endured deep hurts, yet his great goodness, his devotion, and his acceptance of Vera endured to her life's end. When he feels relaxed and accepted by those around him, he is a kind, tender, fun-loving man. Humour is a great leveller.

Postscript: After Vera died, Jennie Painter, an insightful colleague/ friend wrote: "There is something about the loss of a parent that takes us in a new direction... that helps us find or develop a new part of ourselves."

Love, Loss, and Longing

PART TWO

THE BIRTH PARENTS

Carol and newly adopted baby

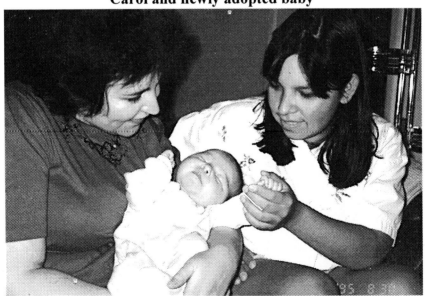

Adoptive mom, baby, birth mom

Chapter Twelve

Working in Adoption

If you follow your bliss, you put yourself on a kind of track that has been there all the while, waiting for you, and the life that you ought to be living is the one you are living.
— Joseph Campbell

Following my reunion with my birth mother, Vera, in the late '80s, the integration of my pre-adoption-reunion self and my post-adoption-reunion self continued. I had been a social worker for about twenty years by the time I found Vera, and I was working mainly in child welfare and the women's movement. As much as I was attracted to working in adoption, I had never dared to venture into it. I knew the field of adoption was simply too psychologically loaded for me; I had too many unanswered questions. Whenever I had attempted to do any reading in the area, I felt depressed and personally criticized as psychological problems of adoptees were identified. But after my reunion, it was different. I completed a thesis on adoption reunion with a dedication and a passion I had rarely before experienced. I could not read enough about adoption. My bookshelves were taking on the look of an adoption library. I wore three hats—adoptee, adoptive mother, and seasoned social worker. Surely these perspectives could be put to good use as I ventured into the adoption field.

I turned from the women's movement to adoption and took a contract with the Children's Aid Society in Ottawa, to conduct home studies for people who wanted to adopt. It was good basic groundwork. After a year, I knew this was the way I could "follow my bliss,"as Joseph Campbell recommends (1988, 113). In 1991 I applied to become an adoption practitioner in the private adoption system, under the supervision of the Adoption Unit of the Ontario Ministry of Community and Social Services. Clients didn't exactly flock to my door in the beginning—there were many capable social workers with private adoption practices already established in Ottawa. A few months after I started my practice, someone asked me how it was going. "Oh, fine," I replied. "I have a few clients." Actually, in the previous three months, I'd earned exactly $50! Then an opportunity came my way from Family and Children's Services, the child welfare agency in Brockville, about an hour's drive from Ottawa. A major sexual abuse investigation in that area had resulted in many children leaving their birth families and coming into "care". As they were made Crown Wards—that is, in the permanent care of the government—the agency needed extra staff to find permanent homes for these children. I was hired to help agency staff to do that. I conducted training workshops with potential adoptive parents and participated in the Adoption Resource Exchange (ARE) to find the best parents in Ontario for these traumatized children. (The ARE is an Ontario government program in which all child welfare agencies may participate to find adoptive homes for the most difficult-to-place children in the province.) A one-year part-time contract stretched to three years, and concurrently, my private adoption practice in the Ottawa area started to take off.

My private adoption practice consisted, in large measure, of conducting home studies for couples, mostly, as well as single applicants who wanted to adopt a child or children either domestically (Canada) or internationally. For many years, the vast majority of couples who sought to adopt internationally went to China to adopt little girls. This was because girls were available in large numbers, and China's streamlined adoption system made the process relatively quick and easy. My role was to prepare families for adoption and assess their suitability for adoptive parenthood. After the usual positive qualities were established, such as a loving, stable couple-relationship, a good understanding of child development, enough money, a strong support system, etc., I found that attitude was everything. I looked for open, flexible, generous confident, yet humble people with a good sense of humour who were neither controlling nor perfectionistic.

At the same time, I counselled birth mothers, and as the years went on, birth fathers as well. I supported and guided them through one of the most difficult of experiences—saying goodbye to the children they love and letting them go. No matter how young the birth parents were, I was struck by their astonishing maturity and caring, as they were given a voice in selecting the adoptive family, and in establishing the kind of contact they would have with their child and the adoptive family as the years unfolded. In the past, birth fathers had been labelled as irresponsible ne'er-do-wells who abandoned birth mothers. I found that if they were treated with respect, they, too, entered into the process with sincerity and caring. Respect involved a flexible approach on my part. If I sensed that a birth parent would be more comfortable meeting at Tim Horton's rather than my home office, then that is where we would meet—even though confidentiality and privacy was more of a challenge in such a setting. Often, birth parents were at a stage in their lives that was neither stable nor settled. It was sometimes chaotic. As I worked with these birth parents, I tried to be flexible and open—the qualities I looked for in adoptive parents. It was essential to obtaining as complete and honest a social and medical history of the birth parents as possible. This was what the adopted child deserved and needed. This sometimes took all the skill I could muster when dealing with an individual on the edge of a psychotic break, or with a serious addiction, or who dodged the meetings I set up because they were operating on the wrong side of the law.

One side of my work informed the other. Walking alongside the birth parents gave me first hand knowledge that I could share with adoptive parents, and vice versa. The pain of parting with a baby you have grown to love and cherish is akin to the pain of losing a baby through miscarriage, or through never having had the experience of pregnancy at all. One side enriches the other's understanding and compassion, and the adopted child is the benefactor.

I did as much adoption-related counselling as came my way. I think of the adoptee who was frozen emotionally and could hardly speak of her birth family or adoptive family at all. As she met with me over the period of a year, she opened up like a flower, and then had the courage to contact her birth family to begin to sort things out. I counselled adoptive parents, fearful that they would lose their adoptive child who was in the early, ecstatic throes of a reunion with her birth mother. I met with birth mothers who longed to find the child they'd placed for adoption years earlier. And I counselled adoptive families who had attachment challenges—the bonding between parents and child.

I learned more from my mistakes than my successes. One huge mistake I made was in recommending a woman for adoption based on how she presented: articulate, open in terms of the childhood abuse she herself had experienced, already the caring mother of a teenage son, persuasive, and brilliant intellectually. I did not recognize the warning signs. She was rigid and had an overpowering inner demand that the child fulfill *her* psychological needs. I wanted so much to arrange a nurturing new beginning for an endearing, abused boy. I did not heed the cautioning voices of agency social workers and the boy's foster mother.   I put their difference of opinion down to a rural-urban conflict. The child was placed for adoption and lived with his new parents for six months with no hint of problems. Then, one day, the adoptive mother asked me to remove the child immediately from the home as he was destroying her family. The adoptive father, who had bonded well with the child, was heartbroken, but chose commitment to his wife above commitment to the child. I learned a big lesson in humility. I picked myself up and tried again for this child. A family came forward who were down-to-earth, full of energy, flexibility, fun, and... they wanted to adopt him. The boy, who was resilient beyond my imagining, responded positively to them instantly. "But they're really nice!" he said. His adoptive parents have written to me every Christmas for over 20 years, telling me how he is doing.

Perhaps the biggest challenge is mental illness and addictions: how to detect these issues and problems, and how to work with them, while keeping the best interests of the child paramount. When birth parents are afflicted with mental illness and addictions, it can affect their capacity to engage in the process of choosing an adoptive family in a predictable manner, and to follow through on their commitment to maintain regular contact with their child in the years that follow. It is not always possible to get an accurate assessment of the problem in advance—all of us tend to put the best possible face on our difficulties, especially if we have a sense of shame about them. Agreements made between the two sets of parents sometimes need to be changed so that the best interests of the child remain paramount. When adoptive parents are afflicted with mental illness and addictions, it is essential to get an accurate assessment from a professional as early as possible in the course of the home study process. A difficult decision must then be made as to whether it is in the best interests of a child to proceed with the home study and recommend the applicant for adoption. An adoption *can* take place, however, if the birth parents are fully aware of an adoptive parent's mental condition (for example, bipolar disorder effectively controlled with medication), and they wish to proceed. The adoption practitioner must determine whether it will be in the best interests of the child, and make a judgment call. Nothing is ever simple.

What guided me in my adoption practice was the voice of the one who has no voice in where she will go, and who will be her parents—that of the adopted child. Although the adoptive parents have their own strong experiences of loss: the loss of a jointly conceived child, the loss of genetic continuity, the loss of the psychological and physical experience of pregnancy, and the loss of control, they do have more power in the adoption equation than either of the other two parties—the adopted child and the birth parent. In recent years, earnest efforts have been made to redress this imbalance of power. Birth parents have been speaking out about their wish for open adoptions, so that the ties between birth family and child are not severed, and extended family relationships are formed and continue over the years which are as varied as relationships with in-laws can be, from one family and one culture to another. I am encouraged by the depiction of the birth mother experience in international best-selling novels, such as *Secret Daughter* (Gowda 2010). Readers learn that the birth mother never forgot her daughter, thinking of her and longing for her on every birth date. This can only increase compassion and understanding for the birth mothers of the world. In my concluding chapter, Reflective Convictions, I address the right of adoptees to know their roots, and the spirit and practice of open adoption.

I was incredibly privileged to walk beside and support many birth parents and adoptive parents on a major part of their life's journey and witness their stories unfolding. I've recorded some of these stories in the next two sections of this book.

Chapter Thirteen

Birth Mother's Day

Our Time

She stirs within me.
"Are you awake?" I say to my bulging belly.
She quiets down and rests peacefully in her cozy bliss.
This is our time.

But later on she makes her appearance known to others around me.
She is not to be ignored.
"Is it a boy or a girl?" they say.
"Do you have many clothes picked out?"
I just smile.

At last, she pushes her way out into the world.
I didn't think she was in a great hurry.
If only she can see how she's lit up the room upon her arrival.
Her presence is overwhelming.

Afterwards, in spite of the looks and the suggestions,
I have her brought to me when all others are resting.
This is our time.

She looks so peaceful, wrapped tightly, sleeping.
She feels my warmth and love (I think).
To hold her forever would be my last request,
Yet I know better.

Soon we must part, go on with separate lives.
I can't bear to,
But when I look at her, as I do now, I know.
This is our time.

I feel her soft, wispy hair with my lips.
I must remember.
And now it's time to perform the unspeakable.

Nothing else matters but us, my sweet.
I'll take one last look, one last kiss,
And forever remember
Our time.

—Written and read by Heather, birth mother
Birth Mother's Day Service, Ottawa, 2001

In late 1994, Ann Goldsmith, an adoptive mother in Ottawa, read a story in the *New York Times* about a vigil that had been held in Cincinnati on the night before the traditional Mother's Day to remember and honour birth mothers who had placed babies for adoption. "What do you think of this?" she asked Liz Kent, her adoption social worker. Liz and I had worked on many adoptions together; in fact, she had welcomed me most warmly onto the Ottawa adoption scene when I was new-kid-on-the-block, and became my unofficial mentor for the next few years. She recognized the loss and powerlessness of the birth mother experience, and became a tireless advocate for the rights of birth mothers in Ontario. I nominated Liz for the National Adoption Award, which she received in 1996. Liz ran the birth mothers' vigil idea by me; then we talked it over with individual birth mothers with whom we'd worked; and finally we approached Sharon Moon, our minister at First United Church. The outcome was a service to honour birth moms at First United Church in Ottawa in May of 1995. It recognized birth mothers as women who love their children with a very special love. It was held the Saturday night before the traditional Mother's Day Sunday, a day when birth moms have felt excluded from the traditional celebrations and rituals of Mother's Day. At the time, it was the only such event that we knew of in Canada, although there were a few services like it held across the United States. A similar honoring service was held one year in Toronto, and there are now gatherings in other Canadian cities—Kitchener, Ontario, for one, to mark the day.

Birth moms took the lead in planning and organizing that first Birth Mother's service, and have continued to do so ever since. Some wondered if it should be held in a church at all. However, as Sharon Moon pointed out and wrote about in the booklet assembled by Brackenbury et al. (2002):

> Women in the past who had become pregnant and who gave their children into adoption for all kinds of complex reasons had sometimes been wounded by labels of 'sin' or 'unclean' as part of some of the church's historic attitude around sexuality. These bigoted attitudes had created unnecessary pain and identity crises for young women already burdened with unplanned pregnancy.

So the birth mothers decided that perhaps there was no better place than a church to honour their stories and heal their sorrow.

The Birth Mother's Day service is a ritual to mark transition, to create an awareness of change, to provide a vehicle to express feelings, to assist in healing, and to provide a public acknowledgment of emotional support. The result is an uplifting, spiritual experience. Native drumming and singing set the mood for an evening of personal stories, poems, songs, reflections, and prayer. One of the highlights is a moving song "Child of Mine" written and sung by Stephanie Coward, the sister of a young woman who had made an adoption plan for her unborn baby. Birth mothers say the song captures perfectly their feelings for the child they gave into adoption. For the deeply meaningful Ritual of Light everyone present is invited to come forward to light a candle for a birth mother or a child placed for adoption, and to name that person, if she or he so chooses. Those who attend are birth parents, adoptees, adoptive parents, birth grandparents and others who are part of or who support the adoption circle.

The service moves from a recognition of the past to a review of the present, and hope for the future. It begins with a dedication to a time in the past when pregnant girls had "gone to an aunt's" (Petrie 1998), a euphemism for being sent away to have their baby in another city, usually with no emotional support or worse—an abundance of condemnation and disapproval or to a home for unwed mothers. It was a time when they didn't have much choice or any options. A birth mother who placed a baby in those times says, "How could you resolve your loss when no one would acknowledge a loss had occurred or that a child had been born?" For the remainder of their lives, many birth mothers lived in sorrow, secrecy and suppressed love for the children they had placed for adoption.

The service also looks at the present. A woman who adopted from China pays tribute to the birth mother she might never meet. New adoption options are highlighted by speakers in semi-open and open adoptions who tell of ongoing contact, of ties not severed, and of strong connections they have made through the years. And in looking to the future, there are reunion stories—those who are hoping for one, those whose reunions have not worked out as they had hoped, and those whose reunions have been and continue to be a source of fulfillment.

A birth mother often feels she has no right to call herself "mother", and instead suffers in shame and silence. She may have hidden her pregnancy from family or friends. She may not be able to find the child she gave for adoption. She might not have been allowed to see her baby, or to know what happened to the baby, and now the child lives on the other side of the world. She may have found her child, but the child doesn't want contact. This annual service breaks the silence, as birth mothers tell their stories publicly, for the first time. This is where the healing begins.

In a letter published in 1995 as "Letter of the Day" in *The Ottawa Citizen,* Judith Kizell-Brans, Chair of the first Birth Mothers' coordinating committee stated, in part, "Family, friends, doctors, clergy, social workers, society, all claimed we would forget. We never forgot." A birth mother who participated in this event said that this public honoring helped her to hold her head high, for the first time ever. An adoptive father said that he learned from attending the service that it is important to understand adoption in the heart.

Over the years, there have been many heartfelt tributes. In 2002, Mark spoke to his birth mother, Elizabeth, who had played a major role in organizing the service:

It has been ten years since that day in May when that door swung open, and I stepped into the warm, strangely familiar embrace of my mom. It was bliss. Her cool hand caressed my brown skin. She watched, entranced as I walked through the room. "So familiar," she said. I searched her face, looking, for the first time, for a glimpse of myself in the face of another. And I found it. And as we talked and laughed and cried, we realized something that I think we had both always suspected. We already knew each other. The Spirit was familiar. We had never been alone.

My mom has given me so much. Love beyond measure. The desire to revel in the magic and mystery of life. The confidence to follow my heart, to take bold steps and make my mark on the world. She taught me how to howl at the moon. And to play. Always play. For you see, she is Strong, Brave, and Gentle.

I had always assumed that our experiences were the same. She had lost a son. I had lost a mother. But our years together have taught me that my mom suffered loss the likes of which I can never comprehend. It has taken me ten years to realize that. Maybe back when she was telling me to be strong and brave, she should have added "perceptive" to her list. But I see it now.

And so I offer these words to all of the mothers who spend years wondering about their daughters and sons. We do think about you. We think about the anguish you must have experienced the day we were taken from you. We hope that the people in your lives were not strangers, but familiar faces and gentle spirits who offered you love, support, understanding, and acceptance. We hope that you have gone on to live and to love. We hope that you know that we think about you on Mother's Day. We think about you on our birthdays. In fact, that is the one day that we know for absolutely certain that we are thinking of each other at the same time. We hope that you know that we love you in a way that we may not even be able to comprehend. We hope that you find peace. We hope you know that we can sense all of the good energy you send us by keeping us in your thoughts and loving us even though we are not there. We know that whatever the reasons for the years and miles between us, that day we were taken from you was the most devastating day of your young life. So—Be Strong, Be Brave, Be Gentle.

There are many different stories represented in this room today. Not all of them will unfold the way mine has. Yet there is still hope. That hope lies in the life you gave your sons and daughters as they make their mark in the world.

> We are your children, we love you in a way that only those who have lost can love.
> We are your children, you need not feel shame.
> We are your children, you will never be alone.
> We are your children and we are changing the world.
> We are your children and we howl at the moon.

I write these words to honour my mom and all birth mothers on Birth Mother's Day. Be Strong. Be Brave. Be Gentle.

In 1999 Judy told her story, which went back almost forty years:

I am a birth mother, and my name is Judy. I feel honoured this evening because I represent birth mothers from the 1960s. My story begins in 1961. I conceived a child when I was 17 years old. My daughter, I suspect, is in Ottawa. She will be 38 in October, and I firmly believe I am a grandmother. I was offered marriage by the father of my baby, but I said "no." In those days, if a young girl got pregnant, she got married. It didn't matter whether [the marriage] was going to work or not. I said "no." This caused a tremendous amount of shame to my family. I spent the fourth and fifth month of my pregnancy at home. I wore a housecoat most of the time. I was hidden. One night a neighbour came over to see my parents, and she said, "What is the matter with Judy? Why is her stomach so distended?" And my parents said, "She's pregnant." The family secret was out, which caused even more disgrace.

In the early '60s when Judy was a birth mother, Freudian analysis was frequently used. Young, unmarried mothers like Judy were stigmatized as they were characterized as delinquent, neurotic, promiscuous, and sinful. No doubt for these women and their families, hiding often felt like their only option. Judy's story continues:

During the time I was at home, my mother made maternity clothes for me as I prepared to go to the Salvation Army home for unwed mothers, located right beside the Grace Hospital on Wellington Street. I entered the home in my sixth month. I found that the home was very strict, but I felt unconditional love, and it was something I didn't have at home. We were responsible for light chores. I shared a room with three other girls. We were not allowed out, but occasionally we were permitted to go to the corner store. We had to travel in twos. I remember going out with two other girls—we must have all been in our eighth month and we were quite big. We were chatting like teenagers—it's who we were—but we wore white gloves to hide the fact to the world that we weren't married. It was quite obvious to other people because we were so close to the home [for unwed mothers], but that never entered our heads. During this time I felt so alone, so scared, and so bad. My mother came to see me on a regular basis, and she always brought me food.

In midsummer the birth father of my baby came to see me. He could not come into the home so he parked the car across the street. I wore a coat to hide my body so he would not see how large I was, and I sat in the back seat of the car. Years later my mother told me he had not wanted to come, but she had persuaded him to visit one time.

I remember feeling very free in the Salvation Army home. I felt I was not judged. I also started to see a doctor. Up until that time, I had not seen one. My parents did not want the family doctor to know that I was pregnant. After the birth in October, I looked after my little girl for ten days. I knew that her eyes were going to be brown, just like her dad's. When the social worker came to pick her up and take her away, she was dressed in a little yellow sweater, and booties and bonnet. She looked adorable. Later I received a notification by mail that my baby had been adopted.

Much of my healing has taken place in this church. In 1996 I rejoined this church and I saw in the bulletin an announcement about a Birth Mother's Service that was to be the evening before Mother's Day. Thinking it was a service to pay tribute to children, I came to pay tribute to my child. I did not dress up. This was a very private experience for me. I had no self-esteem. I saw all these birth mothers, laughing, joyous, dressed up, and proud. I did not identify with being a birth mother, but I realized for the very first time that I had carried my family's shame on my shoulders for over thirty years. A tremendous weight was lifted off my shoulders that night.

I spoke at the service last year. It was the first time to part with the family secret—it was very difficult. I was raised in this church, and there are people here who might know my parents. Since last year, I have been stuck. I have two girls from a marriage of twenty-one years, and I wonder if I should stay with what I have, rather than look for somebody who might reject me. Could I take that rejection? But, you know, maybe my daughter out there wants to see me as much as I want to see her. Is it natural to want to know your daughter? I think it is. Maybe, finally, I will know what it's like to be whole. Just maybe, I won't have this ache in my heart.

Tonight I am celebrating the fact that I am a birth mother because being a birth mother is part of who I am. This year I can honestly say I have no shame. Thank you.

Sharon Moon offered these prayers of reflection at that Birth Mother's Service in 1999:

The Past

Spirit of Life, we thank you for the courage of women like Judy who have gone through the shame of adoption in the past. We thank you for their courage to speak out now and to help create changes for the future. We honour the healing that Judy has experienced, and is experiencing, and will continue to experience, but we honour that healing in many women and in many children who are discovering themselves to be related in these times. We thank you, God, that things have changed and that the shame associated with birthing a child, the gift of life, is something that is not so strong in these days. God of Life, pour your healing on all the women who have given children into adoption in the past and on each of their children. Amen.

The Present and Future

As we celebrate the sacredness of life, we honour those who give it, we honour those who nurture it, we honour all those who have spoken tonight who live it to the fullest, who dare to face into the pain, but also into the joy. God of healing hope, we ask that you pour your grace, your holy presence into each person gathered here at whatever stage of the adoption journey that they find themselves. We ask that the spirit of compassion bathe each one gathered. We ask that the spirit of forgiveness and self-forgiveness bathe each one present, that all may know that they are deeply beloved of you, the Creator, that they are of infinite worth, whichever side of this adoption story they find themselves on. Amen.

I was overjoyed to be able to pay tribute personally to my own birth mother who, at the age of 82, attended the Birth Mother's Service in 1996:

Vera, when you placed me for adoption, you were 22 years old and I was 4 months. You were told that when you signed the papers, you were signing me away for life. I don't think you ever expected to see me again. You waited a lifetime for reunion—a 52-year wait. Over the years you worried and wondered, "Is she all right? Are they treating her right?" And there were no answers. When we finally met, you told me that a great weight had been lifted from your shoulders after all those years to know that I was OK, that I had a good life. You had to wait far too long to know that.

And for me? The gifts that you gave me, Vera, were priceless—my life, my good start in life, and my name. You said that "Carol" meant "a song." If I ever doubted that I had been loved as an infant, that doubt was swept away by this love story that you told me on the day we met: "In the hospital I had no money to buy you anything, so I took a blouse, cut it up, and hand-sewed it into a little dress for you. I crocheted an edging around the bottom and embroidered the bodice. You were the prettiest baby in the nursery."

When we met, I had a million questions about my origins, about my family history, about your life. I cannot thank you enough for how openly you shared your life and your photos after all those years. What a thrill it was to learn that Saskatchewan, the province I had always felt was my spiritual home, was the same province to which my birth grandparents immigrated from Ukraine at the turn of the century!

And the gifts you shared were not just with me. You and I visited my adoptive mom a few years ago, Vera. It was this time of year—close to Mother's Day—and you gave my mom an exquisite ruby-red gloxinia. I will never forget the look of radiance on Mom's face.

How proud I was to learn that, in your late 60s, you began to paint! And when you presented me with this painting of a candle glowing in the darkness [I held up Vera's painting for all to see], you said so eloquently, "This is the light that guided you in your search for me, and this is the light of hope that never went out that I would see you again, and now that we have found each other, the light is brightly shining."

It is with great joy that I welcome Vera who is here with me and with all of us this evening—having come all the way from Winnipeg for the service.

Vera had kept her shame and grief to herself for half a century. Her courage and willingness to risk were evident when she agreed to attend this service. She was welcomed affectionately by many that evening, as if she was the Queen Bee of Birth Mothers. She would not have called it a healing experience—that was not her language—but I did. The main thing was that she was very happy with herself and with me.

At the Birth Mother's Service in 2001, Jacqueline and Marc, adoptive parents, shared a christening prayer which they wrote for their children's birth parents:

We are Jacqueline and Marc, adoptive parents of two beautiful girls: Emma, age four, and Justine, one year old. As we recognize the wonderful contributions this evening, we want to share a prayer that we wrote and read on the occasions of each of our daughter's christenings to two most amazing and courageous young women who chose the path of adoption for their children. This is for you, Barb, whom my daughter Emma calls her 'tummy mummy'; and for you, Pam, my new baby's birth mom. These two women changed our lives forever and we are forever thankful.

The miracle of life has given us Emma and now our beautiful little Justine. Our prayers have been answered. We thank God for the gift of life, for the love we share, and for putting the birth parents of our children—Barb and Bob, Pam and Fred—on our path. It is sad how such pain for them can bring us such happiness. Life is unfair that way. However, today we want to acknowledge the beauty of life and love. May God bless you, Barb and Pam. May God guide you and help you along your journey.

Our daughters, Emma and Justine, are truly blessed, for they have remarkable birth parents who were able to carry out a very difficult decision for the sake of their child, and adoptive parents who wanted these children for many years and who love and cherish them. And today on your christening day, you are especially blessed as you enter Jesus' family, surrounded by loved ones. For you are a child of love, a child of God. Amen.

These Birth Mother's Day services—so powerful, open, and honest—have been held annually these many years. My support of the birth mothers who have given of themselves and my commitment to planning and carrying out these services each year has been a labour of love.

Elizabeth

Chapter Fourteen

Three Birth Mothers—Courage Within Loss

Elizabeth

Life was good—no one knew that inside was a deep, dark place full of pain. —Elizabeth

Elizabeth is an attractive woman in her mid-fifties, with lovely, blue eyes and a gentle smile. She is quiet-spoken, thoughtful, perceptive, and deep. I met Elizabeth at one of the early Birth Mother's Day services, which was a healing experience for her. The next year, and many years after that, she was a leading light in planning, carrying out, presiding, and telling her own story at these annual services. She was keen to tell her story for this book:

> Some time before I became pregnant, I moved from Ottawa to Burlington to start teaching. I was 21, and life was opening up for me. I taught 36 Grade 1's in a beautiful little school, and had good friends and roommates whom I loved dearly. It was my first time away from home, and it was all a big adventure.

Elizabeth had grown up in a loving family as the middle girl child, with one brother older and one younger. She described it this way:

> When we were children, our mom created magic for us: on a hot evening, we slept on mattresses under the stars; we picnicked near a special tree at the Arboretum; we swam at a rented cottage; we grew our own vegetables; and we were encouraged to try drama and take ballet lessons. It was good parenting, albeit with little money.

She met Ian, the birth father, through friends at MacMaster University. He was 19. On a Commonwealth scholarship from Jamaica, he was studying Chemical Engineering and was a first class sprinter. They became good friends and had a lot of fun together. Ian was black and although the mixed-race relationship was accepted by her friends, it was not accepted by his black friends and roommates. It was the time of the race riots in Detroit, and racial tension was flaring in the United States. Ian fell in love before she did. They dated for two years. In those years, he accompanied her to Ottawa to meet her parents and friends.

In June of 1968, Elizabeth knew she was pregnant. Her doctor had told her it was against his moral standards to give birth control pills to unmarried women, and she and Ian had been using condoms and foam. She said, "I just never thought it was 'wrong' because I really loved Ian. He is a true love even to this day."

She went to her family doctor in Ottawa, who confirmed her pregnancy. Walking with her mother at the cottage, Elizabeth heard her say, "Oh honey, I guess we'll have to go tell your dad." Her dad blamed Ian, but her mom did not. They agreed she should talk to the family's United Church minister.

After a big track meet in Toronto, Elizabeth told Ian about her pregnancy. He was devastated, but supportive. Her brother's reaction was to offer an immediate solution to the problem. "Stop crying. You can get an abortion in Montreal," he said. A roommate's boyfriend offered to send her to Denmark for an abortion. "But I felt that my child had to be born," she said.

Some of her friends knew that Ian had a wife and two kids in Jamaica. And all this time Elizabeth had not known. When she confronted him, Ian told her that he and his wife were married young, and the marriage was not going well. He wanted to be with Elizabeth and pleaded with her to wait for him while he returned to Jamaica to end the marriage. "But... he had deceived me for two years. I had serious doubts. How could I base my future on what he was saying?" she thought. Ian was a brilliant student. His professor called her into his office, and said, "You realize you are jeopardizing Ian's scholarship." There was no acknowledgment that Ian was jeopardizing his own scholarship. The university had known he was married.

Elizabeth met with the family's United Church minister. Bewildered, frightened, and hurt, Elizabeth felt somewhat more secure to follow along with what everyone was saying. And they were saying,

"The best thing you can do is to give your baby up for adoption. He'll have a wonderful life—better than you could give him. As an unmarried mother, you would not be allowed to teach. This way you can continue on with your life."

Adoptee Betty Jean Lifton describes the situation: "When I was born, society prophesied that I would bring disgrace to my mother, kill her reputation, destroy her chances for a good bourgeois life. (It didn't raise an eyebrow for my father)" (Lifton 1975, 3).

Elizabeth taught into her fifth month of pregnancy, when the principal advised her to resign. After that, Ian gave her some money, and she lived on toast and grapefruit. She went home for Christmas and wore two panty girdles under her clothes as she sat on the couch with the family relatives. "I was a good actress and no one knew. It was unreal and I felt dissociated from reality," she said. Her older brother knew of the pregnancy and although he pretended he cared, he wasn't truly supportive. Her younger brother did not know.

After Christmas, her mother saw Elizabeth off on the train to Toronto. Taking a taxi from the train station, she arrived, alone, at Victor Home, a United Church home for unwed mothers. Built in 1901, promotional materials of that day described its purpose as: "aiding the problem of the unfortunate girl and tending to the plight of the unwed mother" (United Church Observer, December, 2012). It was a big mansion with a dormitory behind it, a kitchen in the basement, and a chapel. It is still there. Elizabeth rang the bell, and a matron in a nurse's uniform greeted her. The matron outlined the rules:

• Everyone has chores to do.
•A school bell will ring to get you up, after which you'll have breakfast, chapel, chores, and lunch.
•The afternoons will be free time during which you may go outside, but not alone.
•No male visitors are allowed. (Elizabeth was granted special permission for Ian to visit her.)

United Church Women donated prizes for bingo games held on Wednesday nights. A United Church minister came one night a week for a so-called support group. The girls all sat silently without speaking, and some were scared to death. But Elizabeth asked questions to which she didn't get answers. In fact, the minister cut off her questions. He talked about morality and he said prayers. There was no guidance, and no healing. She could not bear to think of the suffering of a 14-year-old girl who had been raped. The only counselling the girls received was from the very helpful workers at the home. Elizabeth recalled, "My social worker had no inkling of what I was going through."

For medical appointments, the girls were sent by taxi to the Maternity Clinic at Wellesley Hospital for Women. The doctor who examined Elizabeth did not speak to her. When she asked if her baby was all right, he became angry. Elizabeth said:

> I knew that women should be treated respectfully, but they were not. One clinic experience outraged me. An intern who had broken his leg while skiing was doing an internal on me. Three of his buddies stood in the doorway, laughing, as he was having difficulty examining me. I wrote a letter of complaint and gave it to the supervisor of Victor Home. She said that the doctor at Wellesley Clinic was on the Board of Directors of Victor Home. If I pursued this, she would have to ask me to leave. I dropped it. The disrespect continued.

The girls were chronically bored at Victor Home. There were no crafts, no school classes, and no pre-natal education. The silence on the part of the matrons about the girls' circumstances felt profoundly disrespectful. They were not allowed to gain much weight, so the chip shop and Dairy Queen were off limits. The girls were known to each other and the staff by their first names only. This kind of secrecy bred shame. Hand-me-down maternity clothes were provided. The chores were essentially busy work: the girls cleaned bathrooms, did laundry and breakfast duty, and vacuumed and dusted every day. The daily chores likely reflected the prevailing sentiment that cleanliness was next to godliness. They started knitting of their own accord. Elizabeth knit a baby sweater—pink with blue flowers—and a pair of booties which she has saved to this day. On her due date, Ian was running a race at Maple Leaf Gardens. She begged to go with some of the girls, and was granted permission. There was a maternity emerald green dress with white lace that was shared by the girls for special occasions. Because this was Ian's race, Elizabeth wore the dress. She vividly remembers all eight girls, sitting on big green garbage bags which the Matron had insisted upon in case their waters broke, watching Ian run!

Elizabeth's teacher friends stood by her. One night they took her to a movie, and then to the Victory Strip Club where they laughed and laughed as "Miss Tangerine" did her strip tease. Dan, a good friend, took her out for dinners. Her parents phoned and wrote letters, but they did not visit her.

The baby's birth was traumatic. Ten days after her due date, her waters broke, and Elizabeth went into labour. None of the staff at the home were there to wish her well. Another girl was also in labour, and the matron on duty that evening was attending to that girl. A light from the dorm shone down on the taxi to take Elizabeth to the hospital. She was sent out the back door of the Home, carrying her own suitcase, in the midst of a heavy snowstorm.

Elizabeth was in labour all night long, and was given an epidural which was intended to deaden sensation from the waist down. But Elizabeth had no sensation from the neck down. She felt panicked. She could not breathe. She remembers that many needles were inserted into her torso to test her sensation. The next day, the labour pains stopped. A nurse who came in to her bedside to make her comfortable, gasped when she saw big bruises, caused by the needles, all over Elizabeth's torso. That evening a doctor who was head of obstetrics came to see her. "We can't send you 'home' because the amniotic sac has broken," he said. "We'd like to try something new." The "something new" was oxytocin which caused huge contractions all night long. As the drug wore off, the hard contractions eased. Her own natural labour began and continued all the next day.

I had been in labour for almost 48 hours. Although I was dilated, I could not push. Finally, the baby came so suddenly that the anaesthetist did not arrive in time for the delivery. Gas was placed over my face, and I gave birth without anaesthetic. An episiotomy was done. They told me it was a boy.

Elizabeth phoned her mother. Her mother asked, "Are you all right? Is the baby all right? I'm so glad it's over." In those days girls who were placing their babies for adoption were not allowed to see them, but for some reason, Elizabeth was given a viewing card. She sat and watched her baby from the viewing window in the nursery. Her baby boy's APGAR was 7:7. This response test, taken one minute after birth and five minutes after birth, runs about 9:9 in healthy newborns. The baby was kept in an incubator for seven days. The birth father came and together, they viewed their baby. She said, "Ian was there for me as much as he could be."

On the seventh day, the social worker was to pick Elizabeth up and together, they would take the baby to foster care. However, the night before, Elizabeth passed a huge blood clot in the bathroom. Nurses began pulling huge clots out of her. While this was happening, the head nurse asked if she would like to hold her baby. "I undressed him, marveled at how lovely he was, checked his toes, and dressed him up again." No more than ten minutes. She became very sick with all the blood clots coming out. She bled and bled, and was transfused with 15 pints of blood. One of the nurses commented, "Don't think this is punishment for what's happened." Elizabeth wondered to herself why she would think *that*. She described what happened next, "Like a true Ben Casey TV drama, they *ran* me down the hall on a gurney to the operating room. A scraping of the womb was performed." The problem was that much of the placenta had remained in her womb.

Afterward, Elizabeth woke up in a dark room, lovely and cozy under the warmed blankets. A nurse washed her down, and said, "Darling, I'm here to take care of you." She was Elizabeth's angel.

Elizabeth remained in the hospital another three weeks. Her friend, Dan, visited and the head nurse called her mother to come. The most caring hospital staff were the custodians who talked to her every day. A doctor came by with a group of interns to do an internal after the hemorrhaging. He commented, "You're not a true redhead, are you?"

The assessment she was given was that her pelvic structure was too small to deliver a baby vaginally. Even after all this time, Elizabeth is in the process of writing a letter to Wellesley Hospital to let them know what happened. She believes that the experimental use of oxytocin was abusive, and that the intern who delivered the baby did not exercise the care necessary to remove all the placenta.

The birth was a major trauma. As explanation of the trauma, Elizabeth's counsellor says that when animals, like humans, need to run but cannot, they freeze in fright. This fear is frozen in cell memory, and it can be triggered by anything.

Elizabeth named her baby Andrew Daniel; his adoptive parents renamed him Mark Daniel. Her friend, Dan, from whom the baby got his second name, knew Mark's adoptive parents, and visited Mark till he was three years of age. That meant a lot to Elizabeth.

Elizabeth says, "I held back my feelings when I said goodbye to the baby. I was playing a part. I shut down. It was as if the bleeding took over and the tears would not come. I thought this was what you had to do to have a baby, and for many years, I minimized it all." After counselling, Elizabeth was able to say, "I almost died."

After she was discharged from hospital, Elizabeth was on a high and dissociated from reality. She returned briefly to her parents' home and her mom bought her some new clothes. Then she returned to Burlington, lived with friends, and supply taught. She had no counselling. Ian was around for another two years. He wanted to continue the relationship, but she tried to cut it off. "Although we still cared for each other, my trust in him was destroyed. I had lost both of them: the man I loved, and our baby," she said.

Elizabeth left the Burlington area to begin a Bachelor of Arts program at Carleton University in Ottawa. After one year she returned to teaching, continuing her B.A. part-time and taking courses in Education. She had the freedom she wanted; she was sharing an apartment with good friends; and she was doing well at university for the first time. She did not date. She says:

Life was good—no one knew that inside was a deep, dark place full of pain. No one asked me how I felt about what had happened. I don't think they knew what to do or say. Some of my friends who had known Ian was married, hated him. When I did begin to date, everything was fine on a certain level, but the experience had lowered my trust in everyone. I could not remember the birthday of my baby. I think the body and mind protect us from remembering.

Several months after her baby's birth, Elizabeth wrote an English exam. But by then, her inner stress had reached such a level that she drew a blank. She sat, frozen. Her parents were shocked, thinking she was "over it." They hadn't wanted to hurt her by asking how she was doing. Those were the days when people didn't raise unhappy, controversial subjects.

Elizabeth was experiencing disenfranchised grief. This kind of grief occurs when an individual's loss is not publicly recognized or acknowledged by others, sometimes not even by the individual. Because their grief cannot be shared, these individuals often experience a complicated kind of mourning in which a roller coaster of anger and depression never lessens. When a relationship is hidden or viewed negatively, it places added burdens on the griever. Accompanying some losses, there is a societal stigma, resulting in shame and embarrassment for the griever, which makes it difficult to talk to others. Thus, the central paradox of disenfranchised grief is that, though the grief is often intense, the social supports that assist other types of grievers are absent. Losses outside of death often go unrecognized; for example, the loss of a life partner to Alzheimer's [or the loss of a child to adoption.] A funeral ritual can be helpful to grievers, but in a loss outside of death, there are no mourning rituals to help the griever (Doka 1992, 5-7).

A year after her baby's birth, the adoption was ready to be finalized by the Court. Elizabeth appeared before a judge to tell her story. The social worker had warned her that the judge was harsh, and might not approve the baby's Crown Wardship. Elizabeth was not prepared for the fact that her baby was in the courtroom, just three rows behind her. The judge lectured her on using birth control. He questioned her closely about why she could not support this child. She told him that she didn't have a job, that she'd had to resign from teaching. He reminded her of the finality of losing her parental rights. Elizabeth thought that was the way it had to be. Now she wishes that the social worker had said, "If you decide to keep the baby, this is what we could do...," and then had given her options from which to choose, and resources to explore. Numbly, Elizabeth filled out the documents and signed away her legal rights. She had no counselling.

After the adoption was final, Elizabeth spent more and more time alone in her room at home. She did not cry in front of her parents, afraid that she would upset them, and afraid they would upset her if they talked together. It was a wall of silence that would last for years. They all needed psychological help and support, and they did not get it.

Ian returned to Jamaica, and he and Elizabeth kept in touch from time to time. About four years after the baby's birth, Ian came to New York City to attend a conference. By then he was in the midst of a divorce, and not living with his wife and children. Elizabeth was sharing living space with a good friend, Kelvin, who knew about her baby's birth and adoption. It was the only time in her life that she was thin. She drank coffee and smoked a lot. When Ian phoned her, Kelvin commented, "I've never seen anyone respond with so much love as when he (Ian) called. I've always wanted someone to love me that much." Elizabeth met Ian in New York City. They went for walks and made love. It was very romantic. Ian had a job in Jamaica with a bauxite company which provided him with a house and car, and he wanted her to join him there. She *was* tempted, but afraid and didn't seize the moment. Now she realizes that if it hadn't worked out, she could have just come home.

After she got back, Kelvin moved his and Elizabeth's relationship along. They were good friends, and she had a lot of fun with him — sailing, camping and cheering at his rugby games. She was quite needy and tried to fill the loss of Ian and their baby with this new relationship. At the time she thought that it did. She and Kelvin were married, but after a while, Elizabeth noticed that Kelvin was becoming extremely unstable. Stress and turmoil for this couple were compounded by Kelvin's parents' acrimonious separation and divorce. Kelvin's instability morphed into emotional abuse, and Elizabeth's self-esteem was so low that she tolerated it. She would tell herself that he was the only man who could love her—a woman who had given her child into adoption. Through counselling Elizabeth came to recognize Kelvin's emotional abuse towards their son, Philip, who was born six years into the marriage.

Before she gave birth to her second son, Philip, Elizabeth had panic attacks: sweats, and heart racing. She believes it was her body's reaction to the fear of having to go through the birth experience again. A spinal was administered before she gave birth to Philip, and she blocked out the first childbirth from her mind. She said:

> Philip was amazing—the best baby there could be. He was huggy, lovable, funny, and affectionate. I parented Philip well. I sometimes thought that if I had kept Mark, I wouldn't have had Philip. A Sophie's choice. I'd give my life for Philip.

When she was 36 years old, Elizabeth's parents were worried enough about her to arrange for her to see a psychiatrist about depression. That psychiatrist was no help at all—he suggested that she could put things [her issues]"in a drawer " and bring them out when she was ready.

Then 25 years after Mark was born, he and Elizabeth had a reunion. The unfolding went like this: Kelvin, Philip and Elizabeth were living in Stittsville. One evening they were watching the NHL hockey finals with Elizabeth's parents when her mother said to Elizabeth, "I have a letter. Do you want to read it? Are you OK?" The letter, addressed to her mother, read, "I am the son your daughter gave up for adoption." The letter also said that when he was 16, his adoptive mother had told him his birth mother's last name. It was a distinctive last name and one that was well known in the Girl Guide community in Ontario. Her son phoned the Girl Guide Office in Ottawa who gave him Elizabeth's mother's address and telephone number. Easy as that. Elizabeth's mother sought the advice of of the Pastoral Care Team at one of the United Churches in Ottawa and was advised not to give her daughter the letter. But her mom felt that Elizabeth had a right to know about the letter. Since there was a return address on the letter from a counsellor in Pennsylvania, Elizabeth was able to make contact with her son. She and Mark exchanged letters, and she learned that he was a nuclear medical technologist living in Toronto, and had sought counselling with Michelle McColm, an adoptee, who has written about adoption reunions (1993). He described the period in his life when he was searching for her: "I wept for days in my room, with a hurricane building inside of me, literally falling apart. I had a deep need to find you." He wrote that the reunion he longed for was meant to be.

A few months went by as Elizabeth and Mark wrote weekly letters. The intensity of the developing relationship consumed her. They then began to phone each other. She could hardly eat, and lost fifteen pounds. All she could eat at a meal was half an egg! The anticipation of meeting Mark took over her life. They agreed to meet at the home of a good friend of Elizabeth's in Toronto. Friends and family were worried. Could he be trusted? Had he lied about everything? Elizabeth hadn't eaten or slept for a week. Mark came to the door and she stood there. He fell into her arms, then presented her with a bouquet of flowers. Elizabeth says the moment of reunion was like memory on a cellular level:

> I could not stop touching him. He sat close, held my hand, and hugged me. I was fascinated by his arms and hands. He even lay with his head on my lap—it goes back to infancy.

As extremely intense as this sounds, it resonates very strongly with my own experience of reunion as an adoptee. The obsessive talking about *nothing else* but my birth mother and almost forgetting to eat, the absolute necessity to meet my birth family *on my own* without my husband or children, and the longing to go back into infancy and be cradled in my birth mother's arms make Elizabeth's mirror-image experience an affirmation of my own overwhelming emotional reaction to reuniting with my birth mother and underlines how primal the reunion experience is.

Kelvin phoned the first night of the reunion—his emotional abuse intensifying. The reunion had to be on *his* terms or not at all. He wrote a letter for Elizabeth to send to Mark asking that Mark not be in contact for two months, that they needed time as a family to sort things out. Elizabeth acquiesced in fear.

Some time later, Elizabeth told Philip that he had a brother. Philip went to Toronto to meet Mark, and they got along well. The whole way back from Toronto to Ottawa, Philip cried, "I don't want to leave my brother." Some time later, Elizabeth hosted a dinner party for Mark to meet Kelvin and her parents. There was pure love and acceptance on her parents' faces when they met him. Mark could not take his eyes off her parents, as though he wanted so much to see himself reflected in them. Her dad took Mark's hand in his two hands, and hugged him when he left. Her dad was not an uncaring person at all. Elizabeth's mind returned to all that heartache so many years before. Although Kelvin was charming as he talked to Mark, Elizabeth felt the tension and sensed that she would pay in some way.

Elizabeth has known Mark for thirteen years now, and the relationship is very complex. They have been together about fifty times: the longest visit was four days. One of their most moving experiences took place at the Birth Mother's service in 2002 when Mark gave an eloquent tribute to Elizabeth and all birth mothers. Now he lives on the west coast of the United States. Elizabeth's counsellor has phoned him about his expectations of Elizabeth: mother? friend? mentor? grandmother? Mark idolizes Elizabeth, saying, "She doesn't realize that she has made me the man I am today. When I met her, it was something profound and spiritual." Elizabeth says:

> When Mark met me, I did have more courage and strength than previously. I hadn't been sick in five years; my career was going well, and I felt good about myself. I was Marg Delahunty (Canadian comedian Mary Walsh's flagrantly outspoken character)! It was this person that Mark met and admired in so many ways.

Elizabeth feels she would have been better prepared if someone had told her that this birth mother/adoption experience would be a lifelong challenge. She says:

The reunion causes heartache. You both have to ask yourselves —how much of a relationship do you want? And work it out together. I believe that the reunion with Mark re-traumatized me 30 years later—like post-traumatic stress disorder.

Life went on, and Elizabeth experienced more losses: death of her parents, divorce, cancer, death of a dear friend, and death of her former in-laws. She learned that Ian was living in the States, that he had remarried and had children.

About ten years ago, Elizabeth was in hospital, nervously awaiting minor surgery. The morning after surgery, the patient in the bed beside her asked, "Why are you crying? Are you all right? A nurse in a white uniform and hat just brought a baby in for you to hold, and then she took him away." Elizabeth's only explanation for this strange incident that may or may not have happened is that a reenactment of the previous loss took place.

Elizabeth has little contact with Mark's parents. She describes them as fundamentalist Christians—good people. She attended a shower for Mark's fiancée, where she felt like a sinner in the presence of Mark's family, and a saint in the presence of his fiancée's family. Mark is now married and has a baby daughter. He did not tell her that he was in contact with his birth father until after Ian had visited him and met his wife and child. Elizabeth reacted intensely to this news. She felt deceived that she had not known that Mark was building a relationship with Ian, and devastated that Ian got to see her granddaughter before she did. Mark had been worried about telling her, but had not expected her to experience such angst over it. Elizabeth feels that this showed a lack of insight, and that before they meet again, the deception issue will have to be worked on with the help of her counsellor. There is a distance between Mark and Elizabeth now.

Elizabeth concludes her story with "Will I meet the birth father again? Maybe, and there could be some healing there." Her journey as a birth mother is ongoing. She says, "I don't think anyone is ever ready for what lies ahead between birth mother and child. It's not always what you want it to be."

Elizabeth's experience as a birth mother has helped to shape her into the deeply sensitive, intuitive, compassionate woman she is. It has brought much suffering into her life in the form of depression, disenfranchised grief, and post-traumatic stress. I sense that she feels some regret and ambivalence about the reunion with her son, but never a moment's ambivalence or regret about her decision to give birth to him those many years ago.

Carol and Micheline

Micheline

I had cared for him in the womb, but when I touched him for the first time, it was instant love.
— Micheline

Micheline is a tall, beautiful young woman with big, expressive, grey-green eyes and a clarity of self-expression that is a joy to experience. She and I met through adoption when she told her story to prospective adoptive parents at workshops I arranged. In the early years of the annual Birth Mother's Day service, she competently chaired the committee of birth mothers, presided magnificently and eloquently told her story at the services. Like Elizabeth, Micheline was eager to share her story:

> I gave birth fifteen years ago to a baby boy named Jules. I was working in a management position with Red Lobster at the time, travelling around Guelph where I'd opened a restaurant. I was 22 years old.
>
> The birth father was the manager of the restaurant in Guelph. He was married and had two kids. He kept trying to get me to go on a date, and I kept refusing—he was quite the guy. I agreed to go out with him, and started the affair. He would tell me he loved me, and I'd say, "No, you don't." I knew it was all wrong, and asked for a transfer back to Ottawa.
>
> He was very sad to see me go, but his big declarations of love didn't ring true. He came to visit me once in Ottawa. At the Champlain Lookout in Gatineau Park he said he was crazy in love with me. But I countered, "I'm not in love with you. And it's time for this to end."

Shortly after that, Micheline realized she was pregnant. The first person she called was her girlfriend, Clarice. And she did tell the birth father. He responded that the only sensible thing to do was to have an abortion. For years after that, Micheline had nothing but anger in her heart for him, for making her shoulder the whole burden alone. Even more years later, she was able to forgive him. "I have a book of photographs by Malak Karsh, signed by the birth father, that I hope some day to give to Jules," she said.

Micheline did see her doctor to schedule an abortion, and asked her general manager for a day off. He somehow knew why, and told his wife, Pat who contacted her. They became good friends. Pat told Micheline about private adoption. Micheline had been considering the three options: to parent as a single mom, to have an abortion, or to give the baby into adoption. "The only thing I knew about the adoption option was that the baby would be torn from my arms, and I would never see him again. I knew that a birth mother would not gain from such an experience," she said.

To backtrack... from the time Micheline left high school until she became pregnant—in her words—she was a "lost puppy." In high school she relied on structure, routine, classes, sports, field trips, teachers and friends. Most of her support, if not all of it, came from high school so that when she left it, she had a hard time figuring out how to be an adult. She didn't know how to make good decisions. She was very lonely and couldn't call home when she felt that way, because she had not shared her feelings with her parents in years.

To backtrack even further... her parents had separated twice during her childhood. Her brother got attention as the squeaky wheel. But she was the kid who kept quiet and was praised for how mature she was and how well she was handling things. She learned that all she needed to do was keep her mouth shut. Her parents would say, "She's the kid we don't have to worry about."

After high school, she made a trip to Brazil where she met a man whom she married and divorced after one-and-a-half years of marriage. She had never learned to share her feelings, and had not even begun to sort out what she wanted in life.

Her parents had not taught her how to make life decisions, and she did not have close relationships with either one of them. She had no role models for intimacy. Her parents' marriage was one of turmoil, inconsistency, and a sharp staccato of fighting. From the age of nine, when her parents first separated, she lived with her mother, and her brother lived with her dad. The roles of mother and child reversed themselves and she became a parentified child. She described her mother as "a very volatile woman, an alcoholic and an insomniac." Micheline did the groceries and the housecleaning. She picked up burning cigarettes off the carpet and watched as her mother drank to pass out and get some sleep. Her mother's life was a downward spiral —slower, and then faster. Her mother felt disdain for men: her father, her husband, her brothers, her son—men in general. She picked on Micheline's brother so that he cut off communication with his mother a long time ago to be free from abuse. Micheline has clear, vivid memories of her childhood while her brother has none. He and her mother have extremely disturbed sleep patterns.

Micheline did not tell her parents about her pregnancy right away. But she did tell her brother. He didn't know what to do or say at first, but later, he supported her through the experience. They shared a lot. He and Micheline have had their differences, but he and his wife seemed to know how important it was not to cut her off. Her dad did his best to be supportive, but he was a worry wart with low self-esteem, and his ability to take a guiding, leading role with her and her brother was limited. She said, "He's a gentle man, without the courage of his convictions. He could never put his foot down." Whenever he got involved in Micheline's life, he felt like he was interfering. He had never intervened when Micheline's mother was behaving in a totally unreasonable manner with her and her brother. Micheline thinks that while she was pregnant, she was on a mission to convince her dad that she was getting her act together, so that he would not fear that she was on the same downward spiral as her mom. Micheline didn't want him to give up on her. She did have some contact with her mother while the adoption was happening, but "Pat was the angel in my life," she smiled.

Micheline found pregnancy an enjoyable, fascinating experience, fully entering into and experiencing each new stage. She was thrilled with the first sensation of movement within her womb, and then to feel the baby kicking. She read book after book about childbirth and how to heal afterwards. She took birthing classes with Pat, and told the couples in the class that she was placing her child for adoption. One woman said, "You think it's going to be OK, but it will not be easy. A lot of memories will come back to you, which you will relive." Some people told her that she was enjoying her pregnancy too much, and that she shouldn't be so explicit about it. Her grandmother told her she should be hiding herself more. But Micheline refused to be miserable through her pregnancy. "I tried to honour myself and my child through the whole thing," she said firmly.

During her pregnancy, she lived by herself in an apartment for a while, and then moved into a townhouse with friends. She quit her job at Red Lobster at Christmas time and gave birth in March.

Micheline chose her baby's parents, Theresa and John, early on in the adoption process—when she was seven and a half months pregnant. There was something universal and welcoming about their written profile that she liked. They would welcome *any* child into their home, they said. She liked the beautiful way they spoke about each other. She met them once with the licensee (a person licensed by the province to coordinate and oversee private adoptions) and her birth parent counsellor, but didn't feel she got to know Theresa and John well enough. She asked if the three of them could go to lunch together. She found it wonderfully reassuring to see how they interacted, and to enjoy their humour. The three of them laughed and cried. Departing from the restaurant, they gave each other big hugs.

The baby was overdue, and Micheline wanted to have a natural childbirth. After many hours of labour, she was only 5 centimetres dilated. She was given an epidural and after one-and-a-half hours, she was fully dilated. "I knew the process of loss was beginning, and I was afraid to start it," she said.

Her mother wanted to be with Micheline in the delivery room, and Micheline had to tell her mother that she wasn't reliable enough to be her birthing coach. So her mother went on the attack, calling her a "crybaby," and accusing her of being incredibly selfish in placing the baby for adoption. Her friend Pat and Micheline's brother were with her in the birthing room. She felt a sense of overwhelming joy to see the child that she had created come out of her. "Hello," she said, "I'm happy to see you." The baby was beautiful and healthy; he didn't make a peep; and he had big, beautiful eyes like hers. "We looked at each other. I had cared for him in the womb, but when I touched him for the first time, it was instant love," she said in wonderment.

Micheline had no idea of the enormity of the impending loss. She spent three days in hospital rooming in with her baby. After a couple of days, a staff nurse gave her a private room. Micheline loved up her baby boy, and got to know him as best she could. Lots of visitors came —her girlfriends, her dad, her stepmother, her stepsister and her husband, her brother and his wife. Her mother did not come. Three or four weeks after the birth, Micheline was back in touch with her mother. Her mother tried to re-write history, pretending that she herself had decided she couldn't be Micheline's birthing coach. Micheline called her on it, and her mother was furious. Micheline's birth parent counsellor was very supportive during the hospital period, warning Micheline about Day Three following the baby's birth. "A new mother will often be weepy and very sad on this day, much of it attributed to raging hormones," she said. Micheline's father came to get her at the hospital the day she was to say goodbye to Jules. Jules was his first grandchild. Micheline remembers:

> There was a moment when Dad looked at me, going through it. I was in tears, but showered and ready. Dad took a picture of Jules and me. Then he left the room for a bit. As I held Jules in my arms, I said goodbye to my baby. But I found that I could not physically put him down. A nurse came in, gently took him out of my arms, placed him in his bassinet, and wheeled him back to the nursery. Dad came back into the room moments later, and we cried, cried, cried. I had not seen my dad cry before. It was powerfully intimate for my dad and me to go through this together.

Micheline made strong connections with the sensitive maternity ward staff. The hospital social worker conveyed the news of Micheline's adoption plan to them. One of the nurses in the nursery became a friend. Having said goodbye to her baby moments before, Micheline was leaving the hospital when she met the social worker in the elevator. The fragile composure she had regained was lost when the social worker wished her well.

Dad drove Micheline to her brother's farm near Ottawa where she stayed for two weeks. Her brother and his wife were very gentle with her. She remembers, "My emotions fluctuated. There were physical reminders of my loss. My breasts were leaking milk onto the floor, and there was no child to nurse. I wailed, I wrote in my diary, I slept, and I talked on the phone to friends for two weeks."

Micheline's resolve to place her child for adoption was firm from Day One. She knew it was the best thing for Jules. Eventually, she came to learn that it was the best thing for her, too. As a young woman who had not learned how to make good decisions, Micheline believes that the first thing she handled well in her life was the adoption of Jules. She said:

It gave me a second chance. The pregnancy and Jules' birth did something very important for me. It stopped me from going down the path I'd been on. I took a different path after Jules' birth. I became university-educated, and a teacher, and I have developed a circle of good friends from high school and beyond. I took a good look at myself and I was not the person I wanted to be. I thought about meeting Jules, say 25 years later, when he might ask, 'What did you do with your life?' I wanted to be able to say I had taken advantage of the fact that I had been given a fresh start. I felt I owed it to my son to get things straight and to work through all the 'crap.' Otherwise, I was destined to have more babies and to repeat the mistakes my own mother had made. I was on a journey of self-awareness, facing all the challenges of life. I knew my own childhood had not been healthy and that I'd been deeply affected by the emotional traumas in my life. I resolved at that moment to make my life healthier, and to heal. I realized then it was a life journey.

In the summer Micheline worked at a temp agency, and when she began university in the fall, she moved in with her dad and stepmother. To finance her university education, she took out student loans, and worked three jobs: caterer for External Affairs, tutor, and teaching assistant. She was 27 years old, had been married, divorced, given birth, and placed a child for adoption. She put all these life experiences into her back pocket as she related to the kids at university. Jules was her motivation, and she was determined to do well. After four years straight ahead, she got her teaching degree.

The relationship with her brother has gone through various phases. She was maid-of-honor at his wedding the year after Jules was born, and was present, joyfully, when his son, Robert, was born five years later. She was able to put Jules' birth and Robert's birth into the proper perspective in her life. However, there was some tiptoeing around her about Robert being the first grandchild. Her brother wondered how she would handle that. She was oblivious to the fact that they were worried about her. But she was *very* disappointed when she wasn't chosen to be Robert's godmother. "You're not in a lasting relationship," her sister-in-law said, "You're just not stable enough." Nor did they choose her to be Robert's guardian in the event of a tragedy that might take both their lives. They did not want to choose someone who was single. Micheline felt rejected, and for many years they did not connect. Could it be that there were lingering judgmental attitudes towards unplanned pregnancy and adoption that surfaced at this point, calling into question Micheline's stability and reliability?

Looking back, Micheline says that even after all these years, she cannot get through the diary that she kept at the time of Jules' birth, beyond a couple of pages. She feels she needs to set up time to reflect on it, to look at the pictures and read the letters that his adoptive parents sent to her. The agreement made between them was that letters and pictures would be sent to Micheline for two years. Some time following his birth, she wrote to his parents (through the licensee), asking if she might meet him when he was five years old. Instead, they wrote and sent her a video. She knew that it must have been hard for them to write and say "no" to her. But surely it was very hard for her to receive their "no." They stated that when he asked about Micheline and wanted to meet her, that would be the time for a meeting. She would certainly want to see him and them as well. She knows that Jules' adoptive mother became pregnant six months after he was adopted, and gave birth to a sister for Jules. His sister is envious that her brother has two mothers and she has but one.

Following the adoption of Jules, when Micheline felt ready, she began to give talks at education workshops to prospective adoptive parents. She told her story simply and powerfully. These talks helped her to heal. "My gosh, you're courageous," some would say to her. She said, "For me, they were encouraging words. They were telling me I'd handled things well, that I'd shared my story and could talk about my memories." As she relived the memories, she recovered. She saw that her desire to share with others, especially other birth moms, allowed them an opportunity to start or to further their healing. For several years, she was an active member on the committee of birth mothers who planned the Birth Mother's Day service. And for several years she presided at the service and shared her story. Then there came a point when it was time to put it to rest.

Some years later, Micheline attended a dinner to honour birth parents who had participated in the Birth Mother's service over the previous ten years. It was there that she realized that she had learned how to survive on her own. But that was not what she wanted to pass on to her kids. When the song "Child of Mine" was played at the dinner and when Ann, an adoptive parent who loves Micheline, asked her, "When are you going to have kids?" it was a moment of clarity and revelation, just as she had experienced when she gave Jules into adoption. She realized that she was terrified to repeat the mistakes that had been made with her. She also realized that she couldn't run from it anymore. Her time to have a child might be up soon. It was not simple. Her man Paul had similar challenges with intimacy. He had been raised by adoptive parents who were both deceased. His adoptive mother had died when he was a small boy. Paul and Micheline were committed to the challenge, and sorted it out slowly. Micheline said:

> I was attracted to a man who understands the coping mechanisms that come from years of loneliness and aloneness. He, too, needs time to be alone. We also have to find ways to share our day and our feelings. When I do share feelings, I feel exposed. I am guarded. I have to force myself to open up.

Paul shares more easily than she does. As an adult adoptee, he enthusiastically tells of speaking to his birth mom. "Paul and I do a lot of talking about our relationship. We need to stop talking *about* it, and live it," she says firmly.

Micheline plans to attend another Birth Mother's service, and bring Paul's birth mother who carried love in her heart for him all the years that they were separated. Micheline would like her to be with people who are respectful and caring of birth mothers. Seeing the relationship between Paul and his birth mother unfold is like a dry run for her. She thinks about her birth son, Jules, all the time. She wonders, "He's probably curious about me and may have some love for me, but I don't know. How far can a birth mother/adopted child relationship go? Does it become more than friendship, admiration, a bond because of physical resemblance?" She is sure that he will contact her, but not anytime soon. It may happen when he starts thinking about marriage and having children. She hopes that he has learned French as Micheline requested. She assumes he's in the Waterloo-London area.

Micheline and Paul tried to conceive, but found it was not going well. They considered the adoption option. "Would we qualify?" Micheline wondered. My heart ached for her. Then sometime later, there was joyful news. Micheline was pregnant with twins. She and Paul had looked into the alternative of having his sperm fertilize her niece's eggs, and implant them into Micheline's womb. And it worked! She had a healthy pregnancy, albeit an uncomfortable one in the final months. The babies, a boy and a girl, Marc and Suzanne, are beautiful, healthy, and lively. Micheline took time off from teaching to be home with them. She and Paul share the parenting, although Micheline takes the lead in her incredible sensitivity to their needs, and in providing the structured care from a mom they can count on.

Maeve

It causes me great pain to let her go.
— Maeve

Maeve was 17, and on the honour roll in her final year of high school. She planned to study English or Drama, and possibly Law, at university. The University of Ottawa had already accepted her on full scholarship. She was brimming with talent, and passionate about drama, debating, writing poems and short stories and singing. She loved family camping vacations, swimming and reading. She had achieved a Bronze Cross in lifeguarding and her black belt in karate. She had created a course for developmentally delayed teens which she taught at her mother's martial arts school. Her favourite colour was blue, and the year before, she had dyed her hair a vibrant midnight blue. She was a dynamite girl.

Maeve also was pregnant, due to have her baby in a few weeks. Maeve had met the birth father, who was also 17, in a karate class. Their relationship did not last; in fact, it soon wore her down to the point of depression. He was shy and seemed a bit lost. His parents had divorced when he was three, and he had lived mainly with his mom since then. He and Maeve continued to be friends for the sake of their unborn child. At first she was torn about what to do, wishing she could raise the child, but knowing she was too young. She spent a few weeks at St. Mary's Home where young women stay with their babies until they can move out on their own. Witnessing the life she and her baby would lead, if she tried to parent, was a wake-up call for Maeve. And yet, "It causes me great pain to let her go," she said. Once she decided to place the baby for adoption, the birth father said he would not stand in her way, even though he wished it could have been otherwise. There was already another young man in Maeve's life, who was devoted to her.

Maeve's mother was an energetic, single woman with five daughters. Maeve described her mother as "easy going and direct, loves music, good with people, a hippie, and a social activist." The marriage of her parents ended when Maeve was 10. Maeve noted, "The births of Heather, age 13, and the twins, Ginger and Gail, age 8, and the adoption of Nancy, age 15, who has mild cerebral palsy and developmental delays, are the major events in my life." Maeve's mother operated her own martial arts school and conducted a children's church choir. Maeve described her family as "close, open, and real." They'd been through a lot together. Her mother was sad about the need for Maeve's baby to be adopted, but was in support of it, especially if it could be an open adoption. Her sister, Heather, did not support the adoption plan and wanted Maeve to keep the baby.

Maeve was interested in finding a gay couple to adopt her child. She had no tolerance of homophobia, and found Jennie Painter, an adoption licensee with whom several same-sex couples had registered. She read through the Jennie's entire set of profiles (resumés that adoptive applicants write about themselves) of prospective adoptive parents, and chose a gay couple in Ottawa who already had a four-year-old adopted daughter named Joy. Maeve was especially drawn to the way they lived their lives and the way they parented Joy. They owned a boutique in a vibrant Ottawa neighbourhood where "it's a great place to be a kid." Joy was a non-stop, outgoing little girl, who loved swimming, gym and cooking classes. "She blew the dust off us," one of her daddies said. As a family, they visited museums and festivals, and took family vacations in big cities. Their love of the arts brought a spiritual dimension into their lives. They described their life: "We really love having company over for a play date, to watch a movie, to have dinner or a waffle breakfast. We think our friends, who, on the whole, are a creative, smart, and talented bunch, are one of the greatest resources we have to offer our child." They said they actually had more female friends than male friends. Each father (Papa and Daddy) had a flexible work schedule, which enabled one or the other of them to be at home full time with a child. They already had an open adoption with Joy's birth family, and thought it "was the best way to go."

The next step in the process was to arrange a "match" meeting for Maeve and her family with the adoptive couple. The purpose of the meeting was to determine whether this really could be a match. They would share information with each other, and if they felt that indefinable connection, they would begin to discuss the details of an open adoption agreement. The meeting was scheduled for February 4 in my home office. However, on the morning of that very day, the birth of the baby intervened! A chubby little girl, 9 pounds 7 ounces, was born three weeks early. Maeve came through the labour and delivery amazingly well, with her mother, her boyfriend and her best friend at her side cheering her on. She declared that she would have the match meeting around her bedside in the hospital that afternoon. There was no stopping her!

The meeting went beautifully... lots of laughter and sharing. Maeve's main concern was the history of bipolar disorder in her family —her father and grandfather had been diagnosed with it, and Maeve thought she might have it as well. She wondered how the adoptive fathers would feel about the child inheriting this disorder. She was reassured to learn from Tim, one of the fathers, that his sister was high-functioning in spite of having both bipolar disorder and obsessive-compulsive disorder. Each family spoke of hoping to invite the other family for dinners and gatherings. They recognized that their family styles differed. The adopting couple had a more formal style— their home atmosphere was fun and somewhat quiet (except for Joy!), and the gatherings were smaller. Maeve's family had a more spontaneous style. Every other Sunday, for example, as many as 40 people—family, friends, and lots of children—would gather for a potluck. It was noisy and fun—a happy hubbub. These differing styles would be taken into consideration when they spelled out the type and frequency of contact between the two families. They discussed the baby's name. Maeve's choice of a first name was "Shannon" and the second name, "Dale", was her best friend's name. Not a lot was said, and it appeared that the adoptive couple would retain these names. When Maeve introduced the baby to the two fathers, the baby was unquestionably the star of the show! Maeve knew she'd made the right choice for her baby, and she asked them to come back that evening to meet her best friend and her boyfriend. It seemed way too much for one day, but this birth mother was taking charge!

Next day, though, Maeve's mother reported that the big birth day had caught up with Maeve. She was overwhelmed and weepy following the evening visit. She would pull back on having so many visitors. It had all happened so quickly... too quickly.

Because of the baby's early arrival on the scene, it was urgent to get the paperwork done immediately, so that the Ministry could approve of this adoption plan. The baby could not go to her new home until this approval was granted. During these few days, Maeve took the baby home and cared for her there. She loved doing that, but it reinforced for her that adoption was the right way to go when she experienced how much time and care it took to look after a baby.

Then it became apparent that the baby's name was an issue. The adopting fathers did not like the first name, and were proposing that the first two names be changed. Maeve was devastated. It was as though she'd lost her baby. She had chosen the names with great care and thought. It was a way to express her love for her child, in one of the few ways that a birth mother could. It was her gift to the child.

The name is a vitally important issue for the adoptee. If there is a name on the child's birth certificate that the adoptive parents don't use, the adoptee has to try to integrate two identities. That can feel like she is two different people. She can see herself coming not from a unified family, but from two families with each giving her a different name.

In open adoption, the child and the child's needs, both short and long term, are made the focus. It is important for the birth mother to name the child, and equally important for the adoptive parents to give the child a name. The significant thing is that the original name is not deleted or altered, only added onto. For the adoptee it means that nothing of her has been lost or left behind. In open adoption, it's about *adding, not subtracting.*

Maeve was willing to accept the adoptive parents' need to give the child a new name, but she was not willing to have them eliminate the name she had given to the child. It was vitally important that the adoptive parents embrace the thinking behind this name issue. The adoptive couple did grasp the importance of the issue and agreed to retain the two names that Maeve had given the baby. They gave the baby a new first name, Tabitha, as well as a new last name.

Vera Fahlberg, an adoption expert on attachment and separation, advocates against re-naming even a young child. Because adopted children do not have a strong sense of who they are, a name change poses a real difficulty to them at any age. In a journal article by Lois Melina (1982, 1), Fahlberg says that a name change does not help an adopted child integrate her past life into her present one.

A "vision" meeting took place next with Maeve (her boyfriend was there to lend support) and the adoptive couple. The specifics of the relationship and the kind of contact the two families envisioned they could be comfortable with were put to paper. It was their Open Adoption Agreement. This was not a legally binding agreement, but rather, a trust agreement entered into by the birth parents and the adoptive parents. Severson describes an open adoption agreement as "based on the assumption that there would be as much communication and contact as possible within the limits of courage, compassion, and common sense" (Gritter 1997, 20).

Things began to go smoothly. The Ministry granted approval for the adoption to go forward, and the adoption placement took place at Maeve's home in the midst of a big snowstorm. The new adoptive fathers were there, eager to see Maeve and to take the baby home. The birth father, Maeve, Maeve's mother, and I were present.

Maeve requested a visit in the baby's new home during the 21-day period of time which is given to all birth parents following the signing of the adoption consent. The thinking behind the 21-day period is that placing a child for adoption is a very important life decision, and those who take it need to be allowed to revoke their consent to the adoption if they cannot live with it. After that visit, Maeve said, "While it was good to see the baby, it didn't feel like she was mine any longer." The baby had been a part of Maeve for nine months, and now she was apart from her.

In choosing a gay couple to parent her child in an open adoption, Maeve played a big part in changing the face of adoption in Canada.

* * *

Open adoption has much to recommend it for the child, the birth parents, and the adoptive parents. But... it is still founded on loss. Over the years the birth parents see for themselves that their child is being well take care of. And they have the comfort and pleasure of having a relationship with their child. Contact between birth parent and child is not to foster or create a parenting relationship, but to create an extended family bond. The birth parents lose their parental rights, and they are reminded of this loss when they visit their child. The child has a strong sense of who she is, and knows through direct experience whether her first parents love her or not. But... the child does not grow up with the mother who gave birth to her. The adoptive parents stand to gain when there is no need to be vague in answering the questions their adopted child asks about her origins. They have an ongoing sense of entitlement that they are the child's parents, which is given to them by the birth parents. Their loss is that the child was born to someone else. Open adoption takes flexibility, maturity and empathy, and a generous kind of love on the part of both sets of parents.

As a result of placing babies for adoption, Elizabeth, Micheline, and Maeve were faced with a number of issues. In the '60s, Elizabeth experienced grief that was disenfranchised—the secret was held behind a wall of silence within the family, shared only with the minister of their church; feelings were not shared with other birth mothers and no counselling was offered in the home for unwed mothers where she stayed. She returned to an outwardly normal life with all of the pain, loss and grief locked inside. Micheline had her baby in the '80s when she was able to share openly the joy of pregnancy with friends and family, and to attend a birthing class with a good friend. After she gave birth, Micheline told her story openly and compellingly to families as part of their preparation for adoption. Yet when she became a teacher, disenfranchised grief emerged as she was unable to share her experience as a birth mother with anyone at school. By the time Maeve had her baby in the new millennium, she was able to be open with family, with friends, with everyone she knew. She experienced grief at not being able to parent her baby, but not the disenfranchised kind. She did not carry the heavy emotional burden into her future that Elizabeth did.

The element of choice: whether to parent, whether to abort the fetus or whether to place the child for adoption differed for these three women. These three options were not presented to Elizabeth: the messages from church, school and family were overwhelmingly against keeping the child, and heavily weighted toward placing the child for adoption. There was no opportunity to choose the family for her baby; a social worker did that. Through the years, she did not receive news directly from the adoptive family about her baby's progress. It was a closed adoption. As for Micheline, she knew she was not ready to parent. She gave careful consideration to the other two options, and found herself emotionally incapable of having an abortion. When she learned that she could choose the parents for her baby, her heart was put at ease. From written profiles, she chose a couple to parent her baby. She had one meeting with the couple, and because she felt she needed to know them better, she asked for a second meeting. This important step resulted in this private semi-open adoption moving in the direction of more openness. Some years after the placement of her child for adoption, Micheline requested a meeting with her child and his parents, but this time, it did not happen. This degree of openness had not been adequately prepared for. Maeve had the freedom, without societal pressure, to carefully consider all three options and decide what was best for her and her baby. She was strong enough in confidence, values, and family support to choose a gay couple to parent her child. By this time in Ontario, open adoption was practiced in a way that enabled the birth family and the adoptive family to create an extended family bond which evolved over the years.

With respect to the support that these three birth mothers received, Elizabeth's family was not with her during her pregnancy. She did have good friends who supported her. She received no counselling and felt little support from staff at the home for unwed mothers or at the hospital. The birth father of Elizabeth's baby was already married and gave Elizabeth as much support as circumstances warranted. But officials at the university they both attended held Elizabeth responsible for the unplanned pregnancy—wanting nothing to stand in the way of a bright sports future for the birth father. In Micheline's case, she received strong support from her brother and from her father. She had good friends who were with her throughout as well. She showed good judgment in keeping her mother at a distance. The father of Micheline's baby was already married and suggested abortion as an easy way out of the situation. This hurt Micheline deeply, and she cut off all ties to him. She made excellent use of the counselling that was offered. In Maeve's situation, she was strongly supported by her mother. Although she was no longer in an intimate relationship with the birth father, she sought his support in his role as the father of her baby. He followed through for her as well as he could.

Elizabeth, Micheline, and Maeve faced the issues integral to the birth mother experience with honesty, dignity, and courage.

Katherine and twin babies, Jocelyn and Julia

Chapter Fifteen

Two Birth Mothers—Wisdom within Chaos

Katherine

I love my girls, but I can't even look after myself!
— Katherine

The stepmother sounded very worried on the phone. Her husband's 17-year-old daughter, Katherine, had given birth to twin girls, Julia and Jocelyn, a month ago, and things were going very badly. Katherine's adolescence had been very chaotic so far, and the twin girls were definitely not settling it down. Katherine was on probation. "She is incapable of following a routine," her stepmother informed me. "Raising one baby would be demanding enough for Katherine, but two? She takes a bus or goes with anyone who gives her a lift, with her twins in tow, to a party which can last for days." It was difficult to track her down. She had no cell phone, and never stayed with anyone for very long. Drinking and drugs were her thing. When the stepmother would catch up with her, the babies would be crying and hungry, their smelly baby clothes encrusted with spit-up, and their bottoms stinging red from lying in sopping, poopy diapers. The stepmother would take the babies home with her, clean them and feed them, begin to set a routine, and then Katherine would go off again, sometimes with them and sometimes without them. "It cannot go on," she said. Children's Aid was sure to be the next step. A phone call is all it would take: "Are you aware that a 17-year-old mother who has just given birth, is hauling her twin babies around from one drug den to another?" And the father of the babies was said to be a drug addict who could get violent.

I went out to meet Katherine at the stepmother's home. She was big, buxom, and beautiful, almost six feet tall, with a tousled mane of gorgeous, red hair. She came across as a happy-go-lucky young woman, who played with the truth. Although Katherine was very unwise about much of her life, she was wise about one thing. She *knew* she was not ready to be a mother. "I love my girls," she said. "But I can't even look after myself! I know I can't look after two babies." That wisdom cannot be underestimated. Many birth mothers with whom I worked did not have it. Katherine was willing to consider an adoption plan for her girls only if they didn't go to Children's Aid, in whose care she had spent too much time as a teenager. If she could meet the new parents and have some kind of contact with them through the years, she would consider it.

We would need a couple who were confident, understanding, and flexible, and who could commit to Katherine empathetically and authentically. The adoption licensee knew of a few couples who might fill the bill, and their profiles were presented to Katherine. She chose Christopher and Caroline—no hesitation there. Christopher was a teacher of teenagers, and understood kids like Katherine who were here one day and gone the next, skirting the law, missing school, and drowning their pain with booze and drugs. Caroline was a teacher of little ones with special needs. She felt drawn to what she knew of Katherine's girls.

Then the inevitable happened. Children's Aid apprehended the twins—hungry, dirty, wet, and crying, from the basement of a crack house. When Katherine's father could not get her to return home with the babies, he called Children's Aid in desperation. At least now the babies would be fed, dry, and safe.

The Children's Aid worker knew Katherine well. Despite her hostility towards the agency in general, Katherine said of this worker in particular, "I just love her. When I was in an out-of-town jail, she came all that way, just to visit me." It just might be possible to work cooperatively on an adoption plan with this overburdened, caring, quiet, young CAS worker.

But I couldn't find Katherine. It was suggested I phone "Mike" at the crack house where the babies had been apprehended. With this lead, I located Katherine. She asked me to drive her to Mike's to pick up some things. As we drove up to the front of the house, I noticed a huge round hole, cardboarded up, punched out of the front window. Timidly, I stood in the front hall beside two big, black, smelly garbage bags as Katherine went downstairs to gather up her things. Mike was heavy-set, grey-haired, and unshaven, with a paunch hanging over his pants. He sat on a beaten-up slouch of a couch, talking on a portable phone, and eyeing me. I wanted out of there.

This was only the beginning. Katherine was not getting down to filling out her social and medical history forms, essential if a private adoption was to take place. I would agree to meet her, wherever, to help her with the forms. But by morning, she wasn't at the address she'd given me the night before. No one answered my knocks or my rings. What to do? I phoned her stepmother who knew who to phone and where to look. She found Katherine, and we arranged another meeting time and place. This time she had stayed at Pete's house overnight, but when I arrived at the appointed time, Pete's mother had kicked her out two hours earlier. I left a message in case she phoned back. And... halleluia! She phoned me. Another address. This time I would make the appointment for as early in the morning as she could tolerate, before she was up and away again. It worked. But she was groggy from sleep and whatever else. I waited till she got dressed. It took forty-five minutes for her to put on her face. "What do you think, Carol? This is record time for me. Do you like it?" she asked, delighted with herself. It was impressive—a work of art, in fact. She wiggled into skin-tight black leggings, and slipped on too-big red stilettos, borrowed from a friend. That tousled mane of gorgeous, red hair really topped it all off.

Off we went to one of her favorite restaurants on Richmond Road. There was a stir as we entered. As I got myself a coffee, she lounged in a chair at a chrome table, her legs crossed high, sipping a coke, and smoking a cigarette. We began to fill out the forms. I asked and she answered. One man after another did a double-take as he entered the place. She was being taken for a hooker. Maybe she was.

She could work on the forms for only so long. The section on family relationships did her in. We would continue tomorrow. But... would I find her again?? If I'd known then what I know now, I'd have relaxed. It is always possible to find a person who *wants* to be found.

The meeting arranged for Katherine with Christopher and Caroline was a great success. Without checking or informing me, Katherine had invited everyone to the meeting—her stepmother, her sister, her young stepsister, and they all came! Christopher and

Caroline took it in stride. They told her they would have no problem sending her pictures and letters about the twins every six months for as long as she wanted. She asked for eighteen years. They said they would be willing to meet with her again, after the twins were settled in their home. She couldn't believe her good fortune! Christopher called her a wonderful young woman, and told her he hoped that the adoption would give her the chance she needed to put her life in order. The couple said they would never forget her, and that her children would be the most precious gifts they would ever receive. They cared about her. She knew they were for *real,* and she was overwhelmed. From that moment on, she wanted them to parent her girls.

The birth father, a drug addict and dealer according to all who knew him, could disrupt the plan that was being made. The adoption licensee advised that if the birth father was willing to sign a consent to the adoption, it would be a stronger adoption plan. At first, Katherine was reluctant to give any clues as to his whereabouts, hoping, no doubt, that it would not be necessary to involve him. Eventually, I convinced her that we had to find him, or at least *try* to find him. We cruised around Mechanicsville, a rough Ottawa neighbourhood, in my old pickup truck. She *did* know exactly where he was hanging out. It was a crack house, boarded up, the only sign of life in the place being a scrawny dog barking at a window. And then, there he was, walking toward the place—a skinny, bent, middle-aged man, in scruffy clothes, with gaunt face and the wild, preoccupied gaze of an addict. Katherine leaped out of the truck to tell him of her adoption plan. An argument broke out. "No f---in' way will I f---in' sign any paper! They're my babies and I'll fight for them in court," he shouted. I feared the fight would escalate beyond words as he poked Katherine in the chest with his forefinger. Heedless of the risk, I got out of the truck and introduced myself. Then I said, "Get back in the truck, Katherine." Did we really think this sad wreck of a man could *successfully* disrupt a adoption plan? No, but we did fear he might *unsuccessfully* disrupt it. He did neither. Since then, Katherine hears stories of his death on a weekly basis. Sadly, sooner or later, one of those stories will be true.

After the paper work was completed, and consent to the adoption was granted by the Ontario Ministry of Community and Social Services, I drove out to her stepmother's house where Katherine was staying with the twins. Together, she and I would drive them to my home where the adoption placement was to happen. The twins were two months old now. Julia was the bigger of the two, a sturdy little girl with big, blue eyes. Katherine clearly favoured her. Jocelyn was smaller and quieter, with a gentle look. There was some concern about Jocelyn, who seemed too quiet somehow. Had she been traumatized or injured? Would we ever know? While she had a few puffs of a cigarette, Katherine let me wrestle the twins into car seats in the back of the small two-door vehicle I'd rented. She sat in the front passenger seat, twirling the radio knob to loud rock music, ignoring her fussing babies behind her. If a soother dropped, she paid no attention until I mentioned it. Mothering instinct and parenting skills were not in evidence and there were no signs of attachment. I sensed that we were doing the right thing for these babies by making an adoption plan for them.

The adoption placement went well. Photos were taken of various combinations: the twins; Katherine and the twins; Christopher, Caroline, and Katherine; Christopher, Caroline, and the twins. Tears were shed, and good wishes exchanged for now and into the future.

Katherine's chaotic lifestyle continued unabated. She phoned one day to tell me that she had been raped, and was in hiding from the rapist. Was it really true? Her phone calls continued from wherever she was. She moved in with a man who lived in a small town in western Quebec until the relationship went belly-up. When she longed for some pictures of her girls, Christopher and Caroline sent some immediately. Then a meeting was arranged for her, her sister, and her mom to meet with Christopher, Caroline and the twins. Katherine couldn't believe how big the girls were. I noticed how loving and attentive Christopher and Caroline were, as they anticipated the little girls' needs. And... the adoptive parents had each lost ten pounds! No small wonder considering they were attending to active twins who were under a year old. It was a bittersweet reunion for Katherine who saw with her own eyes what she was missing. She promised to send the twins Christmas presents and a picture of herself as a baby. That did not happen that first Christmas, but presents were sent the following Christmas.

The twins made good progress as they learned to sit, feed themselves, crawl, and walk. Christopher and Caroline were concerned about how Jocelyn banged into walls without seeming to see them. Her speech was developing slower than Julia's. Christopher and Caroline did wonder, as did I, whether Jocelyn had been dropped and injured on one of Katherine's earlier jaunts. I visited Katherine to ask her if Jocelyn had fallen as a tiny baby, or whether she (Katherine) drank heavily or used drugs during her pregnancy. She told me no. Jocelyn's adoptive mom put her experience with special needs children into play by having the little twin tested for learning disabilities. Jocelyn was placed in a special class in kindergarten and school.

At the Birth Mother's Day service that May, Katherine, Caroline, and Christopher all sat together, holding hands. She told them that she had a wonderful new man in her life who was reliable and hard-working. And, she was pregnant again. The timing seemed right for her to raise this baby on her own. Ezra, a strong, healthy, baby boy was born. When I went out to visit the newly formed family, I saw that she was doing a reasonably good job of raising her baby, with a lot of prompting and filling-in-the-blanks by her partner. Before she could arrange to show off her son to Caroline and Christopher and have the twins meet their brother, Katherine and her partner moved to Edmonton. She phoned a number of times from Edmonton. At first the reports were glowing. She was going to become rich getting a job in sales. Then the phone calls began to tell a different story: the relationship was falling apart, Ezra had had an accident at day care for which Katherine was being held responsible, and she was trying to keep Children's Aid at bay. We lost touch, and I have not had a phone call for many years from Katherine, the beautiful young woman with the tousled mane of gorgeous, red hair.

Jacqueline

Jacqueline

Will anyone adopt my baby?
— Jacqueline

She called out of the blue and she talked very fast. She said her name was Jacqueline, she was 29, and she was seven months pregnant. She'd found my name on a list at a medical clinic. She couldn't keep this baby, she said. She'd done a lot of drugs in the first five months of her pregnancy: crack cocaine mostly, also percocet, oxycontin, morphine, speedballs, some I hadn't heard of, but not much alcohol because it made her sick. For the past while she'd been trying to go straight. She'd moved away from the areas where she knew people who did drugs, and away from her drug dealer. She'd rented a room in a townhouse in the south end of Ottawa, and she had a part-time job cleaning houses. She was going to sign up to do some telemarketing to raise money at Christmas time for a children's hospital in Montreal.

She already had two kids, but in January 2007, the Children's Aid came and took her 11-year-old daughter into foster care, and her 5-year-old son went to live with his father. She'd been trying to hold it together working as an exotic dancer, but her addiction to crack caught up with her. After losing her kids, she stopped caring. She got into prostitution, and was raped by a john. At the rape crisis clinic, she learned she was two-weeks pregnant. That's when she fell into deep despair. Life became a blur... lots of drugs, a short stint in jail, and now she was trying to shape up. She wanted to get her daughter back more than anything. Like Katherine, Jacqueline knew that her life was not stable enough to parent this baby.

Wisdom within chaos.

I asked if she'd considered a Children's Aid adoption. "No," she said, "because for my own peace of mind, I have to meet the people who adopt my baby, and I'm afraid Children's Aid wouldn't let me do that."

Then she said, "Well, Carol, I guess you could call me a 'Jerry Springer Special.' Can you find anyone who would want to adopt my baby?"

"I have no idea," I replied, "but I'll look into it and call you back in a couple of days."

"You will?" she sounded astonished. "Promise?"

"Of course," I said.

I liked her. We talked some more—about what her childhood had been like. Her mom had been an alcoholic and a hooker. "I'm not blaming her," she said. Her mom had been sexually abused by male family members in *her* childhood. Although she drank, sold herself, and abused Jacqueline physically and verbally as a child, her mother was able to hold things together—enough that, in her childhood, Jacqueline didn't go into Children's Aid. Without a trace of self-pity, Jacqueline said, "I took phone calls from men who wanted my mom's 'services', and when they came to our apartment, I often had to go and hang out in the laundry room in the basement. But one thing I can say about my mother—she protected me from being sexually abused by the men who came—often I would go and stay with my grandmother."

Jacqueline was full of rage in her teens: getting into fights at school that got her expelled, shoplifting at shopping malls, and spending time in a Children's Aid group home from which she ran away.

At first she didn't want to tell me much about the birth father. As the trust grew between us, I learned that he was an older man, and her drug dealer, with a big criminal history. He was charming and handsome with lots of women in his life, and... she was afraid of him. She did not want him to find out she was pregnant.

I contacted my colleague, Jennie Painter, an adoption licensee who understands and works well with birth mothers like Jacqueline, to see if there were couples registered with her who might be interested in adopting Jacqueline's baby. What a surprise that she had nine possible couples! Two couples changed their minds quickly for one of two reasons: their fear that the birth father, who had a criminal history, might cause trouble or the implications for the child's health of the birth mother's drug abuse during pregnancy.

Jacqueline described the kind of family she wanted for her baby: a couple who had a good family life, and who would provide lots of love and stability and nurturing—the things she hadn't had. At first she wanted a couple with no children, but she was open to my suggestion that she consider couples who already had an adopted child—to be more sure that they could really accept a child who was adopted.

We completed medical and social histories together. A meeting was arranged for her and the adopting couple that she chose. I could see how smart and funny Jacqueline was, what keenly developed intuition she had, and what a good judge of character she was. She had chosen a traditional family. The adopting father was a good guy, a man who provided for his family, a man who would protect her baby. The adopting mother was an over-involved, over-protective mom, and not very understanding of Jacqueline's circumstances. But they were the parents she wanted. They were worried about Jacqueline's drug use, and did some research on the implications of it. Because of the birth father's history, there could not be a fully open adoption with meetings through the years, or full disclosure of identifying information. But Jacqueline was content with the trust agreement worked out between the adopting couple and herself: letters and pictures of her baby would be exchanged at agreed-upon intervals over the years; they would choose the baby's name together, and she hoped that the couple would be at the hospital for the baby's birth.

Late one Sunday evening in January, she phoned to say she was convinced that she was in labour. In the hospital, she haughtily said to a nurse, "Look, I've already had two babies—I should know if I'm in labour or not". The nurse looked skeptical. She did an internal examination and reported that Jacqueline was only two centimeters dilated. In the wee hours, we had an adventure getting out of the hospital parking lot. The exit bar was down, with no place to insert coins to raise it. To get out, Jacqueline held it up while I slowly drove the car out from under.

The following Sunday evening, same time exactly, she called to say she was in labour. This time *I* was the skeptical one. When I got to her place—one look—and I could see this was real labour. Jacqueline was waddling and could hardly move, stopping every couple of minutes to deal with a contraction. The trip to the hospital was as quick as we could make it, and the baby was born 45 minutes after our arrival. She was frightened of her strong labour pains, wrenching my fingers with each one. Her "aunt" came for support and Jacqueline requested that she cut the umbilical cord. Jacqueline was full of remorse for having used crack in the last 48 hours. She apologized to the delivery room staff. One nurse said, "We're not here to judge you; we're here to help you." It did not go unnoticed by Jacqueline that three handsome young doctors were in attendance for the moment of birth. Two big pushes and the tiny baby boy squished out on the white sheet below. Not one of the three doctors caught him. Ever the show girl, she followed up with "Thanks, guys, you've been awesome." One of the doctors stepped in to cut the cord, and I protested. Her aunt did the honours, and Jacqueline was happy.

Baby Michael was under observation for a few days in the special care nursery to watch for withdrawal symptoms from the drugs that Jacqueline had been using. Miraculously, there were none. Jacqueline fell in love with her beautiful baby. How lovingly she held him, stroking his soft cheek gently with the tip of her forefinger! She changed his diaper and fed him capably and confidently. She knew how to be a mother. It was heartbreaking for her to say goodbye. She said it was the hardest thing she'd ever done, but she knew it was the right thing. She had to get her own life in order in the hope of getting her daughter back. I could hardly breathe when she told me that as soon as she left the hospital, she told the birth father about the baby. I feared that could mess up the adoption. But the birth father said adoption was the right decision. When she showed him the first set of pictures of baby Michael, they cried together as they could see with their own eyes that their baby would be loved and well cared for.

Jacqueline made one attempt since the adoption placement to go straight. She got close to going into treatment, but fell back into old ways. She went to jail again. In spite of her addictions, which she has not yet defeated, Jacqueline loves her baby deeply.

> To love something is to let it go,
> to allow freedom, to grant space,
> to be not heavy clouds but gentle winds,
> to be not the fence but the open path,
> to be not the lock but the key,
> for the greatest of embraces end with open arms,

permitting the ones loved to turn or return as they wish.
This is love.

—Maureen Connelly (1990)

Jacqueline and I lost touch, and I wondered and worried about her. She hadn't seemed genuinely ready to go into rehabilitation and treatment. She told me that if she wasn't doing well, she would not contact me. She didn't want me to see her like that. She would feel too ashamed.

One day she phoned from Innes Road Detention Centre. She'd been rounded up with the other Vanier hookers, she said, and didn't mind being in jail as it was a chance to eat decent food and get healthy.

I went out for a visit. I was nervous as I approached the jail and opened the door to a vestibule. In front of me was a locked door with a window. Through the window I could see a waiting room, and beyond that, a couple of police officers in a bullet-proof glassed-in office several feet above the waiting room. There was a button to the left of the door, so I pushed it. No response. I pushed it again. This time the buzzer buzzed, and I was able to open the door. I approached the window behind which the police officers were working. Again, I saw a button there, so I pushed it. The window slid open and a young police officer leaned out and said in a voice loud enough for the whole waiting room full of people to hear, "Lady, why did you press those buttons? Couldn't you see that I noticed you when you walked in? When you approached this window, why did you do it again? I knew you were here because I buzzed you in!"

That flustered me, but I also felt indignant that this was an intimidation tactic which was disrespectful and totally unnecessary. One of the women in the waiting room kindly showed me the lockers where I was to store my purse. Then I was allowed into the visiting area, where I sat down on a long bench in front of a big window, waiting for Jacqueline. Suddenly there she was, waving and smiling, in a hot pink T-shirt and olive green sweatpants, looking good. "Look, I'm an f---in' watermelon!" she laughed, twirling around. We held up our hands and touched palms together through the window in place of a hug. We had to talk to each other by phone. I read her the story I'd written about her and she teared up, saying, "You really listen to what I say, because it's all true except for one little mistake."

The twenty minutes were up, and just as I was leaving, Jacqueline asked if I could leave a few dollars for canteen at the desk on my way out. I was more than happy to leave the money, but less than happy to have to talk to that same police officer, especially when a sign on the wall said that money was to be left *before*, not *after*, a visit. Undaunted, I approached the same high window and then—was it my autonomic nervous system that kicked in?—I pressed the button again! This time, my officer opened the window, leaned out and in a despairing tone, said, "Lady, you've done it again."

"I'm sorry," I said, embarrassed. "I just don't know the drill around here." How I wish I'd said, "I just can't help pushing your buttons." He *did* allow me to leave Jacqueline some money for canteen.

Jacqueline phoned a bit later to say that when she read this story to the women in the detention centre dorm, they cried along with her.

My support work with Jacqueline was now officially over. Once she was released from jail, she resumed her old ways, and I didn't hear from her for months.

Just before Christmas, there was a phone call to say that she was living with Jason, and she had some wonderful news. She was pregnant—due in a couple of weeks, and was off drugs. She'd been in a methadone program throughout her pregnancy, and was planning on keeping the baby. She invited me to her apartment, noting that she would do that only if she was proud of it, and because she wanted me to meet Jason.

It was a wonderful visit. She was herself—she had more patience, a longer attention span, and could converse comfortably. She was off drugs! We went for lunch and bought a few things for the baby, but she and Jason had accumulated almost everything they needed. They knew that the baby was a girl, and her name would be Hannah. I met Jason who seemed a bit nervous, and couldn't quite meet my eye. And I couldn't quite take my eyes off the tattoos completely covering his arms and shoulders. Jason eventually relaxed enough to speak sincerely about how thrilled he was that he would be a father for the first time and that, at 40 years of age, he had never thought it would happen. Jason had been a heroin user for many years, but had been in a methadone program for longer than Jacqueline. It was Jason who pleaded with his doctor to take Jacqueline into the program. Jason has mental health issues for which he was getting support through individual therapy. His disability pension was enabling them to rent a three-bedroom bungalow. Jason's adoptive parents were giving a lot of support to Jason and Jacqueline.

Jason and Jacqueline were following the methadone regimen faithfully. Each day they walked to the pharmacy to receive their daily dose of the drug. If they followed this without fail for one month, they earned a "carry": that is, one day a week they could take their next day's dose home and drink it there. Jacqueline and Jason had earned six "carries" each.

I saw Jacqueline once more before the baby was born, and that was to receive a Christmas gift from her. She was very excited to be able to do this for me. It was a necklace of vibrantly coloured beads—just the colours I love, and a beautiful music box with space for a photograph. This was all packaged in a fabulous Christmas candy cane box.

Jacqueline's baby was born just after Christmas—a healthy 8 1/2 pound girl. She was considered a special-needs baby because of methadone withdrawal, which made her jittery and irritable. The neonatal nurses kept a watchful eye on her, and Jason and Jacqueline came to visit her every day. Children's Aid, who had to be notified about Jacqueline's baby, did a thorough assessment of the couple—their plans, their new home, their health and how they followed through on commitments. After three very long weeks, the baby was discharged to go home with her ecstatic, loving parents.

I visited the newly formed family in their spotless new home. Jacqueline and Jason had been ingenious at acquiring the equipment and furniture they needed to tastefully furnish it. Jason was nervous about screwing up since Children's Aid would be looking in on them for the next while. It was difficult for him to relax. He didn't want anything to go wrong.

Jacqueline goes regularly for group therapy. She thinks that she and Jason need couple counselling as well. She knows that she needs to learn to be patient with Jason, and that he needs to develop his listening skills. But Jacqueline recounted an incident on the bus when they were taking the baby across town for her weekly appointment with a pediatrician. The baby began to cry and fuss, and Jacqueline panicked. Jason calmly dug the baby's bottle out of their bag and fed the baby on the bus till she was quiet.

"Jason is Super Dad!" says Jacqueline. And I think she's a pretty super mom.

About a year later, Jason began using heroin again. He and Jacqueline separated. When Jason is clean, he is able to have good visits with his child. Jacqueline is a caring, responsible mom.

* * *

In private domestic adoptions, such as were arranged for Katherine and Jacqueline, birth mothers are given the opportunity to choose from a number of prospective adoptive parents. And so they live into the future with the assurance and comfort that comes from doing their own choosing.

PART THREE

THE ADOPTIVE PARENTS

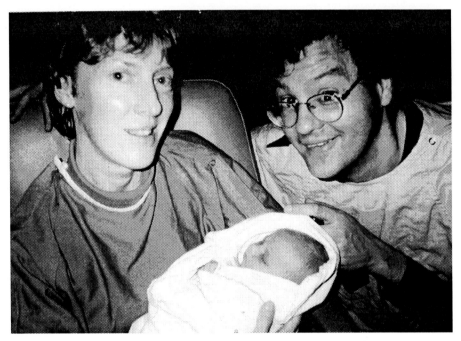

Adoptive mom, baby Julie, adoptive dad

Chapter Sixteen

Three Private Domestic Adoptions

The Angels in Heaven are Singing...

The couple was nervous as they entered my home. They had been trying to have a child for five years—as long as they had been married. They now felt ready to begin the adoption process. She had a prim, earnest manner about her. Her gaze was direct. He was very, very tall, and had a shy, gentle smile. She had chosen to be an at-home wife to make them a life together that was serene and civilized. She was taking piano lessons on an exquisite ebony piano, a pleasure that surpassed all pleasures for her, and she had time now to write poetry. She had lovingly cared for both her parents in their last years. She felt deeply content that she had made it possible for her father to die at home, helping to make his final days happy ones. They didn't have much money. Her husband, although well-educated, was not well-paid. He had a university contract to teach Physics. He loved physics. Their faith in God was strong, and they were active in their church. As we talked, their eyes began to glimmer with hope. As they went out the door, this very tall, very shy man surprised me by bending way down to give me a strong hug, instead of a polite handshake!

As the home study progressed, we talked about the type of adoption they wanted. They were not very comfortable with the idea of meeting the birth parents more than once, or even sending letters and pictures to them for more than the first year or two. But they were studious and so they approached the home study as a learning experience, reading the articles provided and the books recommended. They took it all in, questioned and discussed the issues. They seemed quite deeply moved by the experience of hearing directly from birth mothers at a workshop about how and why these young women had placed their children for adoption. After they attended a Birth Mother's Day service, they decided they wanted a more open type of adoption. They understood and were excited by what a child would gain from it.

One day after sharing a cup of tea with me in their new little house with the red shutters—so perfect for them—the wife said with a confident smile, "Carol, I think that this year ahead will be our year [to succeed in adopting a child]. I just feel it!"

They registered with an adoption licensee with years and years of experience. They wrote a profile, sincere and tender, just like they were. They hoped that a birth mother would like their profile enough to pick them as parents of her unborn child. After a few months, she called, wondering what else she might do to speed the process. At my suggestion, they decided to register with another licensee who lived farther away, and they continued to hope.

A few months later, close to Easter, the second licensee called me with the news that a birth mother, about to give birth in a few days, wanted to review some profiles. It had to be couples who could move *fast*, if chosen. The birth mother had made an adoption plan with her local Children's Aid only to learn that there would be no guarantee that letters and pictures of the child would be sent to her in the years that followed. It was not good enough for her. She turned to a private adoption licensee, chose a couple from the profiles provided, and requested to meet them. It was not to be. The prospective adoptive father had places to go, and people to see. He could not find the time to meet with her. In other words, he was not ready to adopt, and he and his wife withdrew from the "match".

This birth mother then chose my couple from Ottawa! She requested letters and pictures for an agreed-upon length of time, and she wanted the adoptive mom in the delivery room with her. The birth mother was saying, in effect, "I want you to be my child's mother, so you ought to be there for her moment of birth. She was entitling the adoptive mother to parent her child. To agree was no problem for my client. She said, "It is an honour to be asked!" Things often have a way of working out for the best for an adopted child. It had the signs of a strong adoption plan.

There is never a sure thing in adoption, but this one was as good as it gets. The birth mom, who lived in a small northern Ontario town, was married with two young children. She had had an affair and had become pregnant. She could not bring herself to have an abortion, but neither could she keep the child. The whole town was talking, and her marriage was in tatters. Her unborn child's father was harassing her, making life impossible for her and her family. She knew that this would be no life for the child, who deserved a home free of strife. She decided to explain her circumstances in her own words to the couple she had chosen. When the couple read her letter, they knew that they already loved her.

In two days' time the birth mother was scheduled to have her baby induced in a hospital in a large centre in northern Ontario. The adoptive couple and I would fly to meet her there the day before. Before dawn in a snow storm, we set out for the airport. No one told us that the plane would be a 15-seater! The adoptive father, dizzy and pale, with his stomach still in his throat, staggered off the plane. It was a difficult beginning when so much hinged on the meeting with the birth mother going well.

We found the small coffee shop where we had arranged to meet her. It was quiet and bright, like a pretend courtyard. We ordered a coffee while we waited for her. Suddenly there was a big commotion at the counter. A toy Easter bunny erupted into song as its front paws moved stiffly up and down. We were silenced into enduring a raucous chorus of "Here comes Peter Cottontail" before it shut down. An unnerving moment for a couple already unnerved.

The very pregnant birth mother appeared. Friendly and nervous, she and the adoptive mom chatted while the adoptive dad, still a white shade of pale, smiled. What about a name for the baby? The ultrasound had indicated that the baby was a girl, but one never knows for sure until the birth. Julie was the name of the adoptive mom's beloved mother who had died two years ago. Julie was the adoptive dad's grandmother's name; and the birth mother loved the name because it was the name of her favourite aunt. She was Baby Julie for all of them from then on. Annual letters and pictures were offered—for 18 years if she wanted them. That would be wonderful! Wanting to cover all of the bases, I asked about circumcision in case—just in case—the baby was a boy. The birth mother was firm—she would definitely want her baby boy circumcised. The adoptive mom said, "I think it is a good idea; then the baby will look just like his daddy." The adoptive dad, changing from a white shade of pale to a bright red, looked as if he'd like to drop through the floor. Then the Easter bunny on the counter erupted again!

The birth mother had two things on her mind. First, she wanted to be certain that the adoptive mom could be in the delivery room, *for the baby's sake, not hers.* And second, she was worried that the birth father might come into town and disrupt things if he showed up at the hospital. We agreed that we would all go immediately to discuss these concerns with the hospital social worker. More than once the birth mother told the couple, "I'm tough and I can handle things."

The hospital social worker advised that if the birth father appeared in order to see the baby, the hospital commissionaire could be summoned. "No," said the birth mother, "This man is very smart. He might get his girlfriend to pave the way for him with nursery staff before they knew what was happening." The social worker thought that instead of placing the baby in the regular nursery, the baby could go to the intensive care nursery where the door was always locked and where only approved identified adults could visit. It was arranged, and the birth mom sighed with relief.

The adoptive couple met the birth mom early next morning at the hospital. They would be with her from beginning to end—no question of that. She was pleased. She warned them and the nursing staff that her previous two babies had come very fast: just a few hours of labour, one big push, and the babies were out! The induction procedure was working slowly but surely. "I'm tough," said the birth mother, again, "I can take a lot of pain." The adoptive father, well able to read the monitor which etched out the strength and length of the pains, looked into her eyes. She said later how moved she was by his unspoken compassion. A strong bond was in the making. As the pains got stronger and closer together, she drew into herself, sweating and silent.

The babe was coming. Gowning up, the adoptive mom walked alongside the birth mom's gurney to the case room. The adoptive father and I remained in the lounge, but our hearts were in the case room. The baby came fast—too fast—popping out like a champagne cork. In no time, the adoptive mom burst in to the lounge, her eyes shining like stars. "Julie's here, and she's absolutely beautiful! The angels in heaven are singing!" She had no idea of weight or length or anything—the baby had been whisked away so quickly. Tears came to the adoptive dad's eyes. The couple hugged, unbelieving. The birth mom was fine— she had been simply amazing.

Then the female pediatrician appeared, checking out who we were. "There is a problem," she said. "The baby is in difficulty, and is being helped to breathe." Stunned, the adoptive dad asked, "Can we see her?" "No, not yet; she's a pretty sick baby," was the reply. Shock —disbelief—fear. One nurse said the baby had been born with a punctured lung—it was correctable, not to worry. Then we heard the APGAR results, and I went cold. This response test, taken one minute after birth and five minutes after birth runs about 9:9 in healthy newborns. Julie's was 2:4. It was sinking in. The adoptive mother turned to me, her eyes wide with fear and said, "I just can't take another death on this day. I just can't. My mother died two years ago on this day." We sat silently, heads bowed, arms around each other. Minutes passed in silent prayer. Then I voiced a prayer for Julie, for all of her parents, and for the hospital staff who were helping her live. The doctor appeared again. She reported that Julie had had an X-ray which showed no punctured lung; the baby was on a ventilator to receive oxygen. During the precipitous delivery, she had probably swallowed meconium. If so, this was a serious condition in which the newborn somehow breathes a mixture of meconium and amniotic fluid into the lungs.

I left the couple and went down to see the birth mother in a recovery room on the floor below. The doctor had just been in, to give her the news of Julie's difficulties. It hadn't sunk in at all. The birth mother was so relieved that the birth was over, that her thoughts were on her other children—how soon she could rejoin them, and make the seven-hour car trip home. She was ravenous for a chocolate bar, for instant energy. Of course I would get her one. "How are my baby's parents? Are they excited?" I reminded her that the baby was in difficulty. She intended to see Julie before she left the hospital which she hoped to do within the hour. The doctor had warned her of the risk of hemorrhaging if she left so soon. "But I'm tough—didn't I tell you I was tough?" she said. She would stay with a relative who lived not far from the hospital and she would return if necessary. The need to leave and return to "normal" was urgent for her.

In emotional whiplash, I bounced back and forth from birth mother to adoptive parents. The pediatrician was confident that a particular drug would enable the lungs to begin functioning normally. It was agreed that the baby would be given this drug. Julie would need a small dosage of morphine to calm her and prevent her from fighting the ventilator. Finally, the adoptive parents were allowed to see her—a perfectly formed baby, lying still in the incubator with tubes and wires protruding from her body, measuring and keeping her alive. Shock. Agonizing not to be able to hold her. Afraid to even reach in and touch her. But she was tough—like her mother, fighting for her life.

The birth mother visited the baby with wires and tubes attached, and the gravity of Julie's plight began to sink in. She came in once more with her sister before leaving the hospital. The adoptive parents kept a vigil into the long night. They had already become part of the team in the intensive-care nursery, headed by the elegant, competent, reassuring female pediatrician who said to the adoptive mother, "I could see that you were her mother from the moment she was born." This doctor, with one short sentence, had "entitled" a new adoptive mom to be the child's parent! This was further reinforcement of the gift of entitlement the birth mother had given to the adoptive mother by inviting her to be in the delivery room for the birth.

The adoptive parents, knowing that that they had to ration their strength for the days ahead, went back to the motel to bed. At some point, they learned that the baby had swallowed amniotic fluid, not meconium, during her flying trip down the birth canal. Next day, the hospital staff arranged for the adoptive parents to have a room in the hospital. If the couple was worried about the baby at 3 o'clock in the morning, they could walk down the hall to the nursery to check on her. They were included in the daily nursery rounds when Julie's progress was discussed. Their confidence in the competent, caring pediatrician soared.

The birth mother did return home with her mother and children the next day. After seven hours on the road, she was sore and tired. She debriefed the birth experience on the phone with me. It was the bond she felt with the adoptive couple that stood out for her. She had never expected *that*. She was so sure that this was the right thing for the baby. She felt compelled to write an account of the experience for the adoptive parents, which she would fax to me. She wanted to write to Robert Munsch, the Canadian author of children's books, to tell him of the experience. She hoped he'd make Julie's story into a children's book.

Meanwhile, the adoptive parents' days were endless. Julie was making slow progress. It was a day to celebrate when she came off the ventilator and out of the incubator, and they held her in their arms at last! Two more days, and they would be flying home with her. This time the small plane was the least of the adoptive dad's worries. But then—disappointing news. Julie was not feeding quite well enough to go home. It would be a few more days yet. It was very, very hard to take. Would it never end?

It did. Julie and her exhausted, anxious, but very happy parents went home to the new little house with the red shutters. Her progress has been steady ever since. Julie's birth mother expressed her love by sending small gifts. During the 21-day period when she could, by law, withdraw her consent to the adoption, she phoned the adoptive parents. She wanted them to know that they were not to worry—that she was sure of her decision. It was a joyous Easter, a Happy Birthday, and a wondrous Mother's Day for Julie's adoptive mom. At the annual Birth Mother's Day celebration, the adoptive mom joined the procession to light a candle for Julie's birth mother. Then I handed her the Mother's Day card that the birth mother had sent to *her*. It was her first Mother's Day card on her first Mother's Day. Greater love hath no people than these three for their child. Julie's love story had begun.

Time passed. Julie is now 14 years old, in Grade 8—a beautiful, articulate, active teenager. She came third in a national literary contest for a poem she wrote about Remembrance Day.

Over the years two visits have taken place between the adoptive family and the birth mother. When Julie was about three years old, her birth mother came to Ottawa for a visit. And last year, Julie and her adoptive mother were invited to visit her birth mother at a cottage on Lake Nipissing. It was important for Julie to experience her fun-loving birth mother's lifestyle, her outdoor life of hunting, fishing in ice huts, and learning to fly a plane. The visits probably reinforced Julie's strong relationship she has with her adoptive mother.

When Julie was about six years of age, her adoptive parents separated. After a period of mediation, they divorced. Their commitment to their adoptive daughter is strong; a shared custody agreement was struck, and Julie's parents remain devoted to her. The angels in heaven are still singing.

Grace Under Pressure

None of us own our children.
— Jonathan and Ann

Ann was a petite, gentle woman with loving, brown eyes. Music was both her occupation and her love, second only to her husband. Jonathan was a reserved, modest orthopedic surgeon. Both had intelligence and integrity in abundance. It was lovely to see their devotion to each other, and hear of their shared passion for Johann Sebastian Bach. It was in a church in Europe, where Bach was buried, that Jonathan proposed. They seemed so ideal and therefore so deserving, that it was hard to believe.

They loved their nieces and nephews and wanted to be parents. Infertility and the treatment for it had been sad, risky, and alienating. They did not want to continue down that road. They were interested in hearing about open adoption, realizing that the birth family would become like extended family, and the ties between child and birth parent would not be severed. Ann had no reservations about it, recognizing immediately that it would benefit everyone, especially the child who would know who she was right from the start. Jonathan was not so sure. Time to develop trust with the birth family was important to him before he could commit to the concept.

When the home study was complete, they created a profile about themselves, as all adoptive applicants do, attempting to put the essence of who they were on paper. They wasted no time in making connections with a few licensees who arrange private adoptions.

From a licensee in a city two hours away, they learned of a baby girl who had just been born. The birth parents were students of law and kinesiology. Both were Canadian: she was of Scandinavian background, and he was the son of East Indian immigrants. The birth parents had two things uppermost on their minds: they wanted an open adoption, and they were concerned about how a white couple would raise a mixed-race child. The pregnancy and birth had been kept secret from their two sets of parents. The young couple were sure that their parents would reject them and their child if they knew about her. Even more serious, the birth father was sure that his parents would disown him.

Ann and Jonathan arranged to meet the birth couple in a restaurant. The conversation flowed. They adoptive couple liked the birth parents very much, and hoped it was mutual. They loved the name the birth parents had chosen for the baby—Maria. They would not change it. They waited and began to wonder if they would be invited to visit the baby who was still in the hospital nursery. Best not to ask, they thought. Then almost offhandedly, the birth mother said, "Should we go to the hospital to see the baby?" This was the signal they'd been waiting for—that the birth parents wanted to proceed! The baby was beautiful, and they fell in love. Maria bore an uncanny resemblance to the adoptive mother. The adoptive father sensed that a relationship of trust with the birth parents had begun. He was ready to enter into an open adoption with them. The adoptive couple returned to Ottawa and waited.

Meanwhile, the birth mother was bonding with her baby, and the birth father was anxiously wanting to move ahead with the adoption plan. They were at odds. A major rift occurred. The birth mother experienced the birth father's expression of hasty gratitude for her decision to place the child for adoption as extremely insensitive to her underlying heartbreak. Her anger was pushing her toward a decision to keep the child. Her counsellor reminded her that anger and revenge were not a good basis for a decision to parent. In this period of uncertainty, the baby was placed in a foster home and visited daily by the birth mother. She could not make a decision, and was counselled to delay the signing of the consent to the adoption until she *was* sure. In situations of uncertainty like this one, people are encouraged to take things one day at a time, rather than to make a hasty, premature final decision.

Back in Ottawa, Ann, Jonathan, and I went out for dinner. I was amazed at their open-hearted generosity and the complete absence of a need to control the situation. They said, "We know we can live with whatever happens. If Maria is meant to be with us, she will be. I just wish we could support the birth mother somehow to keep her, if that is the best decision." Grace under pressure.

I learned later that the only way Ann could cope with the uncertainty was to return to the state they had been in before this adoption match. So she returned all the baby clothes and equipment they had borrowed. It was her way of not putting pressure on the birth parents to agree to the adoption. Ann repressed her feelings of anxiety, fear, and longing.

On the morning that the consent was scheduled to be signed, the birth parent counsellor felt that it could go either way. The counsellor predicted that the signing would be the defining event. The birth mother signed. The adoptive parents were filled with joy, and "flew" down to meet the birth parents, to take the baby home. It was to be a long, long day. No one was at the licensee's office when they arrived, and it seemed like forever when the four finally appeared—licensee, baby, and the two birth parents—having had a lengthy meeting in the foster home. Another long visit over supper took place, and finally, close to midnight, they bid farewell, knowing they would see each other again soon. Ann and Jonathan began the drive back to Ottawa. But Ann began to shake uncontrollably, and down the road, she had to run into the nearest coffee shop to throw up her dinner. There was no formula or diapers for the baby at home, so Jonathan headed off to the nearest all-night pharmacy. His turn to let go came the next day when he heaved great sobs of relief, and released his bottled-up mix of fear, sadness, and joy.

The birth parents came to visit the baby during the 21-day-period that they are given in order to withdraw their consent to the adoption if it is something they cannot live with. For the new adoptive parents, it was impossible not to worry that something would go dreadfully wrong during the birth parents' visit. The advice they were given to relax and not try to be perfect parents was easier to hear than to follow. The adoptive mother lost 10 pounds over two weeks.

The second visit, which took place following the 21-day period, was much more relaxing and the two couples got to know each another. The adoptive couple were caring and encouraging towards the birth mother and her schooling, and expressed admiration for the birth father's goals and aspirations. The baby's baptism was arranged in a few months' time, and the adoptive parents asked the birth parents to be Maria's godparents. The birth parents gladly accepted the honour, and participated fully in the service. They were warmly welcomed into the extended families of both adoptive parents.

Some time later, the adoptive parents rejoiced to learn that the birth mother had shared her secret with her mother, and instead of the rejection that she feared, it brought mother and daughter closer than they have ever been. A small miracle. But when the birth father told his parents about the baby and the adoption, they reacted as he had feared: hysteria, rejection of the child, condemnation and blaming of the birth mother, and anger and condemnation (but not disowning) of him. The adoptive parents were sad and very supportive of him. They later learned that in the birth grandparents' country of origin, adoption was neither practiced nor approved of. The birth grandparents viewed it as an insult that they had not been asked to raise the baby.

The birth parents moved forward with their careers. and made the important decision to marry. The birth grandparents began to "come around". Ann, Jonathan and Maria were invited to the wedding. Exercising excellent judgment, the adoptive parents arranged a meeting at a hotel restaurant with the birth grandparents a month before the wedding. The meeting over brunch was a great success, and soon the adoptive family were invited to sleep over at the birth grandparents' home where they were "treated like royalty."

At the time of the wedding, Maria was five, and longed to be one of the flower girls. It was not to be. The birth grandparents had not yet shared with their extended family the fact that Maria was their son's birth child and were against it. The birth parents gave in. Maria was heart-broken. Yet at the reception a game of "Spin the Wheel" required the groom to kiss someone of his choosing. He headed right for Maria, not his bride, and gave her a tender kiss. When asked who the little girl was, he proudly replied, "My godchild."

The birth parents showed great consideration for Maria before they tried to have another child. If Maria was too young, would she have a harder time accepting a birth sibling? The birth mother wanted Maria to see her pregnant. When the birth parents came for a visit, Maria sat with her birth mother and hugged her tummy. A son was born to the birth parents. He is now six, and loves to follow his older sister around.

A few years later, a baby girl was born to the birth parents. Shortly after that, Maria's birthday came and went with no acknowledgment from her birth parents. This had never happened before. They had always phoned and sent a card and gifts. It was a crisis for Maria. Had they forgotten all about her? Jonathan and Ann decided to call upon the birth parent counsellor for guidance. She suggested they write the birth parents a letter explaining how Maria was feeling. A phone call came immediately from the birth father. They had been overwhelmed with the care of not one, but two children, and were very sorry about not acknowledging Maria's birthday.

I recall that prior to Maria's adoption, the birth mother had longed to keep Maria. Perhaps she was reliving the loss of her opportunity to parent Maria once she gave birth to another baby girl. Perhaps there was more to the temporary halt in communication between the birth parents and Maria than the fact that they were so busy caring for two children.

Some time later, Maria was invited to sleep over at her birth parents' home. Her birth siblings cried and whined to such a degree that she could not sleep. At age 11, Maria was used to speaking her mind. She stormed into their bedroom, hands on hips, and said, "What are you going to do about these children?" And the birth parents answered, "We're going to let them cry." Sounds like normal family dynamics!

Jonathan and Ann have a family cottage near the city where the birth family live. Many happy family gatherings have taken place there with extended birth family and extended adoptive family members.

The unfolding of this unique open adoption relationship will continue.

* * *

My first impression of an ideal adoptive couple has proven to be true over time. It is a joy to have had a part to play in placing a child who needed a home with adoptive parents like these.

Adoptive mom, Ann, and birth mom, Amber

Like Sisters

They sounded like a family in a Hollywood western: Amber, Jed, and Billy Bob. But they were city people, through and through. Amber was a pretty young woman of 18 who was "cool". Nothing seemed to faze her, even the fact that she was nine months pregnant. She was an only child who had been hurt in her earlier years and had learned not to show it. Her mom was not there emotionally for her, but came through sometimes in practical ways. Her dad, whom she had worshipped, left the family when she was very young, and she learned, from one disappointment after another, that he couldn't be counted on to come for visits when he promised. When he did come, she was ecstatic, and when he didn't, she was devastated. Her cool protected her.

Amber was very proud of her three-year-old son, Billy Bob. She had found a nice home daycare provider for him while she went to school to finish her last few high school subjects. She was living with Jed, who was 17, nice-looking, and wore his ball cap backwards. He wasn't Billy Bob's birth father, and he wasn't ready to be a dad. Jed had very little self-confidence, and his hurt was close to the surface. His dad had died of alcoholism when Jed was 11. Jed had acted out his loss, rage, and grief at school and around the housing project where he lived. He probably had a learning disability, so school was not a fun place to be. "I got into scrapes when I went joyriding in cars with kids who were nothin' but trouble," he said.

Jed and Amber had been together for a year or two. He hung out with a nicer bunch of guys now—they gathered in a different part of town until the wee hours, and he slept in all morning. He wasn't trying very hard to find a job. "And anyways, it would be minimum wage," he said. In a printing shop, the guy in charge would throw his weight around, and make Jed do all the work. Jed had a habit of getting mad and quitting jobs.

Amber had hoped that Jed would mind Billy Bob while she attended school, but that wasn't working out. Getting a good job and having enough money were her goals. She knew that she would be set back indefinitely, if she tried to raise a new baby as well as Billy Bob. She knew Jed well enough to know that he could not be counted on for child care, and that seemed to be OK with her. Amber and Jed cared for and accepted each other.

In reviewing the recent past, Amber shared that her mother "had a fit" when she learned that Amber was pregnant a second time. Amber was willing to consider adoption, so her mom made some phone calls. An open adoption sounded appealing to Amber, and she chose a couple from among a dozen profiles that would-be adoptive parents had written about themselves. "There was just something about Bas and Ann—they sounded nice," she said. Jed, not taking a full part in it, went along with Amber's choice. A meeting was soon arranged for the two couples, but there was a hitch. Bas, a geologist, was up in the Yukon bush for several weeks. The meeting went ahead with Ann, Jed and Amber. Ann was an attractive, friendly, straightforward, warm but not fuzzy woman. The feel of the meeting was cool, and it was hard to tell what Amber thought. To my surprise, she said afterwards that she couldn't imagine liking Ann any more than she did. The licensee thought it was essential for Bas to leave his work in the Yukon and meet the birth parents before the baby's birth. Bas flew home. That meeting went well too; Jed, perhaps, found it a bit intimidating to meet with this older, successful man. As Amber and Ann began to talk about how their contacts might look in the future, Jed was not a bit sure that this would be good. Wouldn't it confuse the child? A child should just have one set of parents, he thought. He was not alone in this way of thinking.

Like Jed, people who are wary of open adoption sometimes confuse it with co-parenting in which a child's parents, following divorce or separation, share in the child's upbringing. The misreading of the situation results from confusion about the boundaries and roles in open adoption. In reality, it is unlikely that the child will be confused about the very distinctive roles of adoptive mother and birth mother in an open adoption. James L. Gritter in his book *The Spirit of Open Adoption* states, "Although each role carries the title of mother, they have little in common. The adoptive mother carries out the boundless role of 'Mom', while the birthmother's role resembles that of aunt or special adult friend." (1997, 22).

In this pre-birth-of-the-baby stage, Amber and Ann met for lunch, and talked about ordinary, everyday stuff. Ann thought Amber was a neat girl, and was impressed that she was such a good mom to Billy Bob. She offered to take Amber to a doctor's appointment. Ordinary everyday stuff from which a strong connection was being forged.

Amber had been raising Billy Bob on her own, with some help from Jed, and absolutely none from Billy Bob's biological father. A few days before she gave birth, she received a contrite phone call from Billy Bob's father, saying that he had a new woman in his life with whom he had a child, and that he wanted to make it up to Billy Bob and to Amber by starting up regular visits with Billy Bob and by providing some child support. Amber was both cautious and hopeful.

Amber gave birth to a baby boy, Brandon, who looked remarkably like his older brother. She was pleased that Jed was with her for the birth. She was also pleased that Bas and Ann liked the baby so much.

When Amber was ready to leave the hospital and go home to Billy Bob with Jed, her step-dad arrived to meet the adoptive parents, see the baby, and drive Amber and Jed home. But Amber was no longer "cool". It was the hardest thing in the world for her to place Brandon for adoption. Seeing Amber's tears, the licensee who made the adoption placement official, dug a tiger-eye semi-precious stone out of her purse and said to Amber:

> My husband died several months ago. I've been carrying this tiger eye around with me everywhere I go to give me the strength to get through each day. I think I'll be OK without it now, and I want you to have it.

Amber took the stone and carried it everywhere, sometimes holding it as she tried to fall asleep.

Her return home from the hospital coincided with Billy Bob's first planned weekend visit with his biological father. They were the worst days of her life—she felt that she had lost both of her children. Jed held her as she wept and wept. Her grief knew no bounds. But she was able to move on—back to life with Billy Bob and Jed, and school.

Visits between the two families continued. Some were special occasions like lunch with Ann's sisters and parents, and Billy Bob's birthday party at the home of Amber's mother with Bas and Ann and the baby invited. Jed was always invited. Sometimes he came and sometimes he didn't.

Ann tells Amber often how proud she is of her. She is proud of how Amber returned to school, of how she was able to get a part-time job, of how she cares for Billy Bob, and of how she saved her money to go on a holiday to British Columbia. Most of the visits are at the home of Ann and Bas, but the relationship is not all one-way: it is one of giving and receiving. Ann suggested that Brandon would love some of Billy Bob's old toys and clothes, so Amber happily brought over a boxful.

Amber graduated from high school and landed a good job with a small company, working her way up to office manager. She went through very bad times as her relationship with Jed went from OK, to poor, to bad, to awful. He began abusing her to the extent that her fellow workers noticed bruises on her face. He cheated on her and flaunted it. He sought the sympathy of other women by telling them that Amber had given their baby away. In retaliation, some of these women wrote abusive letters to her. It was a nightmare. Finally Amber took charge. With the support of Ann, she moved to another apartment with Billy Bob, making sure that Jed would not have the new address, and got an unlisted telephone number. She has since heard that he has done time in jail for drunk driving. It is unfortunate that Jed, who did not ever spend much time with Brandon in the early years of Brandon's adoption, has not visited his son in some time.

Amber has good friends, some of whom are single moms like herself. Together, they plan holidays to an exciting destination each year. Recently, a group of them flew to London, England, where they shopped till they dropped and saw the sights. This taste of freedom had healing power for Amber.

Amber is very proud of the kind of boy Billy Bob is, and of what a good big brother he is to Brandon. Recently, Ann asked Billy Bob to babysit Brandon. Billy Bob's eyes twinkled as he said to Amber, "Just think, Mom, Brandon and I will be all alone in the house. Do you think we'll get into some mischief?" And of course she was sure they wouldn't, and they didn't!

On her 29th birthday, Amber couldn't have been happier, surrounded by friends who lived it up at a club in Montreal. She compared it to her 19th birthday, saying she never wanted to repeat those teen years. She has a wonderful man in her life, and is hopeful and excited about what the future may hold for her and him, and her special relationships with both of her sons. When she is ready—and this will depend on when she can take time away from Billy Bob—she would like to take courses in Psychology and Crisis Management at community college. This could lead to a career change for Amber. She would love to work with pregnant teens in the future. She has walked in their shoes and would love to try to make a difference in their lives. She was profoundly moved when she read about the lives of children in Africa. She immediately signed up to foster a teenage boy in Niger. "I can certainly afford $35 a month," she said.

Amber describes Ann and Bas as wonderful parents to Brandon. He's a boy who never stops moving as he goes from one thing to another, to another, to another. She is impressed that Bas takes Brandon to the gym track before school each morning, so he can work off steam before school begins. This helps him sit quietly and learn.

Visits between the two sides of the family take place about once a month. The women, Amber and Ann, will set up a special day to barbecue and sit around and relax while Brandon and Billy Bob play games. At 16, Billy Bob has grown tall. He is in Grade 10. Brandon is 12, with blond hair and big blue eyes. He loves to play goalie on his hockey team, to swim, and is skilled on the computer, like Bas, his adoptive dad.

For Amber, an only child, Ann is like the older sister she never had. I wonder if Amber isn't closer to Ann than any birth relative she has, the woman she *chose* to be her child's adoptive mother. Having the opportunity to choose for oneself makes the difference. Amber is thriving in this open adoption relationship, as is Brandon, who will always know who he is, and that he is loved and cherished by his birth and adoptive parents as these visits continue through the years. I wonder how much credit Amber would give Ann (and Bas) for the positive changes she has been able to make in her life? And how much credit would Ann and Bas give Amber for what she has given to their family, and for the changes she has made in her own life? Full credit, of that I am certain.

* * *

Private domestic adoption is in an ongoing process of change. It has moved from the closed adoptions of several decades ago, to semi-open adoptions, to open adoptions which are most prevalent today. While adoption practitioners and licensees influence the course of adoption, adoptive parents and birth parents play a major role in changing it. In the first domestic adoption described in this chapter, Julie's adoptive parents began the home study process feeling nervous about contact with a birth mother. But as they sincerely set out to learn about a new way to adopt, they expressed willingness to be with the birth mother for the birth, and received the gift of entitlement from her to be her child's parents. Prior to birth, Julie's birth mother listened to her inner voice in making an adoption plan for her unborn baby. When a Children' Aid agency could not promise information about her child following adoption, the birth mother called a halt to the plan. She then entered into a private adoption plan with a couple who were unwilling to meet with her. She called a halt to that plan, too. Finally, she found a couple who were more than willing to agree to her bottom-line requests.

In the second domestic adoption, Maria's adoptive mother believed from the outset that open adoption was best for everyone, especially the child. Her husband felt he could not commit to such a relationship until a sense of trust had been established. Once Maria's two sets of parents met each other, a trusting relationship began. The end result is a very open adoption—one in which birth parents became the child's godparents.

In the third domestic private adoption, Brandon's adoptive parents, Ann and Bas, had taken a course in open adoption as part of their home study process, and were comfortable with it from the outset. Thus, they were able to move wholeheartedly into an open adoption with Amber who felt Ann's acceptance immediately. There is a particularly strong bond and frequent contact between the two mothers in this adoption—they are indeed, like sisters.

Baby Sam, and Madison, age 5

Chapter Seventeen

Two International Adoptions

And They Waited...

Marika and David came to my home office one autumn afternoon, a married couple in their thirties. They had just experienced yet another disappointment with an infertility procedure. She looked tired and sad. Earnestly and solemnly, he said that they felt the time had come to turn away from infertility treatments and toward adoption as a way to have a child. But they did not seem hopeful. We discussed the possibilities. He had lived and worked overseas, and as he spoke, his sensitivity and interest in other cultures came alive. She was employed by a non-governmental organization (NGO) and worked, perhaps, too long and too hard to make the world a better place for the disadvantaged. They were thinking of adopting from China. They lived in a section of Ottawa surrounded by Asian immigrant families. Growing up, he had had a Chinese-Canadian friend; they both worked with Asians, as well as Indians and Africans. At the end of the meeting, they were daring to hope that their dream might become reality.

They shared their lives with me during the course of the home study. They were very thorough, earnest, and authentic. A home study is never easy. In fact, it is intrusive. They did settle on adopting from China, and chose an international facilitator in Ottawa to help them. Their application was approved by the Ontario Ministry of Community and Social Services, and their file was sent to China.

And they waited... Then she phoned one night. They had just learned that their international facilitator had closed up shop, citing difficulties in working with Chinese officials. They attended meetings with other waiting couples, and breathed huge sighs of relief when their international facilitator reorganized and got under way again, with a new leader.

And they waited... Then she phoned again. They had just heard that China had called a halt to all international adoptions, due to a power struggle between two ministries in China. If their file was in one of those ministries, it would not be read by the other one. Where was it? They had no idea! Worried and anxious, she glued herself to the Internet trying to keep abreast of the situation. The director of their Ottawa international facilitating agency travelled to China, and literally carried files from one ministry to the other.

And they waited... Finally they heard that there was a child being proposed for them. She had been found, healthy and abandoned at the age of three months, at the orphanage gate. They received a picture of Shao Qing, and some medical information. They were over the moon!! They enlarged her picture, made copies, and placed one in every room of the house. Then began a joyful dream about what their lives would be like when she joined them. On the basis of a photograph, the process of attachment to this small child had begun. Their hearts were soaring, but they were still fearful that something else might go wrong.

But things went right! Her sister held a baby shower to celebrate the baby's impending arrival. David and Marika travelled to China and returned with Shao Qing, whom they renamed Madison Mei-Ling. She was just over a year old. They were in love with their child. He loved carrying Madison up to bed on his shoulders. "Madison rules the roost," David smiled joyfully. Marika's voice was richer and fuller than I'd ever heard it and her smile seemed permanent when she spoke of her child. Madison adjusted more quickly than anyone could have predicted. The problems were few. They ached for her as they held her close on the nights when bad dreams took her deep inside herself.

Sleep disturbances are all too common among girls adopted from China. Experts have speculated that this may be due to the abandonment occurring at night when the child is asleep. Thus, the child is at home with her parents one night and wakes up the next morning in an orphanage with strangers.

The background of such abandonments began with the introduction of the one-child policy in 1978, in order to control the population explosion in China. In general, each Chinese family was allowed to have only one child. In adulthood, sons were required to care for their elderly parents, and daughters belonged to the families of the men they married. And so Chinese couples preferred to have sons who would look after them in their old age. When a girl baby was born, her parents had to make the terrible decision to abandon her. This took place likely at night where there was less risk of discovery and in a place of safety—at the orphanage gate or at the police station entrance .

I met Madison again when the couple began to think of adopting again. She was five years old by then—a lovely child with big brown eyes and smooth black hair. She moved quickly and confidently. Madison was creative, adventurous, and intelligent with a wonderful sense of humour. Her parents delighted in her. Her father said, "I love being able to praise her." They described her as a child with a tremendous ability to adapt, a great capacity for empathy, (which is unusual in such a small child), and a zest for new experiences. She loved babies and wanted a baby brother or sister.

Madison's life was full of adventure. She loved school, and she liked artwork and reading. She was taking ballet, swimming, and violin lessons. She could play on her own or with friends equally well. She was especially good at blending new friends with old to make sure everyone was included. She could stand up for herself, and did so on a regular basis.

The family of three enjoyed being together. Their sense of fun shone through their descriptions of outings and activities shared.

Talking about adoption was simply a normal part of Madison's life, and they thought she was very comfortable with the fact of her adoption. Madison said, "We chose each other to be a family."

And they did not forget Madison's other mother, her first mother. They hoped that one day it would be possible to meet, but knew it might never happen. Marika spoke at a Birth Mother's service in 2001 to honour women who had given children into adoption. She called her talk *"To the Birth Mom We May Never Meet"*:

> My name is Marika. A little over four years ago, my husband and I adopted a little girl from China. One of her names is Shao Qing. This is what we would like to say to Shao Qing's birth mother:
>
> Thank you. Thank you for giving us the most precious gift in the world, a human life. From the moment we met your daughter, our daughter together, we were in awe of her courage

and her beauty and, even though she was only a year old, her wisdom. As I've watched our daughter grow over the past four years, I feel that I have begun to know a little bit about you as well, although I don't even know your name. I know that you must have a wicked and wonderful sense of humour. I can see it in our daughter's eyes and hear it in her laughter. I know that you are kind and sympathetic to others. I can see it in our daughter's rushing to comfort anyone she sees in pain or distress. I think that you might also be something of a flirt. I see this in our daughter's daily trip down our street where she catches everyone's eye and makes them laugh and smile, friends and strangers alike, and in our local grocery store, which basically stops functioning the moment we walk through the door. All eyes turn toward Shao Qing and light up in anticipation of hearing her talk about her day or her newest

accomplishment. I wonder if you have very long legs and love shoes as much as she does. How many pairs of high-heeled dress-up shoes do you think are enough for a five-year-old? I wonder if you really did eat noodles with ketchup as our daughter insists you did while you were pregnant. But most of all, I know that you are very brave to have given her up knowing that she carries so much of you inside of her.

Thank you from all my heart. Thank you for loving our daughter and for placing her in a spot where you knew she would be found and well taken care of. Thank you for giving us this wonderful and amazing gift, which we will treasure all of our lives.

I read somewhere that the Chinese believe there is an imaginary red thread which connects people who are meant to be together, and that nothing can break that line—not time, nor circumstance, nor distance. I don't know if I will ever meet you face-to-face, but I do know that red thread will always connect me to you through our daughter. And these are the things my husband and I tell our daughter when we talk about and remember you, her birth mother. Sheshang (Thank you).

In this speech, Marika was affirming the reality of Madison and her birth mother with an open heart and with empathy. An adopted child's loss, hurt, and anger needs to be acknowledged by the adoptive parents. Marcy Wineman Axness (1998), adoptee and mother, believes that what a hurting child needs from a parent is empathy. It can sound something like this:

> I can see that you're hurting. I wonder if you're missing your other mother, that connection you had with her. It was sad for both of you that you couldn't stay together. But it was happy for you and me that we ended up together. I'm here for you and I'm going to stay here with you.

The couple wanted a second child with a heritage similar to their daughter's so the two children would feel closely connected. Madison was as fully a part of the decision to adopt again as they were! The second time around they sought more knowledge about their child's family background. They wanted the process to take less time, and they wanted the child to be as young as possible. They chose to adopt from Korea. In much less time, a beautiful four-month old baby boy, Jin Woo, renamed Sam, was found for them. Their joy knew no bounds, and Madison added her joyous notes to the chorus. Just after Sam arrived, Madison sent special invitations to family and friends to come to a welcoming party for Sam. It was held at the home of a family friend, and Madison was the hostess. She made sure there was lots of candy on the table for the children who came to the party. Madison was thrilled to have a little brother who looked like her, and the connection between them is strong.

The adoptive parents have found ways to help their children develop a sense of pride in their Asian heritage. They hired a young Chinese university student to be the children's caregiver. He is an excellent role model for their children as he reads them stories, draws pictures, sings in Mandarin and teaches them songs. They held a special ceremony on Sam's first birthday with friends and families who also have babies from Korea. Sam wore a special outfit called a *hanbok* for the ceremony. The adoptive mother reads extensively about Korea, works with Koreans, and has taught English-as-a-second-language to Koreans. They have friends of many cultures, including Chinese and Cambodians. The children go to a school with a number of other children who have been adopted internationally. Although the family has moved to a larger house, there are Asian children in their new neighbourhood. As Madison grows up, she is mostly happy with herself, but, as she becomes aware of physical difference, she has said, "I wish I didn't have a flat face." How do they respond? Lovingly. The family plans to travel to Korea and China when their children are older. Interested in both cultures, they read adult and children's books, and enter fully into such cultural events as the Chinese tea ceremony, and celebrate Chinese New Year and special Korean holidays. They have learned some of the language of both countries.

... And they wait no longer. They are a family.

* * *

Bi Yan, age 5, Carolyn, and baby You Bing

That Girl from Canada

Through Carolyn Chang
The life force sang!

I was hesitant to meet Carolyn, the woman who had phoned me a few days earlier. She had told me that she was Chinese-Canadian, age 40, and divorced. She'd had two different kinds of cancer in the past two years, and she wanted to adopt a little girl from China. There's a guideline in private adoption that to be considered a healthy candidate, you must be cancer-free for five years. But... it was a guideline, not a rule. There was something about Carolyn's directness and honesty, her

247

determination and her certainty that her oncologist would provide a positive prognosis and recommend her as a good candidate for adoption that made me agree to meet her.

Her appearance surprised me. She was so tiny—just a shade over five feet tall. She was attractive, with expressive brown eyes, a direct gaze, and short, black hair. There was a strong, positive energy about her.

We got right down to the big issue. Carolyn's ovarian cancer, diagnosed two years earlier, was caught in the early stages; a tumour, the size of an apple, was removed. No chemotherapy or radiotherapy was required. About a year ago, she was again diagnosed with cancer. This time it was cancer of the endometrium. She had a hysterectomy, and again, because the cancer was caught early, there was no need for chemotherapy or radiotherapy. She said that the two cancers were unrelated to each other, and that her oncologist would confirm that she was no more at risk for more cancer than anyone else in the general population.

But how had Carolyn coped with having had cancer twice before her 40th birthday, and how she was coping now? It soon became clear that I was in the presence of a woman of uncommon emotional strength. She was also warm, humorous, honest, and compassionate. She said, "I'm able to put things into perspective. I will not be overwhelmed by sadness about my situation. I could be self-centred and spend my money on trips, but I want to share myself with a child. By adopting a child from China, I am tapping into my deepest life desire." Carolyn could readily share her feelings of shock, anger, and sadness about what had happened to her. But what was striking was her positive outlook, and her capacity not only to accept, but to transcend what she had been through.

There was far more to Carolyn than her cancer. She had returned quickly to the fullness of life with enthusiasm, zest, and vitality. She enjoyed living alone, engaging in such solitary pursuits as pulling weeds in her garden, playing her piano, sewing, walking her small Pug dog, baking, molding a piece of pottery, and in winter, cross-country skiing. She said, "Cancer allowed me to listen to myself about the things that matter." She has written a couple of children's books and taken a course in how to use power tools. She has sung in choirs, danced with a Chinese dance troupe, been part of of an African drum circle, and run two marathons. She gave up the latter, not wanting to stress her body that much. There was almost nothing she would not try!

I was interested in Carolyn's explanation of her Chinese astrological sign. There are twelve signs, and hers is the Rat whose key characteristics are charm, ambition, and the determination to do what is necessary to achieve what one wants. The Rat is a "doer", someone with a lot of initiative, who can be restless and short-tempered when hindered, and can have uneven moods. The Rat is audacious, and can usually convince others when there's a difference of opinion. The Rat aligns with good causes.

All the ducks were lined up, as the saying goes. Carolyn had a well-paid, secure job with the federal government. She could afford to raise a child. Carolyn had good friends in Ottawa. Her family, most of whom lived on the west coast of Canada, strongly supported her in her desire to adopt a child. Some would come to be with her and her child, if that became necessary. If the unthinkable happened, her brother, the patriarch of the family, and his partner would raise her child. While this is a caring, responsible plan, the primary consideration is the adopted child. Because that child has already experienced the loss of a first set of parents, the probability of the loss of a second parent must be kept very low.

As Carolyn had indicated, her oncologist, a leading gynecological oncologist in Ottawa, wrote a letter in support of her application to adopt, stating that her prognosis for the first cancer was "very good, and the prognosis for the second cancer was "excellent". He did indeed confirm that the two cancers were not related to each other, and that Carolyn was no more at risk for any other cancer than the general population.

Carolyn was overjoyed to receive approval from the Ontario government to proceed with an adoption from China. Her file was sent to China to be reviewed and processed by the Central China Adoption Agency (CCAA). In due course, they would forward the proposal of a child to her. To Carolyn's dismay, she received word that CCAA was threatening to reject and close her file. They had placed it "on hold" in their Matching Department. The issue was her history of cancer.

The Rat went into action. She wrote a masterpiece of a letter to a Mr. Li, the Director-General of CCAA, saying in part:

> I ask you to consider my request to adopt a baby girl from China... because I know I would make a wonderful mother, and I would do my utmost, like all Chinese parents, to bring up my daughter to be a productive member of society, and a wonderful human being, proud of her Chinese heritage.... For me, like for all Chinese, family is the most important aspect of my life. By that, I mean having my own family. For me it means adopting a baby girl from China.
>
> The wisdom I have gleaned from cancer serves me well every day.... Cancer has taught me purpose, perseverance and strength.... My oncologist is of Chinese heritage too.... Doctors and patients alike, they all say he is the most skilled, experienced, in short, the very best gynecological oncologist.... A key component of his work is to sometimes tell patients what they do not want to hear. Moreover... he is bound by ethics... by professional integrity and human decency to tell the truth.... His patients conduct the rest of their lives... whether their lives are long or short, based on [his] prognoses of their health.... [My oncologist's] exemplary reputation is built on diagnosing, treating and giving cancer prognoses with breathtaking accuracy and integrity.... Please do not allow recently exaggerated prognoses that other doctors have submitted to the CCAA to cloud your decision....All I ask is that you permit my oncologist's reputation to be judged without prejudice and precedent.
>
> I do realize that the both of us are striving toward the same purpose—that of providing the very best care and home for the baby. I have heard many, many heart warming and wonderful stories of the remarkable and profound work of the CCAA. Your work must bring you and your staff much satisfaction and contentment.

Mr Li, thank you for allowing me the time to express my heartfelt thoughts.

Then she followed her own letter with seven letters of endorsement of her intention to adopt. These were written by

- the Office of the Deputy Prime Minister of Canada;
- her oncologist: "Carolyn's overall prognosis is very good.... There is no reason why [she] should not pursue international adoption, given her health is strong and steadfast";
- The College of Physicians and Surgeons of Ontario, outlining the credentials of her oncologist;
- her family doctor: "the probability that either of these malignancies will ever recur is very low. Currently Ms. Chang's health is excellent, and I regard her as a most suitable candidate for adoptive parenthood";
- her Member of Parliament;
- a senior Citizenship judge, formerly the director-general of Carolyn's department: "[Carolyn] "is a key player on the staff... and entrusted with a particularly heavy and challenging workload.... In the past two years, my encounters with her have been with someone who enjoys good health and appreciates her good luck with early cancer detection and treatment....As a former member of the Ottawa Hospital Board, I underline that Dr. F K F is a wonderful, gifted, and trusted oncologist who has worked at the top of his field of gynaecological oncology at the Ottawa Hospital for 17 years....When Dr. F K F states that Carolyn is in a position to consider international adoption, he speaks knowingly";
- her older brother, appointed guardian of the child, and patriarch of the family: "Our family is a family of tradition and strength....[We] are extremely proud of the way Carolyn conquered cancer. When I look at her now, I see a person glowing with health, quiet confidence, vitality, and humour."

Carolyn also contacted the coordinator of Private and International Adoptions for the Ontario Ministry of Community and Social Services, seeking his intervention with CCAA. To add further challenge to the already challenging situation, support staff at this Ministry were on strike. This coordinator was operating virtually alone.

Nothing happened. Then Carolyn learned that Mr. Li of the CCAA was coming to Ottawa for meetings, and through a contact at the Chinese embassy, she managed to have a few words with him between meetings. That is how he met an articulate woman, glowing with health and vibrant with energy—in person!

And finally, the proposal of Bi Yan came through! The little girl was one year old. The photograph that Carolyn received was of that of a sad little person. When the time came, Carolyn and her brother took a 16-hour flight from Canada to Hong Kong and a tedious bus ride from Hong Kong to Guandong. Bi Yan was already at the office where all of the adopting parents—about 30 in all—were to meet the children. The new parents dared not register any physical discomfort or fatigue. They were balls of raw nerves, speaking too quickly and laughing too loudly. When Carolyn saw a picture of Bi Yan among the mountain of paperwork that she was required to complete—adorable, vulnerable, frightened—the realization struck that she was going to be this little girl's mom. "The gravity of assuming the role of your mother tethered my excitement," she said in an open letter she later wrote to her daughter.

Carolyn described her first moment with Bi Yan:

> Our eyes locked—yours and mine.... It was as if your eyes spoke to me.... I saw fright and panic, then, just as quickly, your eyes told me, "You are my mother. We will be together. I have a mommy now"....In the same moment, I fell deeply in love with you. And so it has been ever since.

They spent two weeks in China getting to know each other. Once Bi Yan knew that Carolyn was her mommy, she would not let Carolyn out of her sight. Carolyn bought a snuggly carrier. Mother and child were inseparable, day and night. Bi Yan was content as long as she was nestled next to Carolyn.

What Carolyn was describing is the beginning of an attachment process between parent and child. Experts like Becker-Weidman tell us that attachment is the base of emotional health, social relationships, and one's world view. It is vitally important for adoptive families to recognize the difference between a child who 'looks' attached, and a child who really is making a healthy, secure attachment. A child may be overly clingy, never wanting the parent out of her sight. She may call someone "Mom" or "Dad," snuggle, cuddle, and say "I love you." But saying "I love you," and knowing what it feels like can be two different things. Becker-Weidman says, "Attachment is a process. It takes time. The key to its formation is trust, and trust becomes secure only after repeated testing" (Becker-Weidman, April 2001, 34).

Bi Yan and Carolyn had begun the process.

When Carolyn, her brother, and Bi Yan arrived in Beijing. they made a mad dash from the airport to the Central China Adoption Agency to meet with Mr. Li, the head of the Agency, and his staff. By then, Carolyn was well known to the CCAA. She was *that girl from Canada.* In Carolyn's words to Bi Yan: "Let's just say, even though Mommy did not go through labour pains, she moved mountains to bring you into her life." Mr. Li and his staff commented on how very beautiful Bi Yan was, and how very happy Carolyn looked.

Carolyn took several months of parental leave from work, and stayed at home full-time with Bi Yan. Carolyn prepared her little one for daycare by reading a loving, gentle book about it, *Oh My Baby, Little One* by Kathi Appelt (2000). She also took the child to her office, so Bi Yan could see "Mommy at work" for herself. Carolyn believed that routine gave her child security. She set two routines for herself and Bi Yan—one for the work week and another for the weekend. Somewhat tentative about trying new things, Bi Yan liked her mummy nearby when she swam in summer or skated in winter. It was a joy to her mother when the child first started painting at her easel and became immersed in her own little world.

In a letter to Bi Yan, Carolyn wrote:

You enjoy being Chinese. You are a girl after your mom's heart, you prefer *dim sum* to French fries.... Yet, not unlike any child, you ran out of the house yesterday morning, bursting to start your day, ponytail in flight, sunglasses perched on your little nose, lips pursed, chin elevated. You had plans to hatch with the kids at daycare!

Life is sweet because you are in it.

The story could have ended there, but it didn't. Carolyn's health became less and less of an issue. Her gynecological oncologist no longer thought it necessary to *follow* her. A year or two later, it was time to add another child to her family. Carolyn felt it would help her little girl be happier and even better adjusted if she grew up with a sibling. She wanted Bi Yan to have a bond with a sibling who came from similar beginnings. And just as much, she wanted a second child for herself and her family.

Because I was taking a short sabbatical from adoption work, I was not able to work with Carolyn on a second adoption. A colleague agreed to work with Carolyn on the reapplication. A few months later, Carolyn phoned to say that things were not going well. Although she and my colleague had a very good working relationship, there was a problem. The reapplication had been written and reviewed by the Adoption Unit of the Ministry of Community and Social Services who were requesting additional information regarding Carolyn's preparation for a second child. It would require a list of readings that Carolyn had completed as well as a home safety check by my colleague. Carolyn had provided this information by email almost immediately to my colleague, but had been unable to contact her by phone or email. She'd left a total of ten voice mail messages, and was becoming anxious and frustrated. She had notified the international adoption agency with whom she was working about the problem. They had also tried to contact my colleague, to no avail. Staff at the Ministry had also left messages for my colleague, which went unanswered. Eventually, Carolyn got an email from my colleague saying that she had been away due to a death in her family. When Carolyn finally reached her by phone, my colleague sounded "overwhelmed". Time went by, and although Carolyn had done all she could to provide the answers to the Ministry's questions, the Ministry had not yet received the required additional information.

Carolyn hoped that I might take over the file—a delicate situation for everyone, at best. I consulted with the Ministry, with the international adoption agency, and my colleague. It became clear that my colleague's health was compromised, and that it would be a relief for her if I took over the file. This time Carolyn applied for a girl *or* boy up to the age of fifteen months. In her presentation letter to CCAA, she wrote: "It is my duty to my family that leads me to ask the Central China Adoption Agency to consider a baby boy first." I completed Carolyn's reapplication as quickly as possible, and it received Ministry approval soon after.

In due course, Carolyn received the proposal of a beautiful ten-month-old baby boy named You Bing. "You" was the first character of his place of birth, Youxian, and "Bing" meant brightness and renown. Carolyn has since renamed him "Bing Walter William". According to the undated *Growth Report of You Bing* written by the Director of the Youxian Welfare Institute, the baby, estimated to be two-and-a-half months old, had been abandoned at the entrance to an orphanage in Hunan province. He was described as wearing white clothing with yellow flowers and a yellow hat with a tiny floral pattern. He had a round face and sparse yellow hair. Baby formula and a feeding bottle were with him. The baby was described as a well- nourished, healthy, active, and lovable little boy.

You Bing adapted quickly to his new family. He loved to snuggle with his mommy after his afternoon nap, and play and imitate his older sister, although he could play independently, too. He slept well, but was sometimes wakened by night terrors (an extreme form of nightmare from which it is hard to awaken the child). He was very much on target developmentally—he walked at 12 months of age, and began to talk at an early stage. He listened to music, which often inspired him to dance. A happy, fun-loving, physical child, he loved to play, both indoors and out.

Carolyn arose at 4:35 a.m. (not 4:30 a.m.!) in order to end her work day at 3 o'clock in the afternoon. This schedule allowed her more time with the children. She has a mental list of things she wants to do when Bing is older—learn to golf, join a book club, and so on. "I'm not interested in doing such things while I work and the kids are at daycare and school. This is not my time. I accept it 100 per cent."

Carolyn says simply, "The family feels rounded and complete.... I love watching the kids smile at each other. It's why I adopted again."

* * *

At the outset, these two families who adopted children internationally had an important choice to make: from which country would they choose to adopt? In Carolyn's case, the choice seems obvious. Of Chinese origin, her pride of heritage and culture is being passed on to her children. As a result, the children stood to lose far less of their identity than they would have if non-Chinese parents had adopted them. Madison and Sam's adoptive parents are neither Chinese nor Korean, but the profound respect they exhibit for the cultures of their children springs from their work in international development, and in their childhood and adult friendships with individuals from these countries. Theirs was a strongly positive choice based on heartfelt experience. As the children grow up, they are encouraged to learn their native languages, and participate in special holidays and cultural events.

A theme that runs through the adoption stories of these two families is their powerful determination to become parents by adoption. Carolyn overcame one obstacle after another in order to become an adoptive mother—her determination knew no bounds. And Madison and Sam's parents never gave up—when an obstacle blocked them, they worked tirelessly to find a way around it. It sounds almost too simple, but I have observed that families who have determination and perseverance in abundance, are the ones who successfully adopt.

Chapter Eighteen

The Adoption That Didn't Happen

Liora, Child of Light

I knocked on the door of their small apartment on the east side of town. The wife, a quiet, slim Sri Lankan woman, in her thirties, with a sad smile, let me in. She said that she wanted to place her child, a little girl about six months old, for adoption. She and her husband had made an adoption plan before the baby was born, but they hadn't been happy with the couple they had chosen, and so they had chosen another one, but they never got the chance to meet the second couple. So they decided to try to raise the child themselves, even though they didn't have enough money.

They did have relatives nearby. Her mother, in fact, lived in the same apartment building, one floor up. Eight years ago, the wife had been the first one in her family to come to Canada to find work. She had learned English quite easily and got a job in accounting. Then she had moved up a notch to be secretary of a women's organization. She had liked that job—the women were nice to her, she said. A man back in Sri Lanka wanted to marry her, and the plan was that she would return to marry him, and then sponsor him to come to Canada.

It was a big wedding in fine Sri Lankan tradition. Four hundred people attended. She wore a beautiful, long, white, jewelled dress. On the second day of the festivities, his parents prepared a feast for two hundred guests. She wore a exquisitely coloured sari on the day of the feast.

After the wedding, she returned to Canada, working and saving to bring her husband here. When he came, he found it difficult to learn English. In Sri Lanka, he had been supervisor of ten men, in a diamond-cutting factory in Colombo. It was steady work and he was proud of what he did. But her husband had been here in Canada five long years and still had no job. Sitting stiffly and quietly, he said, "I want to find a job. She is working and I am in the house. I no like it."

Some years after her husband's arrival, she became pregnant, and had not worked since the birth of their beautiful child. He said, "It is not right for a woman to work when a man does not have a job. A woman can work only if a man already has a job." This was the rule by which they lived. But it meant that they had no money. And this was why they were giving their baby away.

Her dark eyes were luminous and sad. I sensed it would be very difficult for her to do this. Was she withholding something? Was he? I calculated that her husband had been back visiting in Sri Lanka just around the time that the child had been conceived. I wondered if the baby was another man's child—a "love" child. Was it intolerable for the husband to raise another man's child? He was a proud man. Would he feel that people were talking, that he was even a laughing-stock in the small Sri Lankan community? I asked the question as delicately as possible. The answer was, "No, that is not the reason."

The baby was very beautiful with tiny delicate features, dark hair, and a sweet smile. Her name was Liora, which meant "light." She had been breast-fed for three months, and was now on a bottle. Her mother cradled her on a spotless white embroidered pillow, crooning a Sinhalese lullaby, until she fell asleep. A powerful, loving bond. In Sinhalese culture mothers sleep with their children, often until they are grown up.

A child who is six to twelve months of age is very vulnerable to a big change of caregivers, and to a change of environment. It is a difficult age to be adopted. Attachment to the primary caregiver is intense. The child will perceive the loss of this person and grieve. Grief may be expressed by searching behaviour—eyes looking around in agitation; in anger—uncontrollable crying; in depression—withdrawing, sleeping more than normal, no interest in food, play, or people. Finally, hopefully, there will come a feeling of acceptance. These expressions of grief are not necessarily sequential, and may be repeated over and over.

It was important to learn as much as possible about the child's routine in order to replicate it as closely as possible in the new adoptive home. How was she held during feeding? Did she fall asleep following feeding or was she alert? How was she diapered, dressed, and bathed? What sounds and language was she used to—did her parents talk "baby talk" to her? Did they sing to her? What smells surrounded her—curry, for example? Were there transcultural changes to be aware of—a sweetener in the formula, and what *were* the sleeping arrangements?

The adoption planning proceeded. The child's parents were given profiles of couples who were longing to be adoptive parents. They chose one profile. It was arranged that they would meet the couple they'd chosen in my home, accompanied by the couple's social worker. The adoptive parents were as well prepared as it is possible to be. The woman was a school principal and had a lot of experience with children of many backgrounds and needs. The man enjoyed a close connection with his nieces and nephews. They were open to adopting a child of a race different from their own, and a child older than newborn. They felt they could love such a child.

It was nerve-wracking for them. They would be meeting the child's parents, and hoped so much that they would like each other. It would be an awesome thing—to receive a child from her parents after only one short meeting. They said that they would be happy to meet again after the three-week adoption consent period was over, if the child's parents would like that.

The two couples arrived, and the usual format for such meetings was followed. The would-be adoptive parents were asked if they would keep the child's first name—of course they would! Would they give her another name—yes! Were they willing to send pictures and letters for a period of time? Would the birth parents provide a picture of themselves? It was a quiet, subdued meeting.

Throughout this exchange, the child's mother's grief filled the room. She said little; she showed nothing. Her dark eyes mirrored profound sadness. Then I asked the adopting couple a question, "How will you affirm the child's background? Will you try to connect her to the Sri Lankan community in Ottawa as she grows up so she will be proud of her heritage?" "Yes," the adopting couple said, "We will make every effort to do that, although at present, we do not know anyone in the Sri Lankan community in Ottawa." I wondered, then, if the child's father was dismayed as he realized that the adoptive parents were being encouraged to introduce the child to Sri Lankan people who might very well know from whence she came. He showed nothing.

That night, I tossed and turned, unable to sleep. Something was terribly wrong. What would happen to the child's mother if this adoption plan was carried out? I feared she would die, literally, of a broken heart. By morning, I had decided that I would not, could not, play a part in this adoption. If it was to be carried out, it would have to be without me. I phoned the adoptive parents' social worker, who concurred that the grief shown by the child's mother was too great. "Her affect was *dead*," she said.

What happened next never happens. The adoptive parents phoned their social worker to say, "We cannot believe we are saying this, when we want to be parents so much. But...we cannot adopt this woman's child. *We cannot steal the baby out of her mother's arms.*"

I called the child's parents. The mother's voice was so light. "We have decided to keep the child," she said. "We will both try to get jobs, and my mother will help with child care." Such an obvious solution! If my hunch was correct about the real reason for the adoption plan, there would be less family disgrace by keeping the child than by giving her away. And Liora, child of light, would make her mother's eyes shine forever.

The adoption that didn't happen.

CONCLUSION

Chapter Nineteen

Reflective Convictions

As used to be true for women, children's human rights have been largely ignored. They must move from being the "voiceless citizens" to becoming the new kids on the human rights block, especially with respect to their human rights regarding their biological origins and biological families.... [Not knowing their genetic origins] is harmful to children, biological parents, families, and society.
—Margaret Sommerville

Emerging from my personal and work experiences in adoption, I have developed strong convictions, many of which are evident in this book.

One of my strongest convictions is the belief that the right of adopted persons to know the identity of their birth parents surpasses in importance all other adoption issues. In their quest for identity, pioneering adoptees of the past cried out their message. In the early 1970s, Florence Fisher (1973, 112), dubbed the Betty Friedan of the adoptee liberation movement, and the founder of ALMA (Adoptees Liberty Movement of America), an organization dedicated to assisting adoptees to find their birth parents, said:

> How can those secure in the knowledge of who their natural parents are tell me how I should think and feel, when they have never felt or thought the same ambiguity, longing and emptiness? When you know, it means nothing. When you don't know, it means your life.

Drawing from the work of Freud and Erikson, Betty Jean Lifton, another indomitable adoptee pioneer, recognized that hereditary background knowledge is vital to identity formation. Her husband, Robert J. Lifton, an eminent psychoanalyst and author, tells us that the need for origins is more basic to a person than sex drive. A gap in one's identity contributes to a sense of distance from others (Lifton, Betty Jean 1975, 65-66).

I am convinced that the adoptee's desire to know her roots is an undeniable basic human need.

In the past decade in North America, there has been a trend to open records, whereby adoption records are opened to birth parents and adult adoptees. However, it is not as though open records are entirely a new phenomenon. Sweden and Holland, for example, have never had closed adoption records. England has had open adoption records since 1976 with no ill effects. Scotland, Finland, and Israel have records open to adoptees once they reach the age of majority. New Zealand opened its records in 1985. Shortly after that, New South Wales in Australia set into motion one of the most progressive pieces of legislation on open adoption ever written about adoption records. While Australia and New Zealand led the way in adoption reform, it is important to note that they reformed the reforms by eliminating the right to "block" information. Here in Canada, British Columbia chose to fashion its new adoption act, Bill 51, on the legislation of New South Wales (Carlini 1997, 12). Along with British Columbia, the provinces and territories of Alberta, Newfoundland/Labrador, Nova Scotia, Ontario, Manitoba, Nunavut, Northwest Territories, and Yukon have opened their records. Reform groups in Canada such as Parent Finders, which was started in British Columbia by Joan Vanstone, an adult adoptee, have spearheaded the equal rights of birth parents and their children to know and be known for the past 35 years.

In November 2005, Ontario allowed adoption records to be opened to adult adoptees and their birth parents—with the passing of Bill 183, the Adoption Information Disclosure Act. This ground-breaking event was achieved in spite of the Ontario Privacy Commissioner's strong opposition to the Bill. Behind this initiative was Marilyn Churley, a Toronto MPP, often referred to as the "mother" of Bill 183. She was the champion of the "open book" position. For her, the privacy rights of both birth and adoptive parents are trumped by the rights of adopted children when they come of age. Churley herself had been pregnant "out of wedlock" at a time when there were few options to support her to raise her child, and when the culture was oppressive to women. Birth parents of her day were told that when their children turned 18, they'd be able to find their children. Churley had not asked for privacy, did not want privacy, and was not promised privacy. "Quite the opposite," she says. She reunited with her son in 1989 (Elliott 2007, 23).

Bill 183 was the work of Sandra Pupatello, the Minister of Community and Social Services and completed by Madeleine Meilleur, her successor. Ms. Pupatello truly understood the issue and despite opposition, kept working on it. Bill 183 allowed adoptees to obtain copies of their original birth records, which included their original birth names and which possibly identified their birth parents. It allowed them also to obtain copies of their adoption orders that possibly provided their names at birth, their birth registration number, and the names of their adoptive parents. The Bill allowed birth parents access to information from their child's birth records and adoption orders if the adoptee was an adult. Accompanying this, was the right by either party to place a "no contact" notice on their file.

Dr. Michael Grand, a prominent adoption researcher at Guelph University and member of the Coalition for Open Adoption Records, stated that Bill 183, the Adoption Information Disclosure Act would have a profound impact on thousands of people who had longed for years, often decades, to know their roots or the names of their children (Grand 2010).

Three adoptees and a birth father successfully challenged this law, saying it violated their right to privacy under the Charter of Rights and Freedoms because it did not contain a disclosure veto for those who did not want their identity to be released. As a result the legislation was rewritten to include a disclosure veto as well as the existing contact veto. A modified Bill 183, The Access to Adoption Records Act came into effect June 1, 2009. In an article for the *National Post* on Sept. 19, 2007, Katie Rook wrote that The Coalition for Open Adoption Records decried the decision saying, "We are sitting in the backwater of adoption disclosure."

Some individuals in government, and professionals in the adoption field, think that the birth parent's right to privacy trumps the adoptee's right to know. They are doubtless thinking of the disruption and embarrassment it can cause birth parents who keep the adoption of a baby a secret to remain forever in the past. I like how Margaret Sommerville at the McGill Centre for Medicine, Ethics and Law in Montreal, approaches this issue. In an article for the *National Post* on Sept. 25, 2007, she asks this fundamental question: "When biological parents and their children given up for adoption disagree on disclosure, whose claim should prevail?" Sommerville agrees that the privacy of children who don't want contact with their birth parents should trump adults' claims to contact them, and she argues that children's claims to know the identity of their birth parents should trump adults' claims to privacy. "It's true that adults were promised confidentiality, but, as we now recognize, that was an ethical mistake." Sommerville goes on to say that breaching adults' confidentiality is a lesser ethical wrong than intentionally depriving children who want to know their biological origins from finding them. To refuse to disclose an adopted person's identity is to be complicit in deliberately depriving them of knowledge that authorities have and they, the people most affected, do not have— knowledge that is central to their sense of self and well-being.

In the same 2007 article, Sommerville writes:

> Ethics principles such as favoring the most vulnerable person; the person who did not consent to the situation in which they find themselves; and in many cases, the person to whom the most harm will be done, when harm to one or the other person is unavoidable, all favor children's rights of access to knowledge of their biological parents.

Margaret Sommerville recommends that cases where the harms of disclosure outweigh those of non-disclosure should be dealt with as individual exceptions.

Mr. Justice Edward Belobaba, in giving reasons to support his ruling against access to adoption records, wrote that "adoption information is among the most personal areas in individuals' lives, and opening up files against their wishes could be devastating. Lives could be shattered." Sommerville counters his ruling in her 2007 *National Post* article:

Because knowing who one's biological parents are is such important personal information to most people, not opening up files at the request of adopted children can also mean lives are shattered. It's a hard call, but one that should favor children.

In *The Ottawa Citizen* on Dec. 12, 2008, Sommerville provides food for thought on the human rights of children:

> As used to be true for women, children's human rights have been largely ignored. They must move from being the 'voiceless citizens' to becoming the new kids on the human rights block, especially with respect to their human rights regarding their biological origins and biological families.
>
> Children—and their descendants—who don't know their genetic origins cannot sense themselves as embedded in a web of people, past, present and future, through whom they can trace the thread of life's passage down the generations to them and from them. We are learning now that eliminating that experience is harmful to children, biological parents, families, and society.

Advocates for the equal rights of birth parents and adoptees to know and be known to each other note that despite all the knowledge, and all the study, and all the other country experiences, closed adoptions are still the legal norm in Canada. Open adoption agreements are not protected by law.

The modified Bill 183, passed as Bill 12 through Madeleine Meilleur's efforts, has not gone far enough. Humanitarian and just procedures are necessary for those individuals trapped in closed adoptions. The struggle for full human rights for adoptive children regarding their biological origins, not to mention the full human rights of birth parents to know their children, must continue.

Why does Canada lag behind on this human rights issue? Part of the answer may lie in deeply rooted fear-based attitudes towards the truth of origin. Is it the "as if born" concept, still existing in the shadows?

Another strongly held conviction of mine relates to the naming of an adopted child. In earlier adoption days, a social worker usually recommended to the new adoptive parents that the child's name be changed, instead of keeping the first name given to the child by the birth mother. It was intended to be a way for adoptive parents to claim the child as their own, with the new name being one of significance in their own family history. And so "Katherine", the adoptee, would learn that she used to be "Elizabeth," symbolizing the split in her psyche. She used to be one person, and now she was another. This did not help an adoptee integrate her past life into her present one.

In current private adoption practice, the two sets of parents—birth and adoptive—come together before the birth, and agree upon the name for the child. In happy situations, the two sets of parents choose the same name. In other situations, the adoptive parents choose a name dear to them, and retain the name given by the birth parents as the child's second name.

Vera Fahlberg, adoption expert and past medical director of a psychiatric facility for children and adolescents, notes that it was not uncommon for children to think that one name went with being a good person and the other with being a bad person. When older children are adopted, parents should not change the child's first name. It is vital that the child be called the name she identifies as "herself." If re-naming a child is important to adoptive parents, the middle name can be changed, Fahlberg asserts in a journal article by Lois Melina (1982, 1).

I reflect now on the issue of openness in adoption. To counteract the harm that resulted from the secrecy of closed adoption, there has been a growing trend towards more and more openness. Again, this is not a completely new trend, in that there have always been custom adoptions among Inuit and Aboriginal peoples, whereby one family member would raise the child of another family member, with the full awareness of the child, the family and the community. In Michigan, open adoptions have been taking place for decades.

I am a strong proponent of open adoption, convinced through my own woundedness that was the result of living in a closed adoption and through seeing the benefits for adopted children of the open adoption experience in my work. Open adoption addresses the harmful issues of a closed adoption: guilt and shame shrouded in secrecy, fear of the unknown, the lack of information about genetic background, heritage, and personal history that prevents the full formation of identity and the capacity to lead the life one was meant to live.

Put simply, open adoption means that identifying information between the birth family and the adoptive family is shared, but more importantly a relationship between child, adoptive parents and birth family is created and continues over the years. Everyone in the circle stands to gain: the birth parents, the adoptee, and the adoptive parents. James Gritter has observed that if adoptive parents in an open adoption are genuinely filled with the vital quality of openness, they will be able to help their children to process the issues of adoption. Respect for children is always at the core of open adoption (Gritter 1997, 20).

Open adoption embodies a spirit of generosity, openness, and flexibility. When people hold on tight to what they have, when they are not open and generous with each other, when they keep secrets from each other, and when they limit contact with each other, they lose out.

Another strongly held conviction for me is the right of gay and lesbian persons to adopt. Quite simply, it results in many more children finding caring adoptive parents than would otherwise be the case.

About ten years ago, an increasing number of gay and lesbian couples who wanted to become adoptive parents, were coming through my office door. But the doors at many public adoption agencies and private adoption offices were closed to them. In those early discussions we had together, I directed couples to places where adoptions by same-sex clients were actually taking place—agencies in California and Massachusetts for example—so that they were not on a wild goose chase.

Some Children's Aid Societies in Canada had been placing with gay and lesbian clients all along, but it was a question of "don't ask, don't tell." These parents were "in the closet" and paying the big price that people pay when they cannot express who they are in an open, authentic way. If gay or lesbian applicants had applied openly, they would have been turned down. As the tide shifted toward recognition of the rights of gays and lesbians to be married, and to be parents, Children's Aid Societies began to pay lip service to accepting same-sex clients. But reasons would then be given as to why an adoption placement did not take place: there simply were no children whose needs could be met by the same-sex couple, or the agency did not have enough staff to conduct a home study at that time. To be fair, the reasons given were legitimate in some cases. But one had only to ask how many children had been placed with same-sex couples in the past year to learn that such adoptions were not happening.

Similarly in the private adoption field, some licensees were not comfortable working with same-sex couples. They would simply state that no birth parent had ever requested a same-sex couple, but, of course, none had ever been offered. And as for international adoption, the criteria of many countries—China for one—stated that homosexual applicants were not eligible to adopt from their country.

In the past ten years, the climate towards homosexual applicants has become much more moderate and receptive. Some Children's Aid Societies, notably the Ottawa Children's Aid, are leading the way in educating the public and colleagues about gay, lesbian and transgendered parenting. (For some years this agency has staffed an adoption booth at the annual Gay Pride festivities.) They are now openly placing children with same-sex couples. And some licensees are welcoming the registration of same-sex couples, offering birth parents the choice to place their child with them, and making good adoption placements. In seeking a good adoptive home for their child, more and more birth parents are requesting information about same-sex couples who want to adopt.

Sexuality is on a continuum. Some of us are at the far end of the continuum—we are heterosexuals; some of us are in the middle of the continuum with the capacity to express our sexuality either way—we are bisexuals; and some of us are at the far other end of the continuum —we are homosexuals. In the language I use, we are all God's beloved children with the capacity and right to form intimate adult relationships and to nurture and raise children. People who are homophobic fear that placing a child with a person who is gay or lesbian will unduly influence that child to become gay or lesbian. It doesn't work that way. All the psychotherapy in the world cannot make a heterosexual out of a homosexual, and vice versa. However, placing children in an adoptive same-sex home does influence the child *not* to discriminate against people with a same-sex orientation.

It is passionate concern for the voiceless client, the adopted child, that fuels my work. Couples and single applicants often come to me, after having tried through years of fertility treatment to conceive or to carry a child. They are usually discouraged, and filled with longing, anger, and despair at the injustice of being unable to have what other couples seem to achieve so effortlessly. I empathize with these couples, but the adoptive child is the one I must look out for and hold closest to my heart.

I recall a single woman who longed to be an adoptive mother. Her attitude reflected an openness and flexibility that would have stood her in good stead over years of parenting. But her partner with whom she lived was not keen to enter into this type of parenthood at all. He would involve himself to the extent that it was *her* project. I knew this was a "red flag" situation which would not work in the long term. The couple were gently screened out of the process. The woman and I then explored alternatives as to how she might have children in her life some other way such as volunteering to cuddle sick children in hospital, to lead a children's interest group in the community, or fostering the "aunt" relationship within her own family.

One married couple who shared their life story during the home study process impressed me with their sincerity, compassion, and love of nieces and nephews already in their lives. But when they were matched with a baby, something went terribly wrong. The woman's feelings of unworthiness surfaced. She was distraught and felt she could not be the baby's mother. The woman was able to pull herself together, and it was all smoothed over. The couple still wanted the baby. With profound regret, I became convinced that I had to stop the process and recommend psychotherapy to the woman. At that point in time, their opportunity to be adoptive parents could not be realized.

On short notice, another couple asked to meet with me because they had an opportunity to adopt the unborn child of a woman already known to them. They hoped that I would conduct a home study with them, starting immediately. The man was honest about his struggles with alcohol. When I asked when his last relapse had occurred, "two months ago" was not the answer I had hoped for. I had to say "no" to them as I put the unborn child's well-being first.

Concluding Thoughts

The writing of this book has enabled me to explore not only my own experience of wounding and healing, but the experiences of love, loss, and longing of others in the adoption circle. When we share our stories of love, loss, and longing we heal each other.

I have lived adoption as an adoptee who reunited with her birth family, and as a mother whose adopted child reunited with her birth family as an adult. These reunions were experiences of intense personal growth for both of us. Mine was an awakening that freed me to embrace my identity, to open my heart and mind to learn everything I could about adoption, past and present. I could not get enough, and felt compelled to write a thesis about the adoptees' experience of reunion. It became clear as crystal that I would use my new-found knowledge, both personal and intellectual, to work in the field. At age 52, I was a joyous late-bloomer, and learned, experienced colleagues showed me the way.

And so I walk as a birth parent counsellor alongside birth mothers who give their children into adoption, expressing their deep love of their children by letting them go. The emotional cost is unbearable for many. And I witness the pain that couples feel who are unable to bear children and yet long to be parents. I am deeply moved when adoptive and birth families connect with each other and find unimaginably generous ways to care for their child and each other.

I embrace such paradoxical truths in adoption as: adoption is founded on loss; the "as if born" concept is based on legalized deception; adoptees have a right and basic need to know who they are and this trumps the right to privacy of the birth parents and the adoptive parents integral to their adoptive story; those who live adoption by holding on tight to what they have stand to lose it, while those who live it in a spirit of openness and generosity stand to gain. These have become strong, personal convictions which fuel my work.

Spirit-filled words, like the anonymous poem below (Ryan 1994, 95) keep my heart in the right place. And always, what guides me most is the voiceless, vulnerable one—the adopted child who has the unassailable right to a safe, secure, nurturing home.

In soft whisperings from the heart,
The child within offers you always
The thread of your truth.

May you cherish that child, trust
That voice and weave that thread
Richly into the fabric of your days.

EPILOGUE

Chapter Twenty

Searching for Wilf

One of the joyous outcomes of writing this book is that I finally found relatives of my birth father, and in so doing, learned about who he was and the life he led. It could not have happened at an earlier stage. There was no possible way of knowing his identity until I had found my birth mother. His name was not on the Adoption Order with hers. Besides, longing to know who my birth mother was and searching for her held greater importance for me than knowing who he was. Through the years, finding him was not even on the back burner of my mind. However, I think my youthful fantasies about him impacted how I related to young men. I was often attracted to charming, handsome guys who, from the perspective of hindsight, would have been poor choices as life mates. Fantasies, both positive and negative, play a big part in the life of an adoptee before as well as after reunion.

Adoption literature calls the quest for the birth father the Mini-Search. The search for birth mother is of far greater significance because the separation from her is the basis of the adoption trauma. It is through finding her that the wound from the trauma can be healed. The adoptee does not usually embark on the Mini-Search until she has absorbed the reunion with her birth mother. Usually she has expended so much energy on this first quest, that she does not have the psychic energy to pursue the birth father too quickly. She is ready to take on the birth father only when she realizes that to be whole she needs the *whole* family tree (Lifton 1988,152-53).

Around 1954 an adoption social worker for the Manitoba government prepared a non-identifying social history for me. It described two possible birth fathers: One was a Scottish Canadian in his late 20s, dark in coloring, who liked to read and was the leader of a small orchestra. The other was an English Canadian in his early 30s, who had been in the Armed Forces, and who had a weak heart. The first one sounded more appealing, so I "chose" him as my birth father.

More than thirty years later in the early stages of my reunion with my birth mom, Vera set my mind at rest as to which man was my birth father when she said, "The minute I saw you I knew who your father was." It was the man of English origin who had a weak heart. His name was Wilf Noble. This is Vera's story: "I answered the door of my rooming house in downtown Winnipeg one day in 1935 to a handsome, door-to-door salesman. He was selling Watkins or Rawleigh products, I don't remember which. That was how housewives bought items like vanilla and brushes in those days." Vera probably didn't buy any of his products, but no doubt Wilf was attracted to the dark, sensuous young woman. When I asked what he looked like, she said, "He had flashing eyes and was dark and handsome. He looked like the gangster actor, George Raft."

Wilf lived in a rooming house just a few streets away. He invited Vera to dance at the Rainbow Ballroom, and before long they became intimate. He was Vera's first sexual partner and an exciting one. Neither she nor Wilf took precautions against getting pregnant. When did she learn that Wilf was separated from his wife and had two little children? Maybe it wasn't until she told him she was pregnant. Vera did not stay in touch with Wilf during her pregnancy. Instead, she turned to an older woman friend who knew how to deal with such things as pregnancy out-of-wedlock.

After I was born, Wilf came to the hospital nursery to see me. Somehow that means a great deal to me. Yet Vera and Wilf's relationship was over. I know nothing about what they said to each other. I was so grateful that Vera told me as much as she did, that it didn't occur to me to ask for more. Much later in my adoption practice, I learned that many birth mothers are unwilling to speak of the birth father at all due to unresolved pain and anger. Vera seemed to feel no bitterness towards Wilf. Trailing off, she said, "He was a nice man."

There are some striking parallels between the lives of George Wilfred Noble and George Raft. I think Raft might have been Wilf's role model.

George Raft was an American film actor and dancer who portrayed gangsters in crime melodramas in the 1930s and 1940s. One of the three most popular gangster actors of the 1930s along with James Cagney and Edward G. Robinson, he ranked far above Humphrey Bogart in fame and box-office clout throughout the decade. Raft was a stylish leading man who showed a talent for dancing which, with his elegant fashion sense, enabled him to work as a dancer in New York City nightclubs and in London as a chorus boy. He danced in two movies. Fred Estaire described Raft as a lightning-fast dancer "who did the fastest Charleston I ever saw." Wilf loved to dance and won dance contests, especially for his Charleston at the Roseland.

Indeed, Wilf Noble looked a lot like George Raft. Both were well turned out. They had brown eyes, dark complexion and shiny dark hair parted in the middle and slicked down with Brylcreem. A romantic figure in Hollywood and separated from his wife, George Raft was a ladies' man who had affairs with Betty Grable, Marlene Dietrich, and Mae West, to name three. Wilf was too fond of women to remain faithful to his wife who eventually divorced him. He did marry a second time but had many liaisons during and between his two marriages. Vera was one of them. It seems the only parallel path that Wilf did not follow was Raft's association with gangsters of the underworld, such as Bugsy Siegel and Meyer Lansky.

As my reunion with Vera unfolded, I took steps to find Wilf. At the National Archives of Canada in Ottawa, I found addresses for Wilf on Roseberry, Sherbrook, Sargent and Maryland streets in downtown Winnipeg from 1929 to 1945 in the Henderson Directories. I also learned that he had worked for The T. Eaton Co. Ltd, had been a door-to-door salesman for Rawleigh's (this is how he met Vera), a clerk, an elevator operator and a machinist. There were no more entries after 1945. Had he died after that? I wrote to the Winnipeg Free Press and sadly, they sent me a photocopy of his obituary:

> George Wilfred Noble died on November 10, 1947 at Grace Hospital, Winnipeg, late at 350 Maryland, age 42 years. Funeral at the A.B. Gardner Funeral Home, 178 Kennedy St., Interment in Brookside Cemetery.

Why did he die so young? Vera had told me he had a weak heart—the non-identifying history I'd received years before confirmed it. He died when I was only eleven years old. Although I wished I could have met him, somehow it was not the blow it would have been if Vera had died before I could meet and know her.

I set about to find out more about Wilf by writing to the National Personnel Records Office in Ottawa. I learned that Wilf had not served in the Canadian Armed Forces, although he may have been in the Reserve Force. I so wanted to find members of his family, especially his children who would be my siblings. I placed this ad in the Winnipeg Free Press:

> Searching for relatives of George Wilfred Noble, born around 1905, died in 1947, an employee of The T. Eaton Company and in the Army Reserve. Please call Carol collect at 1 613 233 3028.

I received one phone call from a man who claimed to have known Wilf when he worked with him in Eaton's Winnipeg store. There was very little he could tell me, certainly not anything about Wilf's family. I tracked down the funeral home which had been taken over by another funeral home to learn that Wilf had died of a cerebral embolism and that the person who arranged Wilf's funeral was Robert Noble, of Suite 6, Cane Apartments on Assiniboine Avenue in Winnipeg. His father or his brother? This last detail could have led me directly to Wilf's family, but there was no Robert Noble listed on Assiniboine Avenue in the Winnipeg phone book. A dead end.

I decided to write to all the Nobles listed in the Winnipeg phone book, 35 in total, enclosing a self-addressed stamped envelope, and asking if they were related to Wilf. It's amazing that 14 Nobles took the trouble to reply but none was related to Wilf. Another dead end. So in 1989 I put my search for Wilf's relatives on the back burner.

Publishing this book was the spark that reignited my search for Wilf. Just before my book launch in Winnipeg in the fall of 2013, I was interviewed on CBC Radio in that city where I appealed to listeners who might know of a man named Wilf Noble or any of his relatives. Although nothing came from this direct appeal, two people in my life volunteered to help me search: Kathy Stokes, a high school friend, and Will Urban, my son's father-in-law. I was thrilled to receive the help of these skilled genealogists familiar with Ancestry.com. All through the fall of 2013, they sent me documents over the internet—a 1905 Leeds (England) baptismal record listing George Wilfred Noble; a 1916 Manitoba census document listing members of Wilf's family of origin; a June 1, 1926 marriage certificate for Wilfred George Noble and Ethel Adelaide McCaw; and divorce papers for them, dated September 19, 1936. The divorce papers named Wilf and Ethel's two daughters, Doreen age 9, and Joyce age 6, who lived with their mother, and stated that Wilf had committed adultery with an unnamed woman during the year 1936 (this was probably not Vera—her relationship with Wilf ended in 1935.) How exciting to know that I had two sisters!

Genealogists know that the document you're hoping to find is the one that contains a relative's identifying information which can lead you to a live person. They call it "striking gold." My daughter-in-law, Ruth Urban, was becoming interested in her father Will's efforts on my behalf. One of the documents posted on Ancestry.com was an obituary for Joyce Dunn (Beattie) whose first name, birth and death dates matched my half-sister's. She had retired to the hamlet of Yahk, BC, and died only six years earlier. The names of her five children and their partners were listed! These would be my four nieces and a nephew. I plugged the names into Canada 411 and searched for addresses and phone numbers. It was easy— one of the nieces and her husband, Marcy and Brian Eddy, lived in Yahk, BC where Joyce Dunn had lived. Marcy was the daughter of Joyce, my half-sister. I had struck gold! I had to gather my courage and nerve to make the cold phone call. That took a few days.

I made a couple of attempts to phone and got an answering machine message. I decided to wait until a person answered. When a man answered, my call went something like this:

Me: Hello. Are you Brian Eddy? I'm not trying to sell you anything. I'm searching for family members and I have reason to think that I'm related to a lady named Joyce Dunn who died in 2007 in Cranbrook. Did you know her?

Brian: Yes, she was my mother-in-law. I'll put my wife on the phone.

Marcy came to the phone. She was quick to say that she did not think I could be her aunt. The only aunt (Doreen) she had on her mother's side had died some years ago. This was delicate. I said, "Your mom's father, Wilf Noble, had a brief relationship with my birth mother in Winnipeg. I was the product of that relationship and was placed for adoption in 1936. There was a brief pause. Then she exclaimed, "Oh, the little devil!" The tension abated. Marcy spoke of her grandfather Wilf's reputation. "He cheated on my grandmother and broke her heart. My grandmother Ethel divorced him and moved to Vancouver with Aunt Dee (Doreen) and my mother (Joyce). Grandpa was a charming, attractive man, with dark hair and skin, brown eyes, about 5 feet 5 inches in height. He and Grandma loved to dance and won Charleston contests. He was a "player" (womanizer) and a rogue."

Wilf's parents, Robert and Louisa Noble, were born and raised in and around Leeds in the county of Yorkshire in England. He had a younger sister named Marjorie. Robert journeyed by boat to Canada, settling in Winnipeg in 1913. He was joined by Louisa and the two children, Wilf and Marjorie, one year later.

Marcy told me that when Wilf was a child, he came down with Saint Vitus Dance. It is in reference to Saint Vitus, a Christian saint who was persecuted by Roman emperors and died as a martyr in AD 303. Saint Vitus is considered to be the patron saint of dancers, with the eponym given as homage to the manic dancing that historically took place in front of his statue during the feast of Saint Vitus in Germanic and Latvian cultures. Its correct name, Sydenham's Chorea (chorea means "dance" in Greek) is a disorder characterized by rapid, uncoordinated jerking movements primarily affecting the face, hands and feet. It results from childhood infection with a streptococcus bacteria. It is a major manifestation of rheumatic fever, a disease which results from inflammation in the heart, joints, skin or central nervous system. As a result, Wilf was left with a weak heart. He drank and smoked. Family lore has it that his doctor advised him to give up wine, women and song. Wilf's response was, "If I have to do that, life isn't worth living."

A few years after he was divorced from Ethel, Wilf married Edythe who had heart problems like he did. He and Edythe had a daughter named Gladys one year later. And the year after that, Edythe died of heart failure. Tragic. It seems that Wilf did not parent Gladys after Edythe's death. The parenting role was handed on to his sister, Marjorie who was single and had little aptitude for raising a child. Marcy describes her great-aunt Marjorie as loud and outspoken. She smoked and drank too much and liked to party. Little Gladys had a hard time of it. I wonder if anyone really cherished her. She married a man named Al with whom she had children. Life was rough for Gladys especially when Al served time for armed robbery.

Wilf's two families, one in Calgary and the other in Winnipeg, had little contact over the years. For one thing, they lived miles apart. Marcy remembers one time when Gladys came to see her half-sisters, Doreen and Joyce, in Calgary. When Gladys died her sisters were not informed. The tenuous tie had been broken.

Marcy was sorry that her mother had died before I came into the picture. I was, too, and sad to hear that Joyce's first husband mistreated her. I also felt admiration for this sister of mine who separated from him, and drove her children across the country to raise them on her own. Joyce retired from office work in a big Calgary firm to Yahk, BC where she enjoyed the company of her four-legged friends. Sadly, she lost too many people who were dear to her, and her will to live was lost, too. She died at the age of 77. Her daughters miss her still. It was pleasing to learn that Joyce had been left-handed as I am. No one in my birth mother's family was known to be left-handed.

Joyce and Marcy, 1951

Marcy and I stayed on the phone as she briefly outlined the lives of her sisters, her brother and herself. She is the eldest of Joyce's five children. Her first husband who happened to be an adoptee died in his fifties. Marcy fell in love all over again with Brian who had been her high school sweetheart, and they were married in 2009. Then Marcy shared an experience that took my breath away. She and I had led parallel lives. When she was 18, she gave a child into adoption. Several years ago, she and her sister Cindy registered on the Canadian Adoptees Registry Inc. website to indicate their interest in connecting with Marcy's birth child. Time went on and in 2008, Marcy received word from the Registry that a young woman who was probably her daughter had just registered. Marcy was stunned to learn that her daughter lived just a few miles away and that she, Marcy, was a grandmother! Birth mother and daughter did not meet immediately. Then one day a young woman approached Marcy in a restaurant and said, "I think it's time we met face-to-face. I am your daughter." She had recognized Marcy from photos on Facebook. The two women became Facebook friends. Then it went deeper. Marcy learned that her birth granddaughter had cancer. She and her sister Cindy met with Marcy's birth daughter to offer and give financial support to the family. Things are unfolding in a loving way.

JoAnne (Jo) is next eldest. She lives in Fort St. John where she works for an oil company. She welcomed me warmly by e-mail as her new aunt on the scene. JoAnne had a storage box of old photos in a back shed. Rooting through the box on a cold winter's day in northern Alberta, she found photos of my birth father, his sister and his three daughters and sent them to me. At last! After 78 years, I could see what my teenage birth father looked like. He *did* resemble a young George Raft. Jo has been married and has two daughters and four grandchildren. Her first husband was an adoptee. Although his adoptive parents were loving and devoted to their four adopted children, Jo said the children all seemed to be emotionally scarred in some way. Her husband, from whom she was divorced, tragically drank himself to death at the age of 56. Another adoption connection.

Mike, the middle child, has lived in Hong Kong for some years. He is divorced and has a daughter who lives in Calgary. He keeps in touch on Facebook with his sisters and hopes to return to live in Canada. He was understandably surprised to hear about me and asked, "How many more are there??" An amusing comment but beneath my spontaneous chuckle, the comment stung. It felt as though I was laughing *at* my birth father.

Next in line is Karen who has been married to Richard Corley for 30 years. They live in Airdrie, Alberta, and have a son and a daughter.

The "baby" of the family is Cindy whose significant other is Tim. Cindy loves animals and keeps a kind of informal shelter for stray dogs. She even raised pygmy goats a few years ago. If you drove through Yahk, you would see her goats on the grassy roof of the Yahk Soap Company. Cindy has two daughters and a son and a little granddaughter named Summer Lilly. Cindy's former husband is an adoptee as well.

The lives of Marcy, JoAnne and Cindy have all been touched by adoption. That connected me to them.

As Marcy and I talked on the phone, Ken was smiling in the background, timing our conversation which lasted 90 minutes. It ended with a wish that we would meet before too long. After so many years, I was quite simply thrilled with my "find". I spread the word about their new cousins to our children who were very interested. Will, one of my volunteer genealogists, started compiling a family tree.

Then it occurred to me that this "find" had come about through the interview I'd had with CBC Radio Winnipeg just after this book was published. I contacted the producer of the show, and she arranged an interview with Marcy and me that aired just before Christmas, 2013. Excerpts of the interview went something like this:

Me: It would have been wonderful to have been able to meet my sister, Marcy's mother. It's sad really that she died before we got that chance [choking up].
Marcy: Now let's not get too emotional here.
Interviewer: You two sound like "family!"

Interviewer: Do you think you will meet each other?
Me: Yes, my husband and some of my children hope to visit Marcy and the others in Yahk this summer.
Interviewer: What do you think you will do when you meet Carol, Marcy?
Marcy: I'll give her a hug and I'll hug anyone else that she brings with her.

What a lovely welcoming remark! My enthusiasm to meet Marcy and her sisters was building. When close family members and friends heard about my "find," they gave me unqualified support, musing on how this reunion would compare with the reunion I'd had with my birth mother and her family. One somewhat negative comment did not deter me: "Isn't that going a bit too far?"

Ken and I began to plan a trip to Yahk, BC in the summer of 2014. Our son Kevin and daughter Elaine had responsibilities—Kevin to his family, and Elaine to her Native community. They were unable to consider a trip to meet their cousins. However, Ken, Dave, Jill and I were keen to go. We flew from Ottawa to Calgary, rented a car and drove to Marcy and Brian's home in Yahk. It is a big house on the Moyie River with enough beds for us all. We were thrilled that all of my four nieces planned to be there. I knew this reunion would be different in so many ways from my 1988 Winnipeg reunion with Vera, my birth brother Wayne and his family. In Winnipeg I was one person meeting five birth family members for a total of six individuals. This time I was joined by my husband and two adult children who would meet seven birth family members for a total of eleven individuals.

The first reunion was unparalleled in its intensity. I remember having an insatiable craving for information, fearing that if I didn't get the whole story immediately, the door would close and the opportunity would be lost. The literature refers to the experience as "reunion day burnout." I did not expect the same intensity in this Yahk reunion because I was two steps removed from my new relatives: I was not meeting my birth father, nor my birth sister—I was meeting my nieces. Whereas I felt compelled to meet my birth mother alone with no one accompanying me, this time it seemed right that family was meeting family. I was much older for this reunion and knew I would appreciate having my husband at my side. My children and my nieces were close in age and I hoped they would find things in common.

Dave's GPS got us unerringly to Marcy and Brian's house on the outskirts of Yahk. Turning off the highway, we found ourselves on a long narrow trail with bush on one side and a railway track on the other. At the end of the trail was a big, neat three-storey house with gazebo, deck, and water fountain on the property. Ceramic gnomes and frogs peeked out amongst the flowers. Two big dogs barked at us through the window from inside the house. No one answered the doorbell or our knock, so we each pulled out our cell phones. No luck. It was a non-service area. We must have looked silly—four individuals walking around a big, fancy black car, each trying to talk on their cell phones. Then Brian appeared at a window to say that the "girls" had gone to town to shop and he'd be down in a moment. He invited us to sit in the gazebo while five little dogs, wagging their tails, scuttled around our chairs and feet.

Some time later, a van pulled up and four women with grocery bags got out and went into the house. It took a while before anyone came out to say hello. It was not until Brian motioned to Marcy who was in the window that my four nieces, along with the two big dogs—part mastiff and part boxer—joined us. It was a melée—everyone hugging everyone, all talking at once, with five little dogs and two big ones in the midst of us all.

It was not until much later that we learned that Brian was pretty ill with colitis when we arrived, and that my nieces, especially Marcy who was hosting us, had probably felt pretty nervous to meet the four of us (after all, what if they couldn't stand us?). An odd-looking contraption near the gazebo caught our attention. What was it?

Eventually, we took our bags into the house and were shown up some steep stairs with a doggie gate at the bottom. Dave and Jill had a pull-out bed and mattress in an open area, and Ken and I had a bedroom with shared bathroom. In our bedroom there were photos of a very pretty young woman. It was my sister, Joyce, when she was young. Not only that, there was an urn on the chest of drawers with Joyce's ashes in it. It was a sad reminder that she had died before I could meet and know her. Ken thought it was symbolic of the way we were being welcomed into the intimate life of the family. Very moving. The family planned to scatter her ashes at some later stage when Mike could return from Hong Kong.

There is a unique fatigue that comes with adoption reunion which I had experienced many years before in Winnipeg. Reunions are disorienting events. There is no book on reunion etiquette to which you can refer. This time there were so many actors in the play, so much detail and information to absorb and retain. How could I relate to four new nieces at the same time? It was so much more than a social event. We were all trying to connect with family members we'd never met before in a meaningful way. We were checking each other out to see what we had in common, to see if our life values meshed or clashed. It was overwhelming.

I rested on the bed and in no time at all, we were called down for a delicious buffet dinner. Dave and Jill were connecting well with my nieces and Brian. I was quiet, feeling my way into the new role. Karen invited me to look through a photo album created for their mother before she died. We enjoyed some nice moments as she shared the photos with me. She asked if I was tired, and kindly suggested that I could go to bed anytime I wanted. I appreciated her warmth.

Seven dogs and two cats, all obviously well taken care of, friendly, and loved—that speaks well of their people, we thought. The morning dawned bright and clear. A bacon-and-egg breakfast appeared effortlessly on the table, with plenty of good coffee to drink. After breakfast, Jill and Ken tried out a few songs with Brian's guitar. We hardly noticed when Brian slipped away to town. He came back to say that he'd arranged for Dave, Jill and Ken to be the opening act on the open air stage at the Yahk Summer Festival which began that afternoon. The three of them then did some fancy scrambling to decide what songs they could sing. They'd never been an opening act before! Brian was smart to check them out before setting them up to sing at the festival.

The festival kicked off with a parade at noon. First down the road was a kid on a unicycle; then Kootenay Mike, a country singer in the back of a pickup truck; two fire trucks; a couple of cars, a few people walking, and kids riding bikes. Marcy explained that they always had a little trouble getting people to participate. Ken responded with "This is the best parade I've ever watched because I hate long parades." Jill ran off to check out the outdoor band shell for sound. It had a beautiful overhead wooden arch with an elk, moose, and bear carved into it by a local artisan. The ambiance was easy-going and welcoming. We knew we were going to have a great time.

Dave and Jill at Yahk Summer Festival, 2014

On stage, Jill introduced the family, telling the crowd how happy we were to be there. She began with "This Little Light of Mine," adding a verse, "All around Yahk town, yeah, I'm gonna let it shine." This was followed with "One More Dance," an amusing duet by Jill and Ken. Then Ken sang "The Red Corvette" with a funny twist ending. Dave and Jill sang Joni Mitchell's iconic "Both Sides Now." Jill did a swinging solo number "Daisy-A-Day" and ended with her scat version of "Dancing In The Moonlight." Her cherished memory of the event was singing out to the mountains of Yahk. We could tell that our new family liked what they were hearing.

We enjoyed the main feature band "Gone Country," especially Ted who played great guitar with badly arthritic hands and sang like the pro that he was. Our two families did some fancy dancing on a cement pad in front of the bandstand as the band played on. A delicious supper in the church hall was served like clockwork. The evening entertainment was enjoyed by all.

Back at Brian and Marcy's we reviewed the day. Our first family memories were in the making as we sat together in their cozy living room, giggling at photos taken of nieces Jo and Karen and a gentleman with a huge gut in the background. He was the only person in focus! Hanging out with our new family at their summer festival had been a wonderfully relaxing way to get to know each other.

Impressions of our new family were whirling around inside us all—Marcy's warmth and hospitality; Dave was especially delighted to see the fun Marcy and Brian had together; Jill really connected with Jo who is attractive, friendly and full of vitality—a bit vulnerable yet hopeful for the future; Karen, sensitive to how I was experiencing the weekend as she shared photos and comments to help me begin to know the family, and her neat husband, Rick; and Cindy, who loves to laugh and live with Tim and care for animals and dance (as I do.) They were all sad that their mother, my sister, was not there. I was, too.

Ken and I slept well that night.

Next morning Brian made a fabulous pancake breakfast. When I requested that we have a photo shoot on our last morning, they took that as an command performance! Even Tim who seemed shy and Richard who wanted to head back to Airdrie asap agreed to stay for it. We headed down to a lovely spot on the River Moyie at the end of their property. Lots of kidding around made it such fun. Before leaving Ken and I had a great chat with Tim. He was born and grew up until he was four in Belleville, where both my adoptive parents had been raised. Another coincidence. His father, an evangelical preacher, moved his family to Fort McMurray. His father attended to God all his life, but not so much to his children. When they grew up, Tim and his siblings rebelled against church. Tim is a trucker and likes living in Yahk. His father has apologized to his kids for neglecting them, and Tim bears no grudge. He has bought his father a house in Yahk and takes him hunting every fall even though Tim himself is not that keen about hunting.

Back Row: Dave   Ken   Richard   Jill   Marcy
Front Row: Cindy   Carol   JoAnne   Karen

It was a wonderful reunion—music and laughter and a bunch of family members just being themselves. We finally got around to asking what the contraption was near the gazebo. It was a gas-powered margarita mixer which Brian demonstrated to roars of laughter. The note we ended on was that we would see each other again. The reunion was a beginning not an ending.

Brian and Gasoline-Powered Margarita Mixer

There are no established models for post-reunion relationships. We will create our own definitions of who we are in relation to one another. The roles in this reunion may be simpler than in many other reunions: I am their long-lost aunt—will I fill a gap in my nieces' lives in that their mother and aunt have died? My husband is their uncle by marriage, and my children are their cousins.

Adoptee Michelle McColm's insight into reunion explains it beautifully: "Wanting to meet increasing numbers of birth family members even though the original and ultimate goal was to meet her birth mother is evidence of the adoptee's primal need to solidify her identity" (McColm 1993, 162).

My family is now four-fold: birth father's family, birth mother's family, adoptive family, and family with Ken. Jill asks, "Well, Mom, what are you going to do now? Go up and down your street, checking out who else would like to join the family?" I think not. It feels complete.

Wilf, about 15 years old

Chapter Twenty-One

A Letter to My Birth Father

Each of us is more than the worst thing we have ever done.
—Bryan Stevenson

Hello Wilf,

We never had a chance to meet, did we? I was only eleven years old and living in Fort Whyte, five long miles in those days from Winnipeg when you died of a massive cerebral embolism at age 42 in a rooming house in the centre of the city. I knew nothing about you then. I wasn't even trying to imagine who you were. I'd think sometimes about my birth mother, but I had little information about her to build upon except that she was young, unmarried, and couldn't keep me.

This letter to you is based on family lore told to me by your granddaughters (my nieces) Marcy, JoAnn, Karen, and Cindy, which was passed on to them by your daughter Joyce (their mother and my sister) and your first wife, Ethel (their grandmother). I also built upon my birth mother Vera's memories of you, as well as census, marriage, divorce and death papers sent to me over the Internet. Stories and memories take on lives on their own. Truth is elusive. What were you like as a child, a man, a husband, a father?

I will call upon my intuition to guide me. As a social worker, I found I could often discern the truth behind a client's words or silences. However, because we never met, I can't discern directly who you were, who I am in relation to you, what I meant to you or why you weren't there for me and my birth mother. As a young adult adoptee reading into a non-identifying social history, I would have a hunch about something phrased too delicately as I read between the lines. And that hunch would often be "spot-on" when, years later, it was confirmed by a birth family member. So I'm going to go with my hunches and my intuition, Wilf, and the rest stays in the realm of fantasy as I try to imagine who you were.

It's too easy to stereotype you, Wilf, as a "deadbeat" dad, derelict in your responsibilities. Birth parents in the 30s and 40s were judged harshly for their irresponsible, immoral behaviour. Birth mothers bore the brunt of this condemnation because they could not escape bearing their babies. Shame, guilt and sadness followed them as their constant companions. Birth fathers, if they knew of the pregnancy, could protect themselves from the scathing criticism by denying they were the father, by trying to persuade the birth mother to abort the baby with all the attendant dangers of an illegal abortion, or by disappearing out of guilt and shame. This was stereotyped as cowardly behaviour, as deserting the birth mother at a time when she needed his support.

Vera didn't turn to you for support during her pregnancy. Did she even tell you she was pregnant? News of the birth of a baby girl may have reached you indirectly. Like so many birth fathers, you weren't able to provide for your child or the mother of your child, but you didn't disappear from Vera's life immediately. You already had a wife and two little girls from whom you were separated. Like so many birth fathers, you probably didn't know what to do. It must have been overwhelming. But you came to the hospital. and that's a treasure that I carry with me. You were probably not allowed to hold me, but you might have looked through the nursery window while a nurse held me up. You would have noticed that I was a cute baby. Maybe on that hospital visit you confessed to Vera that you were married. How much did you care for Vera, Wilf? She never said a bad word about you. Both of you moved on to new relationships. Vera was broken by giving away her baby.

It is often thought that a young father glories in a pregnancy and a newborn as proof of his machismo. I don't think you did that, Wilf. Instead of allowing yourself to experience feelings of fear, anger, and sadness, you buried those feelings. Dissociation can be a useful coping mechanism in a time of crisis. You already knew how to have a good time. Drinking and dancing the nights away in the Roseland ballroom may have become addictions just as your success at charming women into bed became an addiction. Compulsive sex was a way of trying to forget. Deep inside yourself, were you ashamed?

Maybe you were searching for a kind of divine union with the perfect sexual partner. Or was each sexual encounter merely a temporary boost to your shaky ego as you made another check on your scorecard? I will never know the mysteries that lay buried in your heart, will I?

In her inspiring book *Forgiveness and Other Acts of Love,* Stephanie Dowrick explores the virtue of fidelity. "When sex is taken seriously it leads us into playfulness and laughter, as well as into commitment and intensity. Loveless sex is rarely worth ruffling the sheets for." She quotes Matthew Fox, "There's a stallion of lust inside all of us. There's a stallion of anger inside all of us. Our passions are holy. We can't go any place important without them but we need to bridle them. We need to steer them. If you can't steer them, then they're going to ruin your life." Dowrick asks the question: is there fear where there is infidelity—fear of boredom, fear of intimacy, fear of commitment or truth, fear of being alone, fear of no longer being desired, fear of growing old, fear of being forgotten?

Until recent times, birth fathers were not invited to participate in an adoption. Even today, the birth father is the least represented, least considered, and least heard in adoption. It's the birth mother who tends to get the counselling, and the men are left on their own to deal with the situation. Books about adoption seldom make a single reference to the birth father, a notable exception being a word of advice to adoptive parents about how to ensure that he doesn't interfere with an adoption. The birth father is the most feared and least trusted person inside and outside of an adoption (Martin 1995).

In the past, even if they were invited to be involved in an adoption, birth fathers were reluctant to do so because they were unsure of their role. They did not expect to be treated respectfully and with understanding—quite the opposite. They were often frightened and overwhelmed at the prospect of becoming a father.

However, in the last decade of my adoption practice, there was a growing awareness of the importance of a birth father's participation in an adoption. His participation could potentially benefit everyone in the adoption circle. It could break down the negative stereotype of himself as birth father; it could provide support to the birth mother as he and she went through the loss together, and most significant of all, it could benefit the child by sharing his invaluable history and willingness to participate in the adoption planning. I counselled more and more birth fathers, and found that when they were invited to become involved in the adoption plan, they dropped what was often a belligerent, hostile defense which masked their fear and vulnerability and became cooperative and caring. I learned that they needed support just as the birth mothers did.

The birth fathers I came to know taught me a lot about how they felt about their babies.

Craig, age 20, was happy but a bit bewildered to be in an open adoption. He admitted to having attention deficit hyperactivity disorder and a problem controlling his anger. Craig wrote a letter to his newborn daughter in which he expressed his tender, wistful feelings for her: "When I saw you for the first time in the hospital with your mother, I was very happy. You were so cute and you looked just like your daddy (me!) When I met your adoptive parents, I was kind of sad because I wished it was possible for me to keep you and raise you. But I was happy because they are nice people and they agreed that I can visit you often. I hope you never forget me." Craig's sensitivity to the birth mother shone through when he said, "Since the birth of the baby, I feel [her] pain more than I could before. It's in her voice."

Sandy, age 30, was a musician who had anger and addiction issues. He felt bitter until he became involved in the adoption plan and knew he could meet his child. He told me that this adoption was the most important event in his life. He wrote poignantly to his child, "Fate and life didn't deal a set of cards that would allow you to grow up with me." He found the experience complicated and painful.

Joe, age 28, had many strikes against him. He was abused by his mother throughout his childhood resulting in mental health problems. Joe became addicted to alcohol and drugs. He was a drug dealer and had a police record. His relationships with women always turned violent, His girlfriend was pregnant and planned to place her unborn baby for adoption. As soon as he felt included in the adoption process, Joe dropped his belligerent stance with me. He said, "I want to be able to see my child, for him to know that I did not leave and forget him. My father left my mother and me when I was five years old. I never want to do that to a child of mine." However, Joe was a loose cannon, threatening mayhem if he was not allowed to see his child. It was almost impossible for him to trust anyone so he couldn't believe that the adoptive parents would let him have visits with his child. "It will seriously damage me if I don't get to see my kid," he said. A DNA test showed that Joe was not the biological father of his girlfriend's child. Joe had developed feelings for the child, and it was a big loss for him.

Eric, age 19, was a bright, imaginative high school student with a quirky sense of humour. He sported a nose ring, a lip nail and an arm band fashioned from a coat hanger. His hair was a different iridescent color each time I saw him. Although he and the birth mother had decided to break up prior to knowing about her pregnancy, Eric made a commitment to accompany her to appointments with her doctor, lawyer and social worker. He said, "I am doing everything in my power to help her through her pregnancy." He and the birth mother remained a couple in order to plan for the baby's future. For Eric, the decision to place the baby for adoption was one of the most difficult decisions he'd ever made. He wrote to his child, "We are still kids. I don't think we have the wisdom or life experience needed to raise you. It might sound selfish to you and it sometimes does to me, but I can tell you honestly from the bottom of my heart, that I believe our decision was the best thing we could have possibly done for you." It was heart-wrenching for Eric to carry through with the adoption.

In Mary Martin Mason's book *Out of The Shadows: Birth Fathers' Stories,* a birth father is asked: What parts of yourself were altered by becoming a birth father? He replies, "Try every part. You can't be unaffected by something like this."

Wilf, if you and I were able to sit down and have a glass of wine together, I'd want to ask you about your childhood. You came to Canada from Yorkshire with your mother and little sister when you were ten years old. Your father had come the year before to find a job and housing, I suppose. Was it fun travelling on a big boat, or were you expected to be the little man of the family? Did you keep your Yorkshire accent into adulthood? If so, that must have been part of your charm. The photo taken when you were around sixteen is of a handsome young man with dark skin, expressive brown eyes and dark brown hair close to a shapely head. You don't look much like a young man from Yorkshire. Were you part Roma? There was a significant community of Roma who settled in Leeds in the north of England where you were born. Roma (the more derogatory term is "gypsies") originated in India 700 years ago and have been politically, socially, culturally and economically marginalized by the dominant European population. Did you experience discrimination in the UK and in Canada? Did people ask you if you were part-gypsy just as they asked me if I was part-Indian? When there is covert racism in the question, it doesn't feel good. Did such experiences impact your self-esteem?

If you travelled across Canada by train in the middle of winter to Winnipeg, the Canadian winter would have been a shock. Your family was reunited in Winnipeg, but soon after, your father joined the Canadian army. It was likely a way to earn a good wage. But that meant that your mother was on her own, looking after her two children in a new land. Was that lonely and overwhelming for her? Were your parents strict Baptists? I hope you and your sister weren't strapped when you misbehaved. It was all too common to use physical discipline in the days you were growing up. Did you get lots of hugs? Were your parents proud of you and full of affection, or were you left to fend for yourself as you grew up? I fear it was the latter.

When you were a small boy, you came down with Saint Vitus Dance caused by a streptococcus bacterium. This would have caused you to have jerky, uncoordinated movements, hence the disorder's name. If the onset happened at school, it would have been scary for you. You probably had a high fever and missed quite a bit of school until your symptoms went away. Did the kids tease you when you returned to school? From then on you had a weak heart and were probably advised to take it easy. But you didn't do that, did you? I can't help but connect the fact that you had Saint Vitus Dance when you were a child with how you became a champion Charleston dancer as a young man. You turned something negative into something positive.

I suspect that you were a smart man, Wilf, but you were not able to reach your potential intellectually. You were charming and handsome and I think you capitalized on these traits to make your way in the world. I love the fact that you were a fantastic dancer—you could have taught me some great steps. There was a striking resemblance between you and the gangster actor, George Raft. Was he your role model? He could do the Charleston so well that the likes of Fred Estaire took notice. He was also on the shady side of society, hobnobbing with the mafia, but I don't think you went that far in emulating him.

There is a terrible story about you that was passed on to some of your grandchildren. You were in bed with another man's wife, when he burst in on the two of you. Pulling a knife, he moved to stab you. You shielded yourself and his knife severed the tendons of your left hand. I think you were left-handed like me. Blood everywhere. You didn't have full use of that hand after that. This incident must have shattered and reduced you. One of your last jobs was that of elevator operator, maybe at Eaton's department store where the accordion metal doors could be opened and closed with one hand. You would have been able to do that job reasonably well. As I contemplate this awful experience of yours, I'm holding a truth close in my heart: each of us is more than the worst thing we have ever done (Stevenson 2014).

But about your hand...there is a hand deformity called Dupuytrens contracture in which there is a fixed forward curvature of one or more fingers caused by the development of a fibrous connection between the finger tendons and the skin of the palm. Higher rates of this condition are found in people with previous hand trauma. When I was about 30 years of age, I severed the nerves in the ring finger of my left hand when I picked up a heavy glass milk bottle that slipped and broke. Many years later, I developed this condition. Did this hand deformity happen for you following the knife incident? It could have, but I will never know.

You loved being with a woman, but I don't know if you ever wanted to be a father. Your first wife, Ethel was deeply in love with you. When she learned that you were about to marry another woman, she was heart-broken and moved from Winnipeg to Vancouver with your two little girls. Women liked you, Wilf. Your second wife, Edythe, had serious heart problems like you did. Perhaps you even met in the doctor's office. One year after marrying her, your daughter Gladys, was born. And the year after that, Edythe died. Life must have been tough. You were pretty ill yourself by then and probably very low in spirits. Your wife had just died, you were not well, and you had an infant daughter to look after. Did you try to raise Gladys yourself for awhile?

You spent your last few years living lonely on Maryland Street. Your charm had run out and your health problems were mounting. Meanwhile, I, your little girl, was living in a small village just outside Winnipeg with my adoptive family. In 1947 you died suddenly from a cerebral embolism. Your father Robert arranged your funeral. My guess is that your mom had died before you did. Your youngest daughter, Gladys was given to your sister Marjorie to raise. But Marjorie who loved to party just like you did could not give Gladys the comfort, nurturing and affection she desperately needed. Gladys grew up unwanted and it showed.

It seems to me that you could not keep a commitment either to a woman or a child in your life. We can only give what we receive. I don't think you received steady, enduring love and affection as you grew up, Wilf. It's as though your parents weren't there for you, and you didn't learn how to be a husband and father.

I am grateful that I know as much as I do about you. It is never too late. There is a vital link between us in terms of health history, genetics, race, likeness, personality and interests. Wilf, you had four daughters that I know of: Doreen, Joyce, Gladys and me. We are your legacy, as are our children and our grand children. Something of who you were lives on in each of us.

Frank, 46 years of age

Chapter Twenty-Two

A Letter to My Dad

Go out into the darkness and put your hand into the hand of God.
That shall be to you better than light and safer than a known way.
—M. L. Haskins

Hi Dad,

I'm 80 years old now, and it is a pleasure at this late stage to be reflecting upon what you meant to me. This has come about from having recently learned more about Wilf, my birth father. You were my dad for only twenty-one years of my life. You died just as I was becoming a young woman.

At 21, I knew that Ken and I were serious about each other and you were happy about that. Your blessing meant a lot to me. A few of my boyfriends before Ken would not have received your blessing!

What stands out after all these years is that you were a father I could count on, a dad who was present to his family in spite of chronic illness that sapped your strength.

In our story that follows, trust, patience and nurturance are all expressed by you without fanfare. I loved to play games like hide-and-seek, tag, and Giant step outside on fall evenings with the other kids. The consequences I suffered once I fell asleep at night were worth it. I would begin to cry in my sleep and half-wake up with a "leg ache." It seemed that the cause was over-exertion of my lower leg muscles. You would come into my room with a tin of Watkin's linament and rub it into my legs. The ache would subside, I'd fall back to sleep, and you would return to your bedroom. But almost every time, the pain would rise up again, I'd cry out, and you'd come back to my bedside to repeat the process. There was never an impatient word or gesture on your part. It happened many times over the years, and we never really talked about it. I don't know why Mom didn't attend to me. The only reason I can think of is that she lacked the confidence that she could make it better.

The potential for abuse was there on those nights when you rubbed my legs, Dad. It never entered our minds, yours or mine. As a social worker I have heard many stories of abuse that small children experience in the dead of night when an older family member, usually male, enters their bedroom. I know the lifelong trauma that results. Every child has a right to the kind of trust I had in you, a trust I simply took for granted.

As I contemplate Mom's and your experience of infertility over the eight years before Mom gave birth to Lois, I am reminded of what Elinor Rosenberg tells us in her illuminating book *The Adoption Life Cycle* (1992). It is very difficult to accept the fact of infertility and maintain a high level of self-esteem. Mom assumed that she was the one with the problem as most women did and still do. Couples would often confuse reproduction and sexual adequacy with the competency to parent. I don't think you ever did that, Dad. You seemed very pleased to be a parent; you showed confidence in your parental authority; and you expressed fond feelings for me, your child through adoption. At no time did I feel you were disappointed in me because I, the adopted child, was not the person I was supposed to be; i.e., the biological child.

Even though your chronic asthma stole your breath and weakened you, you managed to teach Lois and me how to ride a bike and how to skate on the little rink across the highway from our house. You always had time to drive me to the end of the bus line so I could go on to my piano lesson, a church confirmation class or a teenage dance near my school in the city.

I sensed that you were proud of me and my accomplishments. I realize now that I was proud of *you* for your competence as Office Manager and Chief Clerk at the Canada Cement, for your gentle authority and the respect that people in the community had for you. You made a contribution to the community of Fort Whyte as a church lay leader, often leading the service for a small group of worshippers in the village school. In later years we made the trip as often as possible on a Sunday morning to a big downtown church. And when the roads were impassable, you led a family worship service for us at home. If you'd had more confidence, opportunity and better health, you might have gone into Anglican church ministry.

You practised your faith through prayer and taught by example. That's where your integrity came in. It was a powerful moment when you gathered us together in the living room to pray for Jean, Auntie Mattie's eldest daughter, who had a life-threatening blood clot following the birth of her second child. For years you helped village men who were illiterate fill out their income tax returns.

You had your emotional struggles, though, didn't you, Dad? I'm sure you were cherished by your mother. In fact, you may have been the favourite of her six children. You were her "poor Frank" as she worried about your breathing difficulties. Did that engender a habit of feeling sorry for yourself? One thing you too often said that caused me to shrink inside was, "You'll be sorry when I'm dead and gone." I think you experienced some loss of confidence when you compared yourself to men who had higher levels of education and better paying jobs than you did.

There were never any open quarrels or obvious tension between you and Mom, but you told me once that Mom had called you "a spineless jellyfish." I was too shocked to ask why. My guess is that she was frustrated that you lacked the confidence to stand up for yourself. Nonetheless, you were a loving partner to Mom throughout your too-short life.

There is no other experience in my childhood to compare it with—the four of us—you, Mom, Lois and I set out from Fort Whyte and walked a dirt road overgrown with willows, poplars, bush and prairie grass. We were not an adventurous family. The outing had to be your idea, Dad. It was a very hot, summer day with bugs and mosquitoes to keep us company. There were a couple of stops along the way to rest, drink water and share a few bars of chocolate to perk us up. Best chocolate I've ever tasted before or since. We walked five long miles until we came to the big stone gate of Assiniboine Park, one of the most beautiful city parks in Canada. We must have met up with the Sinclairs to picnic in the park—Morna and Jack and their two boys, Frank and Bob, who were more like relatives than friends. Mrs. Sinclair would have laid out an oilcloth covering on one of the dozens of picnic tables grouped together. Nearby was a big shelter for when it rained, with a tap to fill a kettle which we set on a wood stove to boil for tea. Then out would emerge the food from the picnic basket. It was always the same delicious fare: cooked ham, fresh bread and butter, home-made pickles, potato salad, tomatoes, cucumbers, deviled eggs, fruit, and cookies. All the vegetables were from Jack Sinclair's back yard garden about as big as a postage stamp. Mrs. Sinclair made the pickles, relish, cookies and cake in the smallest kitchen I've ever seen. Delicious! We played dodge ball, swung high on the swings, and rode the merry-go-round until we felt slightly sick. I have no idea how we got home. We didn't walk to the park again.

Soon after leaving Fort Whyte and moving to the tiny bungalow in the Winnipeg suburb of Fort Garry, Mom knew that time was running out on you. With one partially functioning lung, breathing was even more of a struggle for you. Your poor swollen legs were like logs of wood, and you spent all your time in bed. On one of your last days at home before you went into the hospital, you called me into your bedroom. With tears in your eyes, you asked me to open the top dresser drawer and take out a dollar bill which was to be mine, you said. I was shaken. Was it your way of telling me that you loved me and that you were leaving? I kept that dollar bill in my jewellery box for years after that. When we visited you in hospital, I was numb. I felt that I did absolutely nothing to ease things for you, for Mom, or for Lois.

On the evening of January 4, 1957, Mom came home from the hospital, woke Lois and me, and said simply, "Your dad is gone." You died of malignant hypertension at the age of 51. Lois tells me that I sat on the edge of my bed and wept as Mom put her arm around me. I don't remember weeping. I do remember your burial. It was a bitterly cold January day, and I had a dreadful head cold. Dad, the three of us stood there at your graveside—Lois on one side of Mom, and I on the other. We would carry on.

Life went on for me—my engagement and marriage to Ken, and babies born 1, 2, 3, followed by the adoption of a toddler. You would have been "over the moon" had you had the chance to know and love your grandchildren, their mates and your great-grandchildren. They would have loved you.

For years I felt nothing following your death. I thought that something was wrong with me. How could I not feel sad after losing my father? About 15 years after you died, something happened. I was working for Saskatoon psychiatrist, Dr. Dave Keegan. The research project for which I'd been hired involved conducting a stress interview with cardiac male patients to assess for the presence of Type A behaviour pattern. A renowned cardiologist from San Francisco came to Saskatoon to consult with Dr. Keegan and to train me.

The three of us entered the cardiology ward of the hospital, and with the consent of a few patients, I practised the stress interview. One of the men I interviewed stands out. He was an elderly man with congestive heart failure. As I peppered him with questions, he became visibly upset. All I could see were his sick rheumy eyes looking at me, and hear his struggle to breathe. When the interview was over, I, also visibly upset, walked down the hall with the two doctors. Dr. Keegan asked if I was ok. My reply was, "I don't want this job."

A few days later, Dr. Keegan, who was well aware of my adoptive family history, posed a question in a therapy session. "Did the patient you interviewed remind you of your father?" That was it! The dam burst and I was able to *feel* the loss of you, my dear dad, at long last.

I've worked hard to combine my biological roots and my adoptive bonds to form an identity that is some combination of both. Your legacy lives on in my memories, experiences and heirlooms— both material and psychological, Dad. Most especially, it lives on in the love we shared with each other as father and daughter.

Dad, all those many years ago, you gave me your blessing to marry Ken. I found in Ken a husband who believes in and loves me over the long haul. I found in Ken a nurturing father my children can count on. Yes, your legacy lives on.

REFERENCES

Andersen, Robert S. 1988. "Why Adoptees Search: Motives and More." *Child Welfare* 67 (January-February): 15-19.

Anglican Church of Canada. *The Book of Common Prayer*. Toronto: Cambridge at The University Press.

Appelt, Kathi. 2000. *Oh, My Baby, Little One*. Littleton, NY: Harcourt, Brace.

Axness, Marcy Wineman. 1998. "What is Written on the Heart: Primal Issues in Adoption." *Adoption Insight* 2.

Becker-Weidman, Arthur. 2001. "Notes on Attachment." *Fostering Families TODAY* (April).

Boyce-Tillmann, June. 1996. "We Shall Go Out in Hope of Resurrection." *Voices United*. Toronto: The United Church Publishing House.

Brackenbury, Kathryn, Robin Iraci, Jane Boyce and Debbie Clark. 2002. Birthmothers' Perspective on the Power of Healing Through Ritual and Recognition. Resource paper presented at Ontario Adoption Community Conference. Toronto.

Burke, Rose. 2012. "Birth Pangs." *United Church Observer,* December.

Campbell, Joseph. 1988. *The Power of Myth*. New York: Doubleday, Anchor Books.

Camus, Albert. 1955. *Myth of Sisyphus and Other Essays*. New York: Alfred A. Knopf.

Carlini, Heather. 1997. *Adoptee Trauma: A Counselling Guide for Adoptees*. Saanichton, B.C.: Morningside Publishing.

Carter, Joseph H. 2005. *The Quotable Will Rogers*. Layton, UT: Gibbs Smith.

Coloroso, Barbara. 2007. *Extraordinary Evil: A Brief History of Genocide*. Toronto: Viking Canada.

REFERENCES

Connelly, Maureen. 1990. *Given in Love: Releasing a Child For Adoption.* Omaha, NE: Centering Corporation.

Doka, Kenneth J. 1992. "Grief: Coping with Hidden Sorrow." *Bereavement Magazine,* May.

Dowrick, Stephanie. 1997. *Forgiveness and Other Acts of Love.* Victoria, Australia: Penguin Books Australia Ltd.

Elliott, Trisha. 2007. "Unsealing Hard Secrets." *United Church Observer,* September.

Fisher, Florence. 1973. *The Search for Anna Fisher.* New York: Arthur Field.

Gibran, Kahlil. 1981. First published in 1923.*The Prophet.* New York: Alfred A. Knopf.

Gowda, Shilpi Somaya. 2010. *Secret Daughter.* New York: HarperCollins.

Grand, Michael Phillip. 2010. *The Adoption Constellation: New Ways of Thinking About and Practicing Adoption.* Guelph, ON: Self-published. adoptionconstellation.blogspot.com

Gritter, James L. 1997. *The Spirit of Open Adoption.* Washington, D.C.: CWLA Press.

Haddon, Mark. 2003. *The Curious Incident of the Dog in the Night Time.* London: Jonathan Cape.

Haskins, M. L. 1908. "The Gate of the Year." *The Desert.* www.poeticexpressions.co.uk/POEMS/Gate%20of%20the_year.htm

Johnston, Patricia Irwin. 1983. *Perspectives on a Grafted Tree.* Indianapolis, IN: Perspectives Press.

_____. 1992. *Adoption After Infertility.* Indianapolis, IN: Perspectives Press.

Jones, Chelsea Temple. 2012. "Bernadette's Secret." *United Church Observer*, December.

Kirk, H. David. 1984. *Shared Fate: A Theory and Method of Adoptive Relationships*. Brentwood Bay, B.C.: Ben-Simon Publications.

Kostash, Myrna. 1977. *All of Baba's Children*. Edmonton: Hurtig Publishers.

Lifton, Betty Jean. 1975. *Twice Born: Memoirs of an Adopted Daughter*. New York: Harper and Row.

_____. 1988. *Lost and Found: The Adoption Experience*. New York: Harper and Row.

_____. 1994. *Journey of the Adopted Self: A Quest for Wholeness*. New York: HarperCollins, Basic Books.

Mason, Mary Martin. 1995. *Out of the Shadows: Birthfathers' Stories*. Edina, Minnesota: O.J. Howard Publishing.

McColm, Michelle. 1993. *Adoption Reunions: A Book for Adoptees, Birth Parents and Adoptive Families*. Toronto: Second Story Press.

Melina, Lois. 1982. "Don't Re-name Even a Young Child." *Adopted Child* (July).

_____. 1990. "Seven Core Issues of Adoption." *Adoption Roundup: Journal of the Adoption Council of Ontario*. (Summer).

_____ 1998. "Being Found by Birth Parents Creates Turmoil for Adoptees, but also Sense of Being Blessed." *Adopted Child*. (November).

Miller, Kathryn Ann. 1994. *Did My First Mother Love Me?* Buena Park, CA: Morning Glory Press.

Munsch, Robert. 1986. *Love You Forever*. Willowdale, ON: Firefly Books.

REFERENCES

Paton, Jean. 1954. *The Adopted Break Silence.* Acton, CA: Life History Study Centre.

Perreault, Jean, and Sylvia, Vance, eds. 1993. *Writing the Circle: Native Women of Western Canada: An Anthology.* Portland, OR: Book News.

Petrie, Anne. 1998. *Gone to an Aunt's: Remembering Canada's Homes for Unwed Mothers.* Toronto: McClelland and Stewart.

Piniuta, Harry. trans. 1978. *Land of Pain Land of Promise: First Person Accounts by Ukrainian Pioneers 1891-1914.* Saskatoon, SK: Western Producer Prairie Books.

Rogers, Fred. 1994. *Let's Talk About It: Adoption.* New York: G. P. Putnam's Sons.

Rooke, Katie. September 19, 2007. "Adoption law struck down after two days" *National Post.*

Rosenberg, Elinor B. 1992. *The Adoption Life Cycle: The Children and Their Families Through the Years.* New York: The Free Press.

Rosove, Lori. 2001. *Rosie's Family: An Adoption Story.* Ottawa: Asia Press.

Ryan, M. J. ed. 1994. Untitled poem, p. 156. *A Grateful Heart.* York Beach, ME: Red Wheel/Weiser, Conari Press.

_____. 1994. Untitled poem, p. 95. *A Grateful Heart.* York Beach, ME: Red Wheel/Weiser, Conari Press.

Sachdev, Paul. 1989. *Unlocking the Adoption Files.* Lexington, MA: Lexington Books.

Severson, Randolph. 1991. *Adoption: Charms and Rituals for Healing.* Dallas, TX: House of Tomorrow.

Shawcross, William. 2009. *Queen Elizabeth The Queen Mother: The Official Biography.* New York: HarperCollins.

Shipley, Carol L. A. 1990. Adoption Reunion and After: Women Adoptees' Experience. Master of Social Work Independent Enquiry Project. School of Social Work, Carleton University, Ottawa.

Sommerville, Margaret. September 25, 2007. "Adoptees have the right to know their birth parents..." *National Post.*

_____. December 12, 2008. "The thread of life's passage" *The Ottawa Citizen.*

Sorosky, Arthur D., Annette Baran, and Reuben Pannor. 1978. *The Adoption Triangle: Sealed or Open Records: How They Affect Adoptees, Birthparents, and Adoptive Parents.* San Antonio, TX: Corona Publishing.

Stevenson, Bryan. 2014. *Just Mercy: A Story of Justice and Redemption.* New York: Spiegel and Grau.

Thomas, Dylan. 1952. "Do Not Go Gentle Into That Good Night." *The Poems of Dylan Thomas.* New York: New Directions.

Triseliotis, J. 1973. *In Search of Origins: The Experience of Adopted People.* London: Routledge and Kegan Paul.

Turner, Ann. 1990. *Through Moon and Stars and Night Skies.* New York: HarperCollins, Harper Trophy.

Verrier, Nancy Newton. 1993. *The Primal Wound: Understanding the Adopted Child.* Baltimore, MA: Gateway Press.

Youxian Welfare Institute, Director. Undated. *Growth Report of You Bing.* Hunan Province, China.

ACKNOWLEDGEMENTS

My first thanks goes to three friends—Delia Carley, Rieky Stuart and Ann Qualman—who urged me to "just get started!"; Kate Wilson, who said I had a "real book" and set me on the publishing path; Jennie Painter, Linda Corsini, and Lori Rosove, my supportive adoption colleagues; Alison Beaumont, Sharon Hawkins, Yvonne Harris, and Claire Trépanier who asked important questions and whose enthusiasm spurred me on; Lynne Robertson who lovingly helped me through a difficult patch; Heather Menzies who challenged me to write from a deeper place; Marie and Dave Canvin of Snug Harbour as well as Margaret Maxted and Pat Logan who provided quiet, safe havens to write; Barbara van Gent who came up with the perfect word to add to the title and who entered into my search for a publisher; Hélène Lajeunesse, my hair stylist, for her enthusiastic support; Andrea Nugent who painstakingly proofread the manuscript; Keith Strachan who guided me so capably in developing my website; Estelle Sures who recommended that I contact McNally Robinson Booksellers to publish the book; and to the staff at McNally's for their reliability and expertise.

Three friends died during the writing of this book: Ann Qualman, Dave Canvin, and Pat Logan—each was inspirational in unforgettable, unique ways.

I am profoundly indebted to the unrelenting hard work and encouragement of Frances Wheeler Davis, my editor and life-long friend, who cleaned up the typos and the punctuation in the manuscript and clarified its prose, to my son Dave and Cindy Rodriguez for their genogram expertise, and to my dear friend, Marianne Hodgson for everything. I am deeply grateful to Colleen Lundy, my beloved professor at Carleton University's School of Social Work, who believed in and helped shape the manuscript.

I cannot thank my husband Ken Shipley enough for his patience and encouragement, for his moral and technical support, and for his problem-solving ability. To my children, Kevin, Dave, Jill, and Elaine, and their spouses, thanks for keeping me sane, and for all that they have taught me about being a mother. I pay tribute to my adoptive daughter, my adoptive sister, my birth brother, my nieces on my birth father's side for their love and trust in allowing me to bring their private words and actions into the public domain, and to all the others whose stories grace these pages. You know who you are. And I thank my many clients who kept asking how the book was coming along. It's finished!

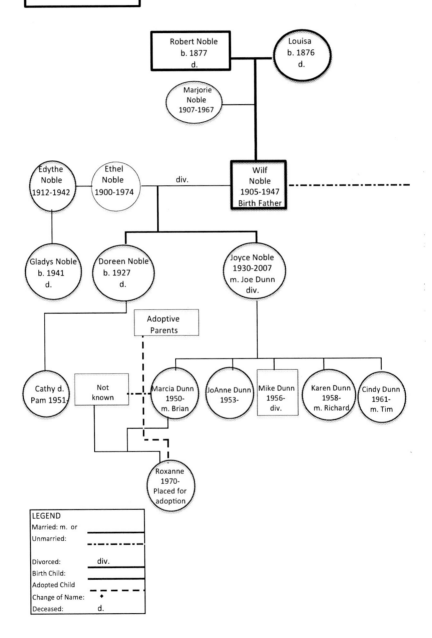

Carol Bowyer Shipley
GENOGRAM

Robert Noble
b. 1877
d.

Louisa
b. 1876
d.

Marjorie
Noble
1907-1967

Edythe
Noble
1912-1942

Ethel
Noble
1900-1974

div.

Wilf
Noble
1905-1947
Birth Father

Gladys Noble
b. 1941
d.

Doreen Noble
b. 1927
d.

Joyce Noble
1930-2007
m. Joe Dunn
div.

Adoptive
Parents

Cathy d.
Pam 1951

Not
known

Marcia Dunn
1950-
m. Brian

JoAnne Dunn
1953-

Mike Dunn
1956-
div.

Karen Dunn
1958-
m. Richard

Cindy Dunn
1961-
m. Tim

Roxanne
1970-
Placed for
adoption

LEGEND
Married: m. or
Unmarried:

Divorced: div.
Birth Child:
Adopted Child
Change of Name: ◆
Deceased: d.

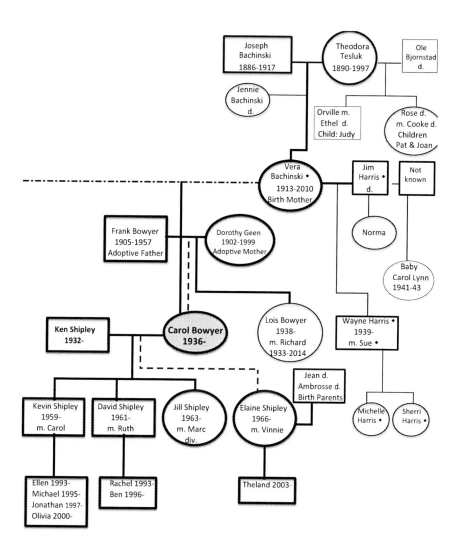

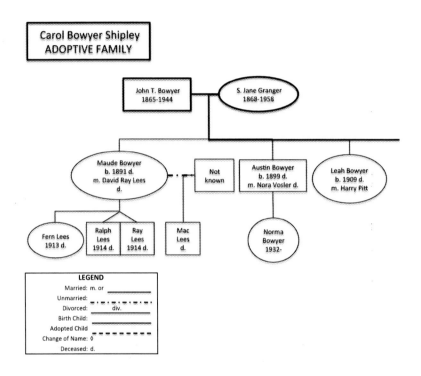

Carol Bowyer Shipley ADOPTIVE FAMILY

John T. Bowyer
1865-1944

S. Jane Granger
1868-1958

Maude Bowyer
b. 1891 d.
m. David Ray Lees
d.

Not known

Austin Bowyer
b. 1899 d.
m. Nora Vosler d.

Leah Bowyer
b. 1909 d.
m. Harry Pitt

Fern Lees
1913 d.

Ralph Lees
1914 d.

Ray Lees
1914 d.

Mac Lees
d.

Norma Bowyer
1932-

LEGEND

Married: m. or	
Unmarried:	
Divorced:	div.
Birth Child:	
Adopted Child	
Change of Name: ◊	
Deceased: d.	